ONE-DISH
DINNERS

ALSO BY JEAN ANDERSON

The Doubleday Cookbook* (with Elaine Hanna)
The Family Circle Cookbook
(with the food editors of *Family Circle*)

The Grass Roots Cookbook

Jean Anderson's Processor Cooking

Half a Can of Tomato Paste & Other Culinary Dilemmas**
(with Ruth Buchan)

Jean Anderson Cooks

The New Doubleday Cookbook (with Elaine Hanna)

The Food of Portugal***

Micro Ways (with Elaine Hanna)

Jean Anderson's Sin-Free Desserts

The New German Cookbook (with Hedy Würz)

The Nutrition Bible (with Barbara Deskins, Ph.D., R.D.)

The American Century Cookbook****

*Winner, R. T. French Tastemaker Award, Best Basic Cookbook of the Year
(1975) and Best Cookbook of the Year Overall (1975)

**Winner, R. T. French Tastemaker Award,
Best Specialty Cookbook of the Year (1980)

***Winner, Seagram/International Association of Culinary Professionals Award,
Best Foreign Cookbook of the Year (1986)

****Finalist, James Beard Cookbook Awards and Julia Child
Cookbook Awards (1998)

JEAN ANDERSON

ONE-DISH DINNERS

275 Great-Tasting, Easy Recipes Using Fresh, Frozen, Canned, and Other Convenience Foods

Previously published as *Dinners in a Dish or a Dash*

WILLIAM MORROW

An Imprint of HarperCollinsPublishers

Originally published by HarperCollins in 2000 as *Dinners in a Dish or a Dash*.

ONE-DISH DINNERS. Copyright © 2000 by Jean Anderson. All rights reserved. Printed in the United States of America. No part of this book may be used or reproduced in any manner whatsoever without written permission except in the case of brief quotations embodied in critical articles and reviews. For information address HarperCollins Publishers Inc., 10 East 53rd Street, New York, NY 10022.

HarperCollins books may be purchased for educational, business, or sales promotional use. For information please write: Special Markets Department, HarperCollins Publishers Inc., 10 East 53rd Street, New York, NY 10022.

First William Morrow paperback edition published 2004

The Library of Congress has catalogued the previous edition as:

Anderson, Jean
Dinners in a dish or a dash / Jean Anderson.
p.   cm.
Includes index.
ISBN 0-688-14572-8
1. Casserole cookery.   2. Quick and easy cookery.
3. Dinners and dining.   I. Title.
TX693.A57 2000
641.5'55—dc21
99—049514

ISBN 0-06-073421-3 (pbk.)

04   05   06   07   08 ❖/ RRD   10 9 8 7 6 5 4 3 2

CONTENTS

INTRODUCTION

When I was a food editor at *The Ladies' Home Journal* some years ago, one of our best-loved features was a monthly column called "Shelf Magic."

The idea was to help busy moms get dinner on the table on the double. No fuss, no muss. Of course, our recipes ran heavily to creamed-soup casseroles, beefed-up macaronis, and eggy skillet scrambles. We used a lot of hot dogs and processed cheese, stuffing mixes and bottled dressings, not to mention a ton of canned goods (even, I now shudder to think, canned asparagus, green peas, and mushrooms). Particular favorites, I remember, were canned Chinese noodles and French-fried onion rings—jiffy casserole toppers with plenty of crunch.

Our short-order dinners were hugely popular and remain so in many parts of the country. Indeed, I can scarcely riffle through a community cookbook (one of those little spiral-bound club or church fund-raisers) without spotting a recipe that dates back to my *LHJ* days.

That got me to thinking. With both parents working these days, we're busier than ever. We're more stressed out, less inclined to cook after hard hours at the office. There's fast food, of course, but many of us feel guilty about settling for burgers, pizza, fried chicken, or "Chinese" night after night. Even "gourmet" takeout soon becomes boring (not to mention expensive).

How much nicer to toss together something at home with the greatest of ease. Surely, I thought, there must be more modern, more imaginative, more healthful one-dish dinners than those Shelf-Magic meals of old. No-sweat one-dish meals that don't rely so heavily on highly processed foods. Ones that take advantage of the variety of fresh produce now available at every good supermarket, much of it washed, peeled, chunked, sliced, or shredded and ready to use. Quick and easy dinners that make the most of frozen foods (not just meat, fish, fowl, and vegetables but also filo sheets and puff pastry leaves). Recipes that confine the use of canned goods to a select list of "acceptables," that recognize the time-saving potential of bottled salsas and so many foreign foods and seasonings unknown a few years ago.

Recipes that recognize, too, that the one-dish dinner doesn't begin and end with the casserole. There are main-dish soups and stews, for example, that don't have to simmer the whole day long. Wonderful salads—toss-togethers, put-togethers—that are meals in themselves.

Then there's pasta. Its possibilities (to say nothing of the ready-made tortellini, ravioli, and pasta sauces now proliferating in supermarket frozen and refrigerated food sections) are nearly endless. Stir-fries, quiches, and pies are equally versatile and the short-cuts here—beginning with frozen pie shells—are nearly as impressive. Finally, let's not forget microwave meals.

The trouble with the microwave is that in the beginning, we tried to make it do everything. It can't. At least not well. What I've done here is let it do what it does best: nourishing casseroles, soups, and stews. And hearty risottos brimming with vegetables.

In creating these one-dish dinners, I've followed the lead of restaurant chefs. That is, I've learned to be flexible, to improvise, and even more important, to prep ahead—not only the basics, which can be frozen, but also ready supplies of chopped onions, bell peppers, parsley, and so forth. If a chef had to stop mid-recipe to mince a tablespoon of parsley or chop an onion, he'd never send plates into the dining room on time. So, too, the home cook.

Properly stored, these make-aheads keep "fresh" for a week or more. And how handy just to reach in and scoop up a tablespoon of minced garlic, a cup of chopped onion, a dab of duxelles (mushroom paste), or a pint of broccoli florets that require nothing more than a fast final warm-up with seasoning or sauce.

The list of ingredients in some of my recipes may seem long, but there's good reason for this. If you trim cooking times—especially those of soups and stews—there's less chance for flavors to build, to balance. To compensate, I've punched up the seasonings, tasting as I tested. Many ingredients, thus, are herbs, spices, and condiments—pinches of this, dashes of that—that require little or no prep.

Many of the one-dish dinners that follow are ready to serve in 30 minutes. Very few take as long as an hour and these longer ones cook virtually unattended. There's no need to prod and poke, to stand and stir the whole enduring time. And certainly no need to dirty every pot and pan in the kitchen.

May these 275 recipes and the dozens of professional tips salted throughout the book show you how to produce delicious one-dish dinners.

HOW TO USE
THIS BOOK

Read each recipe carefully before beginning.

Do not make ingredient substitutions in recipes unless alternates are given.

Use casserole and pan sizes and shapes specified; they are essential to the recipe's success.

"Cool" means to bring something to room temperature.

"Chill" means to chill until refrigerator-cold.

Preheat the oven a full 20 minutes.

Preheat the broiler a full 15 minutes.

Always use microwave power levels and cooking times specified.

Always cover microwave dishes with materials specified (casserole lid, plastic food wrap, waxed paper, etc.).

Use freshly squeezed lemon, lime, and orange juices only.

Broth vs. consommé vs. stock: If you are a dedicated cook who keeps a supply of homemade beef, chicken, and/or vegetable stock in the freezer, and if your stock is good and rich, by all means substitute it for the canned broths called for in these recipes. Do not, however, substitute beef stock for canned beef consommé unless you first boil it down to concentrate the flavors (the reduced stock can be substituted measure-for-measure for consommé). Canned beef consommé, available in every supermarket, is double-strength and injects a simmered-for-hours depth of flavor into quick soups and stews—a valuable shortcut. My best advice is to sample several brands of beef consommé, pick the one you like best, then stick with it.

Whenever a recipe calls for "freshly grated Parmesan cheese," use only imported Parmigiano-Reggiano (its name appears in an all-over pattern on the rind). Only it has a perfectly balanced nutty flavor that's a little bit sweet, a little bit salty. The grated "Parmesan" sold in little glass jars or plastic tubs tastes like salty sawdust. I buy a large wedge of Parmigiano-Reggiano, chunk half of it, then grate in the food processor as coarse or fine as I like. Stored in a tightly sealed glass jar in the refrigerator, it keeps for weeks. The rest of the wedge I wrap in plastic food wrap to "shave," dice, or slice. Tip: Save the Parmesan rinds and drop into soups or stews. The tag ends of cheese melt, spreading their goodness and thickening the mix ever so slightly.

Unless otherwise indicated:

- Black pepper is freshly ground.
- Butter is unsalted.
- Cornmeal is the yellow granular type available in every supermarket.
- Eggs are extra-large.
- Flour is all-purpose flour sifted before being measured.
- Garlic cloves are medium-size.
- Onions are medium-size yellow onions.
- Potatoes are medium-size all-purpose potatoes.

GETTING SET

I've never cooked in a restaurant but I apply many professional prep-ahead techniques to my own kitchen and find that they, together with a well-stocked pantry, refrigerator, and freezer, save worlds of time. Indeed, for me, they're the best way to cook on fast-forward.

What follows is a highly subjective list of pantry, fridge, and freezer items that I've found particularly useful over time: "acceptable" canned goods (broths, salsas, and tomatoes, for example), essential condiments and dry staples (lentils, pastas, grains, and such) and not least, high-quality refrigerated and frozen foods (fresh slaw and salad mixes, frozen chopped greens, and whole-kernel corn) that can be pressed into service whenever I need to rustle up a meal. You perhaps have your own roster of "old reliables," but these are the ones that have never failed me in a pinch.

Many appear in recipes in this book because they are versatile, they lend themselves to improvisation, and they have rescued me time and again. Finally, I include my own favorite time-saving make-aheads, which I keep at the ready in refrigerator and freezer.

STOCKING PANTRY AND CUPBOARD

CANNED AND BOTTLED GOODS

BROTHS
> *Indispensables*
>> beef broth
>>
>> demi-glace or concentrated beef broth
>>
>> beef consommé
>>
>> chicken broth and concentrated chicken broth
>>
>> vegetable broth
>
> *Useful Extra*
>> clam broth or juice

DAIRY PRODUCTS
> *Indispensables*
>> evaporated milk (skim/regular)

JUICES
> *Indispensables*
>> apple cider
>>
>> tomato juice
>>
>> vegetable juice (mild/hot)
>
> *Useful Extras*
>> pineapple juice
>>
>> Thai coconut milk, unsweetened (light/regular)

MEAT/FISH/FOWL
> *Indispensables*
>> corned beef
>>
>> chicken
>>
>> boiled or baked ham
>>
>> tuna (chunk light or white)
>
> *Useful Extras*
>> anchovy fillets (flat)

THE FASTEST WAY TO
MELLOW GRAVY, SAUCE,
SOUP, OR STEW IS TO
BLEND IN 1 TO 2 TABLE-
SPOONS CREAMY PEANUT
BUTTER.

clams (diced/minced)

crab (lump/flake)

salmon (pink)

sardines

shrimp (tiny/medium)

OILS/DRESSINGS

Indispensables

mayonnaise

mayonnaise-type relish sandwich spread

extra-virgin olive oil

vegetable oil

Useful Extras

bottled tartar sauce

peanut oil

Asian roasted sesame oil

Szechuan chili oil

SAUCES/PUREES/PASTES

Indispensables

barbecue sauces (mild/hot)

pasta sauces (Alfredo, marinara, pesto)

peanut butter (creamy)

salsas (mild/hot fruit and chunky vegetable)

tomato paste

tomato puree

tomato sauce

Useful Extras

anchovy paste

pasta sauces (Bolognese, puttanesca)

tahini (sesame seed paste)

CONDIMENTS/SEASONINGS/VINEGARS

Indispensables

capers

chili sauce

chutney

horseradish

hot red pepper sauce

India relish

ketchup

mustard (Dijon, honey, whole-grain, yellow)

soy sauce

steak sauce

teriyaki sauce

vinegar (balsamic, cider, red wine, white wine)

wine (dry red, dry white)

Worcestershire sauce

Useful Extras

Asian fish sauce

Asian oyster sauce

dill pickles

gherkins

ginger (candied/pickled/preserved)

hoisin (fermented soybean/red rice sauce)

hot green pepper sauce

Szechuan hot spicy sauce

tamari (dark Japanese soy sauce)

Thai peanut sauce

dried tomatoes in oil

vinegar (rice, tarragon)

dry vermouth (it can double for dry white wine in recipes and unlike wine, doesn't sour overnight; in fact, it keeps for months on a cool, dark shelf)

BOTTLED SWEETENERS

Indispensables

corn syrup (light/dark)

honey

molasses

Useful Extras

maple syrup

marmalade (ginger, orange)

CANNED VEGETABLES AND FRUITS

Indispensables

artichoke hearts (plain/marinated)

beans (baked beans, black beans, black-eyed peas, chickpeas, kidney beans, navy beans)

caponata (Italian eggplant appetizer)

corn (cream-style/whole-kernel)

olives (oil-cured black, pimiento-stuffed green)

peppers (whole/diced roasted red peppers, whole/diced
jalapeños, whole/diced pimientos)

tomatoes (whole/crushed/crushed in tomato puree/diced/
diced with green chilies)

Useful Extras

bamboo shoots

beans (cannellini)

beets (whole/sliced)

carrots (sliced)

hominy or posole

olive salad (chopped pimiento-stuffed green olives)

sauerkraut

water chestnuts (whole/sliced)

STORAGE TIPS FOR CANNED AND BOTTLED GOODS

- To extend shelf life, keep in a cool, dark, dry place.
- If a can bulges or leaks, or if a bottle oozes, discard immediately, making sure it's out of harm's way for both people and pets.
- Once open, many canned and bottled goods must be refrigerated. Read labels carefully.
- Each time you use molasses, syrup, or honey, wipe top of bottle clean with paper toweling moistened with hot water, using detergent if necessary. And pay particular attention to the cap and threads at the top of the bottle. I've been doing this for years and, as a result,

have never had to battle ants, roaches, weevils, or mice.

DRY FOODS

It goes without saying that every cook will stock such staples as flour, sugar, cornmeal, and cornstarch, also such good "pantry vegetables" as garlic, onions, and potatoes. Listed here are other dry foods that I like to keep on hand.

BOUILLON CUBES AND GRANULES (these are the fastest way to pump up the flavor of sauces, soups, and stews)
> *Indispensables*
>> beef bouillon cubes or granules
>> chicken bouillon cubes or granules
> *Useful Extra*
>> vegetable broth cubes or granules

DRIED FRUITS AND VEGETABLES
> *Indispensables*
>> dried currants
>> prunes
>> raisins
> *Useful Extras*
>> dried apples
>> dried apricots
>> dried peeled Italian chestnuts
>> dried mushrooms (especially porcini and shiittake)

GRAINS AND LEGUMES
> *Indispensables*
>> bulgur (tabbouleh)
>> couscous (quick-cooking)
>> dry-roasted peanuts
>> rice (Arborio for risotto, converted white, brown)

Useful Extras
    falafel mix
    kasha
    lentils
    yellow (saffron) rice mix
    rice/macaroni mix
    wild rice
    wild rice/white rice mix

PASTA (PREFERABLY BOTH WHITE AND GREEN OR SPINACH)

Indispensables
    egg noodles (medium)
    elbow macaroni
    fettuccine
    fusilli
    linguine
    shells (small/medium)
    no. 9 spaghetti
Useful Extras
    capellini (angel hair pasta)
    farfalle (bow-ties)
    gnocchi
    no-cook lasagne noodles
    orzo
    penne
    ravioli
    spaetzle
    tortellini (cheese)

HERBS

Indispensables
    basil
    bay leaves
    dill weed
    marjoram
    oregano

poultry seasoning

rosemary

sage

tarragon

thyme

Useful Extras

chervil

mint flakes

parsley flakes

summer savory

SPICES

Indispensables

allspice (whole/ground)

chili powder

cinnamon (stick/ground)

cloves (whole/ground)

curry powder

ginger

mustard (seeds/powder)

nutmeg (whole/ground)

black peppercorns

ground hot red pepper (cayenne)

red pepper flakes

Useful Extras

anise (seeds/ground)

caraway seeds

cardamom (seeds/ground)

Chinese five-spice powder

coriander seeds

Creole seasoning

cumin (seeds/ground)

fennel seeds

ground mace

poppy seeds

saffron threads

ground turmeric

NOTE

I DON'T LIKE THE TEXTURE OF "INSTANT RICE" AND PREFER TO COOK A BIG BATCH OF CONVERTED WHITE RICE AND STORE IT IN THE REFRIGERATOR OR FREEZER; IT REHEATS IN SECONDS AND REMAINS REMARKABLY LIGHT AND FLUFFY—SEE PAGE 35.

SHOPPING/STORAGE/PREPARATION
TIPS FOR DRY FOODS

- Store flours, meals, grains, legumes, pastas, and sugars in tightly capped, wide-mouth, half-gallon preserving jars with cooking instructions cut from the label and tucked inside. The reason for wide-mouth jars is that you can dip measuring cups into them.

- Buy "leaf" herbs, not ground, which have lost much of their punch by the time they go into the jar. Two exceptions: poultry seasoning (a blend of ground herbs) and sage (best in the "rubbed" form).

- Buy whole spices and seeds whenever available (they last far longer than the ground) and grind as needed. I have a little electric coffee grinder that I use exclusively for pulverizing whole spices and seeds (allspice, nutmeg, cinnamon sticks, cardamom and poppy seeds). The difference in flavor is truly remarkable.

- Transfer tinned herbs and spices or those in plastic bottles to half-pint jelly jars with dome lids that practically vacuum-seal. Herbs and spices packed in glass jars keep well in their original containers.

- Store herbs and spices on a cool, dark, dry shelf and replace whenever they begin to fade or lose flavor. Note: herbs go stale much faster than spices.

- To intensify the flavor of aromatic seeds and spices (both ground and whole), warm briefly in a dry skillet over moderate heat or spread in an ungreased pie tin and set in a preheated 350°F. oven for a few minutes (your nose will tell you when they're done).

- Each time you withdraw something from a spice or storage jar, wipe the jar clean with a damp cloth, using a little detergent if necessary.

STOCKING THE REFRIGERATOR

I see no point in listing the obvious—fresh eggs, butter and margarine, milk, sour cream, plain yogurt, sliced bacon, cold cuts, sliced or shredded cheeses, assorted lettuces, bell peppers, tomatoes, oranges, lemons and limes, etc.— which belong in every well-stocked refrigerator. I list here the other perishables that help me get dinner on the table fast.

BREADS
> *Indispensables*
>> refrigerator biscuits
>> refrigerator pizza dough
>> firm-textured bread (white/whole wheat)
>> French or Italian bread
>> English muffins
>
> *Useful Extras*
>> rye bread
>> refrigerator cornstick dough
>> refrigerator crescent rolls

DAIRY/EGGS
> *Indispensables*
>> half-and-half cream
>> ricotta cheese (part-skim)
>> light cream cheese (Neufchâtel)
>> blue or Roquefort cheese
>> Cheddar (wedge/shredded/sliced)
>> feta cheese
>> Gruyère or Swiss cheese
>> Monterey jack (wedge/shredded/sliced)
>> mozzarella (whole/shredded)
>> Parmesan (Parmigiano-Reggiano only; wedge/freshly grated)
>> hard-cooked eggs (see page 19)
>
> *Useful Extras*
>> crème fraîche
>> heavy cream

Fontina cheese

Jarlsberg cheese

ricotta salata (an aged cheese similar to feta)

shredded mixed Mexican-style cheeses

FRESH HERBS/SPICES

Indispensables

basil

chives

cilantro

ginger

parsley (flat-leaf or curly)

rosemary

thyme (preferably lemon thyme)

Useful Extras

dill

lemongrass

marjoram

mint

oregano

sage

tarragon

MEAT/FISH/FOWL

Indispensables

ground lean beef chuck

boiled or baked ham

kielbasa

boneless, skinless chicken cutlets

Useful Extras

chicken drummettes

chicken thighs

chorizo

thinly sliced prosciutto

smoked salmon

Italian sausage (sweet or hot)

PASTA/GRAINS

Indispensables

refrigerated fresh fettuccine or linguine

refrigerated fresh ravioli or tortellini (cheese or mushroom)

Useful Extras

polenta

other flavors of fresh tortellini and/or ravioli

PASTA SAUCES

Indispensables

Alfredo

marinara

pesto

Useful Extras

Bolognese

mushroom

VEGETABLES

Indispensables

broccoli

cabbage

carrots

celery

white mushrooms

salad greens

scallions

yellow squash or zucchini

tomatoes (cherry, Italian plum, sweet grape)

Useful Extras

asparagus

arugula

bean sprouts

cauliflower

cucumbers (especially Kirby or small pickling cucumbers)

leeks

mesclun (mix of baby salad greens)

mushrooms (cremini, portobello, shiitake)

watercress

NOTE

Also see Make-Aheads
(page 19) and Produce
Counter Shortcuts
(page 22).

STORAGE TIPS FOR REFRIGERATOR PERISHABLES

The majority of perishables are now stamped with "sell by," "use by," or expiration dates, and although there's a little leeway here, the best policy is to abide by these. I suggest here maximum storage times for undated perishables only.

STORAGE TIPS FOR FRESH PRODUCE

- Salad greens: Wash in several changes of lightly salted cool water (fill sink with water, add greens, and slosh gently up and down so dirt and grit sink to the bottom). Spin greens dry in a salad spinner, then layer with paper toweling in large plastic zipper bags, keeping different types of greens separate, and refrigerate. Maximum storage time is 1 week.
- Vegetables (asparagus, bell peppers, broccoli, carrots, celery, cucumbers, yellow squash, zucchini, etc.). Do not wash before refrigerating. If vegetables seem unusually wet (often the case with supermarkets automatically spritzing produce bins), pat dry on paper toweling, then layer in plastic bags with dry paper toweling. Fold tops of bags over and store in refrigerator crisper drawers. Maximum storage time is 7 to 10 days.
- Herbs: The best way to handle parsley and tender-leafed herbs (basil, chervil, cilantro, dill, tarragon, etc.) is to unband the bunched herb, separate the sprigs, and discard any that have broken stems or are yellowing or going soft. Do not wash herbs. With a sharp knife, slice off base of each stem slightly on the bias just as you would if readying roses for a vase. Fill a large glass or small jar with cool water three-fourths of the way, then stand herb springs in jar just as if you were arranging flowers. Pop a soft plastic bag upside-down—loosely— over bouquet of herbs, do not secure around bottom

of jar, and set in refrigerator. Maximum storage time is 10 days to 2 weeks for parsley, 3 to 5 days for basil (it tends to blacken as moisture accumulates), 7 to 10 days for other herbs.

- Fresh ginger: Slip whole, unpeeled ginger into plastic zipper bag, press out air, seal, and store on refrigerator door shelf where plainly visible. When ready to use, whack off the amount you need (a 1-inch cube, peeled and minced = about 1 tablespoon). Maximum storage time is about 1 month, but check ginger from time to time and if molding, softening, or shriveling, discard.

- Eggs: Leave fresh eggs in original carton and store in coldest part of refrigerator, not in door "egg-keeper." Store hard-cooked eggs unpeeled in plastic storage container with tight-fitting lid. Also label eggs "hard-cooked." Maximum storage time for hard-cooked eggs is 7 days if eggs were very fresh, 3 to 5 if not.

- Milk: Transfer to glass bottle; it will last nearly twice as long as that kept in paper or plastic cartons. Glass, moreover, is inert and imparts no off flavors to milk.

- Parmigiano-Reggiano: Chunk a large wedge of cheese, then grate in food processor. Stored in a tightly sealed glass jar in the refrigerator, it keeps for weeks. Wrap wedges or blocks of Parmigiano-Reggiano in foil or plastic food wrap, pop into plastic zipper bags, and store in the "meat-keeper" drawer of the refrigerator. Maximum storage time is several weeks for grated cheese, several months for properly wrapped wedges.

MAKE-AHEADS
FOR THE REFRIGERATOR

- Broccoli florets: Divide broccoli into small florets (no more than $1\frac{1}{2}$ to 2 inches across the top), leaving $\frac{1}{2}$ inch of stem on each and trimming to a thickness of $\frac{1}{4}$ inch. Blanch florets 2 minutes in large pan of rapidly boiling unsalted water. Drain florets and quick-chill 5 minutes in large bowl of ice water. This stops the cooking and sets the bright green color. Drain florets well, then layer with paper toweling in a plastic zipper bag and store in the refrigerator until ready to use. Maximum storage time is 5 to 7 days.

- Hard-cooked eggs: see page 19.
- Minced garlic: Separate 2 or 3 bulbs of garlic into individual cloves and peel. The easy way to do this is to whack each clove with the broad side of a large heavy chef's knife; this loosens the skin, which can be quickly stripped away. Mince garlic moderately fine. (I use a food processor, pulsing to just the right degree of fineness; if you mince by hand, sprinkle chopping board with salt—that way the garlic won't stick to the knife or your hands.) Spoon minced garlic into a glass or porcelain ramekin and press plastic food wrap flat over surface of garlic. Slip ramekin into a small plastic zipper bag, press out all the air, seal, and store in refrigerator. Every time you dip into the garlic, reseal as carefully as you did the first time around. Because most recipes call for garlic by the clove, here's a handy table that translates minced cloves into teaspoons:

  1 small clove garlic = $1/2$ to 1 teaspoon minced

  1 medium-size clove garlic = 1 to 1 $1/2$ teaspoons minced

  1 large clove garlic = 2 to 2 $1/2$ teaspoons minced

- Dumpling/Biscuit Topping Mix: see page 31.
- Fresh lemon juice: It's a pain to have to stop and juice a lemon mid-recipe, so I like to keep a little jar of "freshly" squeezed lemon juice in the refrigerator (and sometimes separate jars of orange and/or lime juices, too). My favorite storage container is a half-pint preserving jar with a dome lid because the jar fits directly underneath the spout of my electric juicer and holds the juice of about 6 lemons (or 8 limes or 2 medium-size oranges). I squeeze the juice directly

into the jar, cap it tight, and set in the refrigerator. It remains amazingly fresh and is infinitely superior to bottled juices (I won't give them house room). Maximum storage time is 2 weeks for lemon or lime juice, 1 week for orange juice.

- Chopped yellow onions: You'll save tons of time if you chop 2 or 3 pounds of yellow (all-purpose) onions whenever you have time and store them in the fridge. But I recommend this only if you have a food processor. Here's the technique that has served me well over the years: Halve each onion lengthwise, slip off the peel, then cut each half in two both crosswise and lengthwise. Drop onion chunks into food processor fitted with the metal chopping blade and pulse briskly until moderately coarse—further chopping may reduce the onions to mush. So will trying to chop too many at a time; for best results, no more than half-fill the processor work bowl. Once the onions are chopped, bundle into a large plastic zipper bag (a heavy-duty freezer one), press out all the air, and seal. Place this bag in a second large, heavy-duty plastic zipper bag, press out the air, and seal. Store in the refrigerator. Whenever you need onions, simply reach in with a measuring spoon or dry cup measure and retrieve the amount you need. Carefully reseal both bags as before after each use, pressing out all air (this keeps the onions from smelling up the fridge and/or absorbing refrigerator odors). Many recipes call for onions by the piece (2 medium-large yellow onions, chopped), rather than by the cup (2 cups chopped onions). No problem. Here's a handy conversion table geared to today's onions, which tend to run large:

    1 small yellow onion = $1/4$ cup chopped
    1 medium-small yellow onion = $1/2$ cup chopped
    1 medium-size yellow onion = $3/4$ cup chopped
    1 medium-large yellow onion = 1 cup chopped
    1 large yellow onion = 1 $1/2$ cups chopped

NOTE

PRE-MINCED GARLIC SOFT-ENS SOMEWHAT AND ALSO GATHERS STRENGTH, SO MY ADVICE IS TO USE IT IN COOKED DISHES ONLY; FOR SALADS AND OTHER RECIPES REQUIRING RAW GARLIC, MINCE CLOVES TO ORDER. MAXIMUM STORAGE TIME IS 7 TO 10 DAYS.

USE PRE-CHOPPED ONIONS ONLY IN COOKED DISHES; IF A RECIPE CALLS FOR RAW CHOPPED ONIONS, CHOP THEM AS YOU NEED THEM. MAXIMUM STORAGE TIME IS 1 WEEK.

CERTAIN MINCED FRESH, TENDER-LEAFED HERBS CAN ALSO BE STORED SUCCESS-FULLY—CHERVIL, CILANTRO, DILL, AND TARRAGON BUT NOT MINT OR BASIL, ALAS, WHICH WILL BLACKEN. MAXIMUM STORAGE TIME (IF YOU DAMPEN THE PAPER TOWELING LIGHTLY AS IT DRIES) IS 7 TO 10 DAYS FOR PARSLEY, 4 TO 5 DAYS FOR OTHER HERBS.

- Minced parsley: Here's a trick I learned some years ago. Unband the parsley but do not wash. Discard the stems, also any wilting or discoloring leaves, then mince the parsley as coarse or fine as you like. Place in a small fine-mesh sieve and set under cool running water to clean. Bundle washed parsley in several thicknesses of paper toweling and squeeze as dry as possible. Next spread the parsley on several thicknesses of dry paper toweling, fold left and right sides of toweling in, then roll parsley up in toweling. Slip roll into a small plastic zipper bag and set in the refrigerator.
- Chopped bell peppers: Wash peppers, pat dry, then quarter, core, and seed. If chopping by hand, score each quarter lengthwise, starting about $1/4$ inch from the top; stack 3 or 4 scored quarters and slice crosswise, spacing the cuts about $1/4$ inch apart. This will give you a good even chop. Even easier, cut quarters into 1-inch chunks, drop into food processor fitted with metal chopping blade, and pulse quickly until coarsely chopped.
- Cooked rice: See Al Dente Make-Ahead Rice (page 35).

PRODUCE-COUNTER SHORTCUTS

These are the partially prepped fresh vegetables that I find especially useful and like to keep in the refrigerator.

broccoli and cauliflower florets
carrots (peeled baby-cut/shredded)
celery hearts
coleslaw mixes (including one made with broccoli)
mushrooms (pre-sliced fresh white mushrooms, creminis, portobellos)
potatoes, Red Bliss (washed, chunked, partially cooked)
romaine hearts

salad mixes (European, Italian or Caesar, mesclun)
baby spinach (washed)

DELI/MEAT COUNTER SHORTCUTS

Without these items in my refrigerator, I'd find it hard to cook dinner on a deadline.
fully cooked crumbled bacon (a recent meat counter arrival)
corned beef
roast beef
fully cooked carved chicken breast (another new item)
rotisserie or barbecued chicken
freshly cooked shelled and deveined shrimp
roast turkey

STOCKING THE FREEZER

For me, these are the frozen foods that speed cooking.

EGGS
Indispensable
frozen egg product (often erroneously called "egg substitute") is actually made of egg whites and natural food coloring and is nothing to shy away from because there's nothing fake or phony about it. I find frozen egg product extremely useful because 1 to 2 tablespoons, thawed, enriches and thickens salad dressings, sauces, soups, and stews. Formula to remember: $1/4$ cup thawed frozen egg product = 1 whole egg.

FRUITS
Indispensables
cranberries
frozen orange juice concentrate

NOTE

I LIKE TO KEEP BOTH CHOPPED GREEN AND RED BELL PEPPERS ON HAND—IN SEPARATE BAGS—SO THAT I CAN DIP INTO THEM AS NEEDED. AND SOMETIMES I CHOP A BATCH OF YELLOW PEPPERS, TOO. THE DIFFERENT BELL PEPPERS CAN BE USED INTERCHANGEABLY IN RECIPES. FOR THE RECORD, 1 MEDIUM-LARGE PEPPER EQUALS ABOUT 1 CUP CHOPPED, 1 MEDIUM-SIZE, ABOUT 1/2 CUP CHOPPED. MAXIMUM STORAGE TIME IS 1 WEEK.

Useful Extras
frozen limeade concentrate
frozen unsweetened sliced peaches
frozen unsweetened raspberries
frozen unsweetened strawberries

MEAT/FISH/FOWL

Indispensables
chicken (breasts/cutlets/drummettes)
ground lean beef chuck frozen in 4-ounce burgers
shelled and deveined small raw or cooked shrimp (sometimes called "cocktail" or "salad" shrimp)
frozen snow crab

Useful Extras
cooked seasoned beef strips
cooked chicken breast strips/dice
chicken thighs

PASTA

Indispensables
ravioli (cheese or mushroom)
tortellini (cheese or blue cheese)

Useful Extras
sausage or chicken ravioli or tortellini

PASTA SAUCES

Indispensables
Alfredo
marinara
pesto

Useful Extras
Bolognese
mushroom

PASTRY

Indispensables

deep-dish pie crusts

pizza crusts

Useful Extras

filo leaves

puff pastry sheets

NUTS

Indispensables

almonds (sliced/slivered)

pecans

walnuts

Useful Extras

hazelnuts

pine nuts

VEGETABLES

Indispensables

artichoke hearts

asparagus cuts

bell peppers (frozen stir-fry mix)

cut green beans

corn (whole-kernel/cream-style)

greens (frozen chopped collards/kale/spinach)

baby lima beans

onions (frozen chopped/peeled whole)

tiny green peas

hash brown potatoes

Useful Extras

black-eyed peas

chopped broccoli/mustard greens/turnip greens

Southwestern-style corn with roasted peppers

O'Brien potatoes

snow pea pods

succotash

NOTE

EVEN THOUGH MANY VEGETA-BLES ARE NOW LABELED "WASHED," I WASH THEM AGAIN JUST BEFORE I USE THEM UNLESS THEY LOOK ESPECIALLY FRESH AND CLEAN. EASIEST FOR ME IS TO PLUNK THEM INTO A LARGE FINE-MESH SIEVE OR COLANDER, SET IN THE SINK, AND SPRAY WELL WITH COOL WATER. I SPIN-DRY THE GREENS, SHREDDED CARROTS, AND SLAW MIXES IN A SALAD SPINNER, THEN PAT DRY ON PAPER TOWEL-ING. MUSHROOMS SHOULD ALSO BE PATTED DRY—VERY DRY.

STORAGE TIPS FOR FROZEN FOODS

IN GENERAL

- Do not try to freeze or store food at less than 0°F.
- Keep a freezer thermometer handy and check freezer temperature from time to time.
- Never put hot food in a freezer.
- Never refreeze frozen food that has thawed.

COMMERCIAL FROZEN FOODS

- Transfer at once from shopping bags to freezing surface of 0°F. freezer and leave there several hours.
- If any packages were ripped in transit, overwrap in plastic food wrap, slip into plastic zipper bag, press out air, and seal.

HOME-FROZEN FOODS

- Always cool hot food before setting in freezer.
- Spoon cooled food into 1-pint or 1-quart freezer container, filling to within 1/2 inch of top.
- Snap on lids, label, date, and set on freezing surface of 0°F. freezer.
- When solidly frozen, move to upper freezer shelves.

FREEZING FRESH HERBS

1. Mince herbs, then spoon 1 tablespoon into each compartment of an ice cube tray, keeping different herbs separate.
2. Add 2 to 3 tablespoons water to each compartment and freeze.
3. Pop frozen "herb cubes" into plastic zipper bags, label, date, and store in freezer. Maximum storage time is 3 months.
4. To use, drop solidly frozen cubes into sauce, soup or stew, remembering that 1 cube = 1 tablespoon freshly chopped herb or 1 teaspoon dried herb.

FREEZING FRESH GINGER

1. Wrap unpeeled "hand" of ginger in plastic food wrap.
2. Slip into plastic zipper bag, press out air, seal, label, and date.
3. Store on freezer door shelf. Maximum storage time is 4 months.
4. To use, cut off the amount you need. A 1-inch square = 1 tablespoon minced ginger.

MAKE-AHEADS FOR THE FREEZER

Al Dente Make-Ahead Rice (page 35)
Soft Bread Crumbs (soft white/whole wheat/buttered/ seasoned) (page 36)
Fine Dry Bread Crumbs (plain/buttered/seasoned) (page 37)
Homemade Croutons (plain/buttered/seasoned) (page 39)
Dumpling/Biscuit Topping Mix (page 31)
Duxelles (mushroom paste) (page 33)
Basic Meatballs (page 29)
Basic Tomato Sauce (page 30)

TIME-SAVING KITCHEN EQUIPMENT

CUTLERY

Indispensables
paring knives
8-inch and 10-inch chopping knives
swivel-bladed vegetable peeler
rotary hand grater
Useful Extras
kitchen shears
12-inch chopping knife
serrated slicing knife
mandoline (for fast, uniform thick and thin slicing/grating)

ELECTRIC APPLIANCES

Indispensables

blender

can opener

citrus juicer

food processor

microwave oven (600 watts or more)

Useful Extras

electric coffee grinder (for grinding whole spices)

mini food processor

immersion blender (for pureeing soups and sauces in the pan)

MISCELLANEOUS

Indispensables

salad spinner

sieves (large and small fine-mesh for washing and draining herbs/pasta/vegetables)

Useful Extras

pasta pot with perforated inset to facilitate draining

RECIPES TO MAKE AHEAD AND KEEP "ON ICE"

Despite the huge array of fully and partially prepared foods available at every good grocery, I still like to make many items "from scratch" when I have a little extra time. I stash them in the refrigerator or freezer to use when time is short: bread crumbs and croutons, for example (far fresher tasting than the store-bought), meatballs from a favorite recipe, tomato sauce.

I also like to keep boiled rice and hard-cooked eggs on hand, both of which are endlessly versatile and help me get dinner on the table fast. I've even developed an accommodating mix that I can turn into toppings or dumplings in seconds.

The recipes that follow, then, are my freezer/refrigerator staples.

BASIC MEATBALLS

MAKES ABOUT 4 1/2 DOZEN (1-INCH) BALLS

I find I'm way ahead of the game if I have a supply of frozen meatballs on hand to pop into pasta sauces, soups, stews, and casseroles. This multi-purpose recipe has served me so well over the years. I often make triple batches of it. There's no need to thaw the meatballs before cooking them; in fact they'll hold together better if you don't.

MAXIMUM STORAGE TIME: 6 WEEKS IN 0°F FREEZER.

1 pound lean ground beef chuck
¼ pound fresh sweet Italian sausage, removed from casings
½ cup soft white bread crumbs
¼ cup milk
3 tablespoons freshly grated Parmesan cheese
2 tablespoons finely minced yellow onion

1 small garlic clove, minced
2 tablespoons minced fresh parsley
1 teaspoon dried marjoram, crumbled
½ teaspoon dried thyme, crumbled
¾ teaspoon salt
¼ teaspoon freshly ground black pepper

1. Mix all ingredients together with hands and shape into 1-inch balls.

2. Arrange, not touching, on foil-lined 12-inch pizza pan, set on freezing surface of 0°F. freezer, and freeze until firm.

3. Peel frozen meatballs off foil and bundle into large plastic zipper freezer bag; seal, date, and label. Store in 0°F. freezer and use as recipes direct.

BASIC TOMATO SAUCE

MAKES ABOUT 2 QUARTS

NOTE

I LIKE TO FREEZE THIS
SAUCE IN 1- OR 2-CUP
CONTAINERS—AMOUNTS
RECIPES ARE MOST LIKELY
TO CALL FOR.

An easy, all-round tomato sauce that can be made ahead of time—when you have time—and stored in the freezer. This is a singularly versatile tomato sauce, one that can be used in place of bottled marinara sauce or canned tomato sauce in any recipe in this book or, for that matter, in any favorite recipe of your own.

¼ cup extra-virgin olive oil
2 cups coarsely chopped yellow
    onions (about 2 medium-large
    onions)
2 large garlic cloves, minced
1 tablespoon dried basil,
    crumbled
2 teaspoons dried marjoram,
    crumbled

1 teaspoon rubbed sage
Two 28-ounce cans crushed
    tomatoes in tomato puree
One 8-ounce can tomato puree
    or sauce
1 cup dry white wine
1 teaspoon salt
½ teaspoon freshly ground
    black pepper

1. Heat oil in medium-size Dutch oven over moderate heat for 2 minutes. Add onions, garlic, basil, marjoram, and sage; reduce heat to moderately low and cook uncovered, stirring often, until soft and golden, 15 to 20 minutes. Do not brown or sauce will be bitter.

2. Add tomatoes, tomato puree, wine, salt, and pepper; adjust heat so mixture bubbles gently, cover, and simmer slowly, stirring occasionally, until flavors mellow and merge, 1 to 1½ hours. Taste for salt and pepper.

3. Cool sauce to room temperature, then ladle into 1- or 2-cup freezer containers, leaving ¾-inch head room. Snap on lids, label, and date. Store in 0°F. freezer and use as recipes direct.

DUMPLING/ BISCUIT TOPPING MIX

MAKES ABOUT 10 CUPS

A wonderfully versatile mix to have on hand because it can be used to top a variety of casseroles or to make featherweight dumplings. For each level 1 cup of mix, lightly fork in 4 to 6 tablespoons milk — just enough to make a soft dough. (Note: Because flours vary from one part of the country to another, from brand to brand, and even from season to season, you may find that it takes 8 or 9 tablespoons of milk to turn 1 cup of mix into a soft dough.) These proportions are good for dumplings and small casserole toppings (no more than 10 inches in diameter). For larger casseroles, double the amounts. Use this mix with your own favorite stews and casseroles or use as recipes in these pages direct.

One 2-pound bag (8 cups)
   sifted all-purpose flour
¼ cup baking powder
4 teaspoons salt
1 cup firmly packed vegetable
   shortening or lard (rendered
   hog fat), chilled well

½ cup (1 stick) unsalted butter
   (no substitute), chilled well
   and cut into slim pats

1. Pulse flour, baking powder, and salt briskly in large food processor to combine.

2. Add chilled shortening by teaspoonfuls, distributing evenly over dry ingredients, then drop in butter pats, again distributing evenly. Pulse briskly until texture of uncooked oatmeal.

3. Spoon into 2½-quart freezer or refrigerator container and snap on lid. Or spoon into jumbo zippered plastic freezer bag, press out all air, and seal. Label and date and store in freezer or in refrigerator.

continued

MAXIMUM FREEZER STORAGE TIME: 10 WEEKS. MAXIMUM REFRIGERATOR STORAGE TIME: 6 WEEKS.

NOTE

I BUZZ UP THE MIX IN SECONDS IN A LARGE, HEAVY-DUTY FOOD PROCESSOR. IF YOU HAVE A SMALLER MODEL, MAKE IN TWO BATCHES. AND IF YOU HAVE NO FOOD PROCESSOR, COMBINE ALL DRY INGREDIENTS IN A LARGE SHALLOW MIXING BOWL, ADD FAT, THEN CUT IN WITH A PASTRY BLENDER UNTIL THE TEXTURE OF COARSE MEAL.

TIPS

When preparing mix by food processor, cover work bowl with plastic food wrap before snapping lid into place. This way the floury ingredients won't fly all over the place. To quick-chill vegetable shortening, pack into a 1-cup metal measure, level off the top with the edge of a spatula, then set on the freezing surface of a 0°F. freezer for 20 to 30 minutes. Quick-chill butter by setting unwrapped stick in freezer.

For dumplings

Drop dough from a rounded teaspoon into gently bubbling liquid, spacing evenly, cover, and steam 15 minutes—no peeking!

For biscuit topping

Drop dough from rounded tablespoon on top of casserole ingredients, spacing evenly, then bake uncovered at 425°F. until puffed and tipped with brown, about 15 minutes.

DUXELLES (MUSHROOM PASTE)

MAKES 2 BUTTER-STICK-SIZE BARS (16 TABLESPOONS)

MAXIMUM STORAGE TIME: 3 MONTHS IN 0°F. FREEZER.

I make this rich mushroom paste with mushroom stems, which would normally be thrown away (but you can use whole fresh white mushrooms). The beauty of duxelles is that it can be frozen and dipped into as needed to flavor soups, stews, and sauces (including those used to bind casseroles). Several recipes in this book call for it. Because duxelles is so concentrated, one to two pats (tablespoons) are usually sufficient.

Stems from 2 pounds mushrooms (or 1 pound whole mushrooms), wiped clean and very finely minced

6 tablespoons unsalted butter

½ cup very finely minced yellow onion (about 1 medium-small yellow onion)

4 medium-size shallots or scallions (white part only), very finely minced

½ teaspoon salt

¼ teaspoon freshly ground black pepper

1. Bundle mushrooms in clean dry dish towel and wring as dry as possible; set aside.

2. Melt butter in medium-size heavy saucepan over moderately low heat, add onion and shallots, and cook, stirring often, until very soft and golden, about 10 minutes; do not allow to brown because duxelles will taste bitter.

3. Reduce heat to low, add mushrooms, and cook, stirring now and then, until very thick and pastelike, about 15 minutes. Mix in salt and pepper.

4. Shape half of duxelles on double thickness of foil into butterstick-size bar; wrap snugly. Repeat with remaining duxelles. Label, date, and set in 0°F. freezer.

5. To use, slice off ¾-inch pats (each equal to 1 tablespoon) and add to soups, sauces, casserole binders, and stews. Taste as you go and continue adding duxelles until flavor suits you.

HARD-COOKED EGGS

MAKES ½ DOZEN

So many casseroles and salads call for hard-cooked eggs I like to keep a supply of them on hand to shell and use as individual recipes specify. Cooked and stored this way, they won't develop that ugly green ring between the yolk and white.

6 extra-large eggs
Cold water to cover

1. Place eggs in large, heavy saucepan (preferably stainless steel or enameled metal; aluminum will discolor). Add enough cold water to cover eggs by 1 inch.

2. Set uncovered pan over moderate heat and bring water to boiling. Remove from heat the instant water begins to bubble, cover, and let eggs stand 20 minutes.

3. Drain eggs, plunge at once into ice water, and chill 5 minutes. Drain well.

4. Mark egg shells "HC" (for hard-cooked) and place unshelled eggs in small bowl. Slip bowl into large plastic storage bag (do not seal) and set in refrigerator.

MAXIMUM REFRIGERATOR STORAGE TIME: 7 days if eggs were very fresh, 3 to 5 if not.

TIP

IF YOU FORGET TO ID YOUR HARD-COOKED EGGS AND CAN'T TELL THEM FROM THE RAW, HERE'S A QUICK TEST: PLACE AN EGG ON ITS SIDE ON THE COUNTER AND GIVE IT A SPIN. IF IT SPINS NEATLY, IT'S RAW; IF IT WOBBLES, IT'S COOKED.

AL DENTE MAKE-AHEAD RICE

MAKES 16 CUPS

Many years ago I learned to cook rice ahead of time and stash it in refrigerator or freezer. The trick is to cook it just until al dente (firm-tender) so that the grains remain separate instead of clumping. Few staples are handier to have because cooked rice can be slipped—refrigerator cold, even solidly frozen—into casseroles, soups, salads, stews, and stir-fries. Then, too, it can be reheated and used as a backdrop for dozens of other recipes. This is the method I've evolved for cook-ahead rice. It continues to serve me well.

2 quarts water
4 cups uncooked converted
    white rice (no substitute)

1. Bring water to rapid boil in large (at least $4^{1}/_{2}$-quart), heavy saucepan over high heat.

2. Add rice, stir well, then return to rapid boil. Adjust heat so water stays at gentle but steady ripple and cook uncovered until all water is absorbed, about 20 minutes. Do not stir.

3. Fluff rice gently with fork and cool 1 hour. Do not cover.

4. Fluff rice gently again, then spoon lightly—do not pack—into plastic storage containers, snap on lids, label, and date. Set in refrigerator or freezer.

5. To reheat refrigerated or frozen rice, pile rice in large fine sieve, fork lightly apart, and balance sieve in top of large, heavy saucepan over 2 inches boiling water. Cover loosely with lid or foil and steam just until heated through, 3 to 5 minutes, but times will vary according to amount of rice being reheated and whether it's refrigerated or frozen. Fluff with fork and serve.

MAXIMUM REFRIGERATOR STORAGE TIME: 7 TO 10 DAYS. MAXIMUM FREEZER STORAGE TIME: 3 MONTHS.

NOTE

WHEN FREEZING RICE, USE 1- OR 2-CUP CONTAINERS SO IT'S EASIER TO WITHDRAW AMOUNTS YOU'RE MOST LIKELY TO NEED (FROZEN EN MASSE, RICE TENDS TO FORM A SOLID BRICK).

SOFT WHITE BREAD CRUMBS

Makes 6 cups

Maximum Storage Time: 3 months in 0°F. freezer for white bread crumbs, 2 months for whole wheat.

NOTE

If you don't have a food processor, stack the bread, three slices at a time, and rub endwise over the second coarsest side of a four-sided grater.

I bless my food processor every time I make bread crumbs because in seconds it can whiz chunks of bread as coarse or fine as I want. These crumbs are "medium," perfect for casserole toppings, for meatballs, and myriad other uses. Resist the temptation to add grated Parmesan or herbs to fresh crumbs—they'll only hasten the staling (not the case with dry crumbs; see page 37). I keep a big plastic zipper bag of fresh crumbs in my freezer so that I can dip into them as often as needed.

12 slices firm-textured white bread

1. Do not remove crusts. Tear bread into largish chunks directly into the work bowl of food processor fitted with metal chopping blade.

2. Pulse 6 to 8 times until crumbs are "medium"—not too coarse, not too fine.

3. Empty into large plastic zipper bag and press out all air. Seal, label, and date. Store in freezer and use as individual recipes direct.

VARIATIONS

Whole Wheat Bread Crumbs: Substitute firm-textured whole wheat bread for white.

Buttered Bread Crumbs: Place 1 cup solidly frozen crumbs (white or whole wheat) in food processor and briskly pulse in 1 tablespoon melted unsalted butter. Use at once. Makes 1 cup.

Garlic Bread Crumbs: Melt 2 tablespoons unsalted butter with 1 minced small garlic clove in butter warmer over low heat. Strain, then pulse melted butter briskly in food processor with 1 cup solidly frozen white bread crumbs. Use at once. Makes 1 cup.

Italian Bread Crumbs: Place 1 cup solidly frozen crumbs (white only) in food processor and quickly pulse in 2 tablespoons freshly grated Parmesan cheese, 1 tablespoon coarsely chopped Italian (flat-leaf) parsley, 1 tablespoon extra-virgin olive oil, and $^1/_2$ teaspoon crumbled dried oregano. Use at once. Makes about 1 cup.

Herbed Bread Crumbs: Place 1 cup solidly frozen crumbs (white or whole wheat) in food processor and briskly pulse in 1 tablespoon melted unsalted butter or extra-virgin olive oil, $^1/_2$ teaspoon crumbled dried oregano, and $^1/_4$ teaspoon crumbled dried thyme or rosemary (thyme for poultry recipes, rosemary for red meat). Use at once. Makes 1 cup.

FINE DRY BREAD CRUMBS

MAKES 3 TO 3$^1/_2$ CUPS

The crumbs you make yourself will always taste fresher than the commercially packaged, which may have been languishing on store shelves for months.

6 slices firm-textured white bread

1. Preheat oven to 300°F.

2. Arrange bread slices, not touching, on ungreased large baking sheet. Set on middle oven rack and toast until uniformly crisp and golden, 25 to 30 minutes.

3. Cool, break into small chunks, and pulse in food processor or electric blender until uniformly fine. Or place in plastic bag and crush with rolling pin or cutlet bat.

continued

IF YOU HAVE HOMEMADE CROUTONS (PAGE 39) ON HAND, THEY CAN BE BUZZED TO CRUMBS IN A JIFFY (1 CUP CROUTONS = $^1/_2$ CUP CRUMBS).

MAXIMUM STORAGE TIME FOR PLAIN BREAD CRUMBS: 3 MONTHS IN 0°F. FREEZER.

MAXIMUM STORAGE TIME FOR
HERBED BREAD CRUMBS:
6 WEEKS IN O°F. FREEZER,
4 WEEKS FOR ITALIAN BREAD
CRUMBS.

4. Empty into large plastic zipper bag and press out all air. Seal, label, and date. Store in O°F. freezer and use as directed.

VARIATIONS

Herbed Dry Bread Crumbs: Proceed as directed, but in step 3, pulse 2 teaspoons crumbled dried marjoram and $1/2$ teaspoon each dried crumbled rosemary and dried crumbled thyme along with chunks of bread. Package and freeze as directed.

Italian Dry Bread Crumbs: Proceed as directed, but in step 3, pulse $1/2$ cup freshly grated Parmesan cheese and 1 tablespoon crumbled dried oregano along with chunks of bread. Package and freeze as directed. Makes $3^1/2$ to 4 cups.

Buttered Dry Bread Crumbs: Place $1^1/2$ cups solidly frozen dry crumbs in food processor and briskly pulse in 1 tablespoon melted unsalted butter (or, if you like, substitute 1 tablespoon fruity extra-virgin olive oil for butter). Use at once. Makes $1^1/2$ cups.

HOMEMADE CROUTONS

MAKES ABOUT 4 CUPS

Store-bought croutons always taste rancid to me, especially flavored croutons. Making your own couldn't be easier.

8 slices firm-textured white bread

1. Preheat oven to 300°F.

2. Stack 4 slices bread, trim off and discard crusts, then with sharp serrated knife, make 5 vertical cuts straight through stacked slices, spacing about $1/2$ inch apart. Now make 5 cuts at right angles to vertical cuts, also spacing $1/2$ inch apart. Repeat with remaining 4 slices.

3. Spread croutons on ungreased large baking sheet. Set on middle oven rack and toast until uniformly crisp and golden, about 20 minutes, stirring well at half-time.

4. Cool, empty into plastic zipper bag, and press out all air. Seal, label, and date. Store in 0°F. freezer and use as directed.

VARIATIONS

Buttered Croutons: Prepare as directed, but brush 1 side of each slice of bread with melted unsalted butter (you'll need about 3 tablespoons) before stacking and cutting. Also reduce baking time to 15 minutes. Maximum Storage Time: 6 weeks.

Italian Croutons: Prepare as directed, but brush 1 side of each slice of bread with extra-virgin olive oil before stacking and cutting. Also reduce baking time to 15 minutes. Maximum Storage Time: 6 weeks.

Garlic Croutons: Melt $1/4$ cup unsalted butter or heat $1/4$ cup extra-virgin olive oil with 1 minced small garlic clove in butter warmer over low heat, 2 to 3 minutes. Strain, brush slices of bread. Also reduce baking time to 15 minutes. Maximum Storage Time: 4 weeks.

MAXIMUM STORAGE TIME FOR PLAIN CROUTONS: 3 MONTHS IN 0°F. FREEZER.

NOTE

SAVE BREAD TRIMMINGS, BUZZ TO SOFT CRUMBS, AND ADD TO YOUR STORE OF CRUMBS IN THE FREEZER.

MAIN-DISH SALADS

In the beginning, salads were a handy way to recycle roast meat and poultry, to dress up leftover fish, shellfish, and vegetables, even macaroni—bland combos bound with mayonnaise or gelatin. As for seasonings, minced onion was about as inventive as we got.

With the rise of the counterculture in the '60s and '70s, cooks became more creative (make that intrepid). Many had traveled to Europe, the Middle East, and beyond; they sampled salads unheard of here, then returned home to improvise.

Who knew tabbouleh before the 1970s? Or yogurt or orzo or lemongrass? Indeed, who knew extra-virgin olive oil, to say nothing of walnut, hazelnut, and roasted sesame seed oils?

In Grandmother's day, vinegar was either white (sharp distilled vinegar used for pickling) or brown (apple cider vinegar used for everything else). Then along came wine vinegars (red and white), herbal vinegars (with tarragon a particular favorite), fruit vinegars. Today's favorite? That mellow brown aged Italian grape vinegar known as balsamic.

In this new millennium, salads are no longer also-rans. They're the focal point of the meal, as carefully planned and prepared as a pricey piece of meat.

The collection of main-dish salads that follows is truly global, with nearly every continent represented. I haven't forsaken Grandma's best, however. But I have given them new life (check out the Macaroni and Cheese Salad and the Warm Hoppin' John Salad with Ham and Greens).

NOTE

THIS IS THE DISH TO MAKE
WHEN YOU HAVE LOTS OF
LEFTOVER RICE. SEE AL
DENTE MAKE-AHEAD RICE
(PAGE 35) FOR DIRECTIONS
ON COOKING RICE SPECIFI-
CALLY FOR FRIDGE OR
FREEZER.

WARM HOPPIN' JOHN SALAD WITH HAM AND GREENS

MAKES 4 SERVINGS

Down South it's considered good luck to eat hog jowl, black-eyed peas, and turnip greens on New Year's Day. I've assembled them all in a salad and taken some liberties with Southern tradition. Instead of hog jowl, I use ham. Instead of boiling the greens half the day with a chunk of fatback, I use frozen chopped greens and cook them only until tender. Finally, I dress the salad with olive oil and add a hefty dose of garlic. Many Southerners will consider this blasphemous; I think it's delicious.

FOR THE SALAD

2 tablespoons bacon or ham
    drippings
6 large scallions, trimmed and
    thinly sliced (include some
    green tops)
1 large garlic clove, minced
1 cup finely diced baked or
    boiled ham (about 4 ounces)

2 cups frozen chopped turnip
    greens or collards (do not
    thaw)
One 15½-ounce can black-eyed
    peas, drained and rinsed
3 cups leftover cooked rice, at
    room temperature (see Note)

FOR THE DRESSING

¼ cup extra-virgin olive oil
2½ tablespoons cider vinegar
1 teaspoon salt

½ teaspoon hot red pepper
    sauce
¼ teaspoon freshly ground
    black pepper

1. For the salad, heat the drippings in large, heavy skillet over moderate heat 1 minute. Add scallions and garlic and cook, stirring often, just until limp, about 2 minutes. Add ham and cook until lightly golden, 3 to 4 minutes. Add greens and cook, stirring frequently just until tender, 3 to 4 minutes.

2. Dump skillet mixture into large bowl, add black-eyed peas and rice, and toss lightly.

3. For the dressing, bring all ingredients to a boil in same skillet, scraping up browned bits.

4. Pour dressing over salad, toss well, and let stand at room temperature 10 to 15 minutes to mellow flavors. Toss again and serve.

MACARONI AND CHEESE SALAD

MAKES 6 SERVINGS

An old favorite family casserole in a new guise. Have all ingredients prepped and measured at the outset, and this hearty salad goes together at the speed of light.

FOR THE SALAD

½ pound elbow macaroni, cooked al dente by package directions and drained

½ pound sharp Cheddar cheese, cut into ½-inch dice

One 10-ounce package frozen tiny green peas, thawed and drained

FOR THE DRESSING

¾ cup mayonnaise (use light, if you like)

¾ cup sour cream (use light, if you like)

1 medium-size lemon, juiced

½ cup freshly grated Parmesan cheese

1½ tablespoons minced fresh tarragon or 2 teaspoons dried tarragon, crumbled

½ teaspoon salt

½ teaspoon freshly ground black pepper

½ teaspoon hot red pepper sauce

1. For the salad, place all ingredients in large bowl and toss lightly.

2. For the dressing, whisk all ingredients together, pour over salad, and toss well.

3. Let stand at room temperature 15 to 20 minutes, toss again, and serve.

VARIATIONS

Ham and Macaroni Salad: Prepare as directed, substituting ½ pound finely diced baked or boiled ham for cheese. In dressing, use ½ cup relish/mayonnaise sandwich spread and ¼ cup mayonnaise instead of ¾ cup mayonnaise; also substitute 2 tablespoons freshly snipped dill or 1 teaspoon dill weed for tarragon and add 1 tablespoon Dijon mustard. All other dressing ingredients remain the same.

Shrimp and Macaroni Salad: Prepare Ham and Macaroni Salad as directed, substituting ½ pound fresh or thawed, frozen "salad shrimp" (cooked, shelled, and deveined small shrimp) for ham. Also, if you like, omit green peas and add 1 ½ cups blanched small fresh broccoli florets or asparagus tips. In dressing, omit Parmesan and mustard, using ½ cup each relish/mayonnaise sandwich spread and mayonnaise. Finally, add ¼ cup each ketchup and well-drained small capers and 2 teaspoons prepared horseradish. All other dressing ingredients remain the same as for Ham and Macaroni Salad.

Shrimp, Artichoke, and Macaroni Salad: Prepare Shrimp and Macaroni Salad as directed, substituting two well-drained 6 ½-ounce jars marinated, quartered artichoke hearts for green peas (or broccoli or asparagus). In dressing, reduce ketchup to 2 tablespoons and horseradish to 1 teaspoon. All other dressing ingredients remain the same as for Shrimp and Macaroni Salad.

PASTA, BROCCOLI, AND RED PEPPER SALAD WITH LEMON-GINGER DRESSING

There's a bit of chopping and slicing here, still this is a fast and winning one-dish dinner. If you have everything ready, this salad will go together even faster.

FOR THE SALAD

1 cup diced red bell pepper (about 1 medium-large)

4 large scallions, trimmed and thinly sliced (include some green tops)

2 tablespoons peanut or vegetable oil

1 tablespoon Asian roasted sesame oil

2 pounds broccoli, trimmed of stems and divided into small florets

1/3 cup pine nuts, toasted (see Note)

3 cups small shell pasta, cooked al dente by package directions and drained well

4 ounces feta cheese or ricotta salata, coarsely crumbled

FOR THE DRESSING

1 large garlic clove, halved (finely minced if whisking dressing by hand)

One 1/2-inch piece fresh ginger, peeled and halved (finely minced if whisking dressing by hand)

1 teaspoon sugar

1/2 teaspoon dried marjoram, crumbled

1/2 teaspoon dried basil, crumbled

1/2 teaspoon salt

1/2 teaspoon hot red pepper sauce

1/4 cup peanut or vegetable oil, or more as needed

2 tablespoons Asian roasted sesame oil

1/4 cup fresh lemon juice

1. For the salad, place bell pepper and scallions in large salad bowl and set aside. Heat peanut oil in large, heavy skillet over high heat 2

minutes. Add sesame oil and broccoli and cook, stirring, just until crisp-tender, 3 to 5 minutes. Dump into salad bowl and add all remaining ingredients except feta cheese. Toss lightly.

2. Churn all dressing ingredients together in food processor or electric blender (or whisk vigorously by hand) until smooth.

3. Add feta cheese to salad, drizzle dressing over all, and toss well; let stand at room temperature 15 to 20 minutes and toss again. If mixture seems dry, add 1 to 2 tablespoons additional peanut oil, and toss. Also taste for salt, fine-tune seasonings, and serve.

NOTE

FOR ME, TOASTED PINE NUTS ARE A STAPLE I KEEP IN THE FREEZER. THE EASIEST WAY TO TOAST THEM IS TO SPREAD IN A PIE PAN, THEN SET UNCOVERED IN A 300°F. OVEN FOR 12 TO 15 MINUTES; STIR OCCASIONALLY.

AVOCADO, BLACK BEAN, AND TOMATO SALAD

MAKES 4 SERVINGS

Take advantage of the salad green mixes now available in most super-markets. But wash and spin them dry before using.

2 tablespoons fresh lime juice
3 tablespoons extra-virgin
  olive oil
2 large scallions, trimmed and
  finely chopped (include some
  green tops)
1 large garlic clove, minced
1 firm-ripe Haas avocado,
  peeled, pitted, and diced
One 15 ½-ounce can black
  beans, rinsed and drained
One 10-ounce can diced
  tomatoes with green chilies,
  drained well

½ teaspoon salt
¼ cup coarsely chopped fresh
  cilantro
¼ cup coarsely chopped fresh
  Italian (flat-leaf) parsley
One 10-ounce bag European
  salad mix (iceberg, romaine,
  escarole, endive, and
  radicchio)

1. Whisk lime juice, olive oil, scallions, and garlic in large bowl until "creamy." Add avocado and toss lightly.

2. Add beans, tomatoes with green chilies, and salt. Toss lightly again and let stand at room temperature 20 minutes to combine flavors. Taste for salt and adjust as needed.

3. Add cilantro and parsley, toss again, and let stand 5 minutes. Meanwhile, bed greens on large deep platter.

4. Spoon bean mixture on top of salad mix and serve.

ROMAINE AND RAVIOLI SALAD WITH ANCHOVY-LEMON DRESSING

Makes 4 to 6 servings

TIP

Make the dressing first so that its flavors have a chance to mellow while you proceed with the salad.

Fresh refrigerated pastas now stocked by every supermarket are hugely versatile. Why not, for example, use them to boost a crisp green salad into the main-dish category? This one is reminiscent of the classic Caesar salad. But ravioli substitutes for croutons and crisp bacon crumbles (real bacon), a new entry at the meat counter, add additional crunch. To save on prep time, I pick up a bag of ready-to-use romaine at the produce counter.

For the dressing
3 tablespoons fresh lemon juice
2 teaspoons anchovy paste
1 teaspoon Worcestershire
  sauce
1 small garlic clove, finely
  minced

1/4 teaspoon salt
1/4 teaspoon freshly ground
  black pepper
1/3 cup extra-virgin olive oil
  (the fruitiest you can find)

For the salad
6 cups bite-size pieces romaine
One 9-ounce package four-
  cheese ravioli, cooked al
  dente by package directions,
  drained well, and patted dry

1/3 cup packaged crumbled
  cooked bacon (see headnote
  above)
1/4 cup freshly grated Romano
  or Parmesan cheese

1. For the dressing, whisk together lemon juice, anchovy paste, Worcestershire sauce, garlic, salt, and pepper in large salad bowl. Drizzle in oil, whisking hard, until creamy.

2. For the salad, add romaine, ravioli, and bacon to bowl and toss gently but thoroughly with dressing.

3. Sprinkle with cheese and toss again. Taste for salt, pepper, and olive oil, adjust as needed, and serve.

EASY SKILLET SALAD WITH ITALIAN SAUSAGE AND VEGETABLES

A terrific way to use up leftover corn and green beans. If you have none, no problem. Simply reach into the freezer and scoop up one cup each of frozen whole-kernel corn and cut green beans. You can even use canned corn and beans—the 8-ounce can is about right, but drain well. As for the rice, I keep on hand a supply of Al Dente Make-Ahead Rice. For the lettuce, I use packaged, washed romaine hearts.

3 sweet Italian turkey sausages, casings removed (about 6 ounces)

2 large scallions, trimmed and thinly sliced (include some green tops)

1 cup whole-kernel corn (leftover cooked, thawed frozen, or drained canned)

2 cups Al Dente Make-Ahead Rice (page 35)

1 cup green beans (leftover cooked, thawed frozen, or drained canned)

One 10-ounce can diced tomatoes with green chilies, drained

1 medium-size romaine heart, sliced crosswise at 1/2-inch intervals

6 tablespoons extra-virgin olive oil

1/4 cup cider vinegar or red wine vinegar

1 small garlic clove, finely minced

1/2 teaspoon salt

1/4 teaspoon freshly ground black pepper

1/3 cup coarsely chopped Italian (flat-leaf) parsley

1. Crumble sausage into large, heavy skillet, set over moderately high heat and cook, stirring often, until nicely browned, 3 to 5 minutes.

2. Add scallions, corn, and rice and cook, stirring often, until heated through, about 3 minutes. Dump skillet mixture into large

heatproof salad bowl along with green beans, tomatoes with chilies, and romaine.

3. Add olive oil, vinegar, garlic, salt, and pepper to skillet and bring to boiling, whisking constantly.

4. Pour over salad, add parsley, and toss well. Taste for salt, pepper, and vinegar, adjust as needed, and serve.

NOTE

IF YOU SHOULD HAVE LEFT-OVER WILD RICE ON HAND, OR BULGUR, SUBSTITUTE MEASURE-FOR-MEASURE FOR WHITE RICE.

NOTE

Ricotta salata is a semi-hard, aged Sicilian sheep cheese. Most high-end groceries and specialty food shops carry it. The best substitute: feta, although it's saltier.

ROASTED ROOT VEGETABLE SALAD WITH COLLARDS AND RICOTTA SALATA

Makes 4 to 6 servings

Nothing improves the flavor of vegetables like a stint in a hot oven. This salad can be enjoyed as is. But since it also takes kindly to leftovers, 1½ to 2 cups diced roast meat or poultry, baked ham, even leftover boiled or grilled shrimp can be substituted for cheese.

For the salad

- 2 tablespoons extra-virgin olive oil
- 2 cups peeled baby-cut fresh carrots, halved crosswise
- 1 medium-size red onion (about ½ pound), cut into 1-inch chunks
- 10 large garlic cloves, halved lengthwise
- 1 pound golfball-size red-skin potatoes, quartered but not peeled
- 1 small celeriac (celery root; about ½ pound), trimmed, peeled, and cut into ¾-inch cubes
- Two 3-inch sprigs fresh rosemary or ½ teaspoon dried rosemary, crumbled
- 1 teaspoon salt
- ¼ teaspoon freshly ground black pepper
- 8 ounces (half package) frozen chopped collards or turnip greens, thawed and drained well
- 6 ounces ricotta salata or feta cheese, coarsely crumbled

For the dressing

- ⅓ cup extra-virgin olive oil
- 2 tablespoons fresh lemon juice
- 2 tablespoons balsamic vinegar
- 1 tablespoon honey
- ½ teaspoon salt
- ¼ teaspoon freshly ground black pepper

1. For the salad, preheat oven to 450°F. Place oil, carrots, onion, garlic, potatoes, celeriac, rosemary, salt, and pepper in large, shallow roasting pan. Toss well and roast uncovered, stirring now and then, until vegetables are firm-tender, 35 to 40 minutes. Meanwhile, place collards in large heatproof bowl; set aside.

2. For the dressing, when root vegetables are nearly done, bring all dressing ingredients to boiling in small nonreactive pan and pour over collards.

3. Dump in roasted root vegetables, remove rosemary sprigs, and toss well.

4. Sprinkle crumbled cheese on top, toss, taste for salt and pepper, and adjust as needed. Toss well again and serve.

TIPS

IF YOU HALVE GARLIC CLOVES LENGTHWISE BEFORE YOU PEEL THEM, THE SKINS WILL SLIP RIGHT OFF. CELERIAC IS A ROOT FULL OF BUMPS AND CREVICES AND, UNLESS YOU KNOW HOW, THE VERY DEVIL TO PEEL.

HERE'S THE TRICK: WITH YOUR SHARPEST CHEF'S KNIFE, SLICE OFF TOP AND BOTTOM, STAND CELERIAC ON A CUTTING BOARD, AND CUT FROM TOP TO BOTTOM, FOLLOWING THE CURVATURE OF THE ROOT AND REMOVING ALL WARTS AND SKIN.

THE EASIEST WAY TO THAW FROZEN CHOPPED COLLARDS (OR OTHER GREENS) IS TO PLACE IN A LARGE FINE-MESH SIEVE AND SET UNDER THE HOT WATER TAP; DRAIN WELL AFTER THAWING. FINALLY, IF YOU CAN'T FIND GOLFBALL-SIZE RED-SKIN POTATOES, USE LARGER RED-SKINS AND CUT INTO 1/2-INCH CHUNKS. DON'T PEEL—THE SKINS ADD COLOR AND FLAVOR.

Use only Parmigiano-
Reggiano for the Parme-
san curls; only it has
the proper nutty flavor.
The fastest way to make
curls: Draw a swivel-
bladed vegetable peeler
across a ¾-inch-thick
wedge of cheese.
The dressing can be
buzzed up in a food
processor or electric
blender a day or two
ahead and stored in the
refrigerator. If you have
neither processor nor
blender, mince the garlic
fine, then whisk with
remaining ingredients
until smooth and creamy.

NOTE

This recipe needs no salt.

PUMPED-UP CAESAR SALAD

Makes 6 servings

To make this a satisfying meal, I've added hard-cooked egg, two cups Parmesan curls, and twice the amount of croutons. I prefer croutons that I've made and stored in the freezer (see Homemade Croutons, page 39) because the store-bought usually taste stale. I also like to keep hard-cooked eggs in the fridge (see page 34 for directions on hard-cooking eggs perfectly). Hard-cooked eggs make the salad safe, as does adding thawed frozen egg product to the dressing. The original Caesar salad, created in the 1920s by Tijuana restaurateur Caesar Cardini, called for softly coddled eggs—risky in this age of salmonella.

FOR THE DRESSING
1 garlic clove, halved (finely minced if whisking dressing by hand)
2 teaspoons anchovy paste
⅓ cup extra-virgin olive oil
¼ cup thawed frozen egg product

Juice of 1 medium-size lemon
1 tablespoon freshly grated Parmesan cheese
1 teaspoon Worcestershire sauce
¼ teaspoon freshly ground black pepper

FOR THE SALAD
One 10-ounce package hearts of romaine salad mix, washed and spun dry, or 9 to 10 cups broken romaine leaves

3 cups plain croutons
2 hard-cooked extra-large eggs, peeled and finely chopped
2 cups Parmesan cheese curls (measure loosely packed)

1. For the dressing, churn all ingredients in food processor or electric blender until smooth (or whisk in small bowl until creamy); set aside.

2. For the salad, place romaine, croutons, and eggs in very large salad bowl, add dressing, and toss well. Add cheese curls, toss lightly, and serve.

ALL-ARUGULA SALAD WITH TWO CHEESES AND GARLIC CROUTONS

Makes 2 servings

With four cups of greens per person, this jiffy tossed salad is a nourishing, satisfying meal.

1 large garlic clove, smashed
8 cups arugula (measure loosely packed), washed and spun dry
1 cup Garlic Croutons (page 39)
2 ounces ricotta salata or feta cheese, moderately finely crumbled
⅓ cup freshly grated Parmesan cheese

1 tablespoon finely chopped fresh basil or 1 teaspoon dried basil, crumbled
½ teaspoon dried marjoram, crumbled
⅛ teaspoon freshly ground black pepper
¼ cup extra-virgin olive oil
2 tablespoons balsamic vinegar

1. Rub large salad bowl well with garlic, then discard any garlic pieces.

2. Pile arugula, croutons, ricotta salata, and Parmesan in bowl. Sprinkle with basil, marjoram, and pepper and toss lightly.

3. Drizzle olive oil evenly over all and toss lightly. If every leaf doesn't glisten, add 1 to 2 more tablespoons oil and toss gently again.

4. Drizzle vinegar evenly over salad and toss once again. Taste for pepper and vinegar, adjust as needed, toss lightly, and serve.

Note: The salad will be better if the croutons have been made with extra-virgin olive oil instead of butter. But those made with butter are perfectly acceptable. Because of the saltiness of the cheeses, this recipe needs no salt.

TIP

To save last-minute prep, I prepare a huge batch of greens ahead of time (whenever I have time) and store in the fridge so all I need do is reach in at the last minute and retrieve whatever I need. Here's my method: Wash an assortment of greens—keeping types separate—in several changes of lightly salted cool water, spin dry, then layer in a large plastic bag between double sheets of paper toweling. Again, keep the different greens separate. This way it's easy to make an all-arugula salad or an all-romaine one. Press air from bag, fold top over, and set in refrigerator. Stored thus, greens will stay crisp for a week or more.

SALAD OF ARUGULA, PORTOBELLOS, PROSCIUTTO, AND PARMESAN

MAKES 4 SERVINGS

On a sultry night a giant green salad plumped with mushrooms, ham, and cheese is filling and refreshing. Many supermarkets sell washed and trimmed arugula. If it looks fresh, by all means buy it and save yourself the job of trimming it, but give it a quick wash and spin dry in a salad spinner.

4 cups crisp young arugula leaves, washed well and spun or patted dry

4 cups baby spinach leaves, washed well and spun or patted dry

1/4 cup extra-virgin olive oil

3 large scallions, trimmed and thinly sliced (include some green tops)

One 6-ounce package portobello mushroom slices, coarsely chopped

1/2 teaspoon minced fresh lemon thyme or 1/4 teaspoon dried thyme, crumbled

1/2 cup finely julienned prosciutto

2 tablespoons fresh lemon juice

1 tablespoon balsamic vinegar

1/2 teaspoon salt

1/4 teaspoon freshly ground black pepper

1 cup Parmesan cheese curls

1. Pile arugula and spinach in large bowl and set aside.

2. Heat oil in a skillet over moderate heat for 1 minute. Add scallions, mushrooms, and thyme and cook, stirring, until mushrooms give up their juices and these evaporate, 5 to 8 minutes.

3. Add prosciutto, lemon juice, vinegar, salt, and pepper. Heat just until mixture steams, 1 to 2 minutes. Pour over arugula and spinach and toss well.

4. Add cheese curls and toss lightly. Taste for salt and pepper, adjust as needed, and serve.

MIDDLE EASTERN SALAD WITH CRACKLY BREAD AND YOGURT-MINT DRESSING

I've enjoyed salads like this throughout Greece, Turkey, Lebanon, Israel, and Jordan and few are more sustaining, colorful, or refreshing. For proper crunch, use Armenian flat bread, bagel crisps, toasted pita bread or, if you can find them, "Crak'ets"—shatteringly crisp shavings of oven-baked bread.

FOR THE DRESSING
1 cup plain yogurt
3 tablespoons extra-virgin
   olive oil
3 tablespoons coarsely chopped
   fresh mint
2 tablespoons minced Italian
   (flat-leaf) parsley

1 tablespoon fresh lemon juice
1 small garlic clove, finely
   minced
Salt and freshly ground black
   pepper to taste

FOR THE SALAD
One 10-ounce bag Italian salad
   mix (romaine and radicchio),
   washed and spun dry
One 4-inch Kirby cucumber,
   peeled, seeded, and diced
2 medium-size Italian plum
   (Roma) tomatoes, peeled,
   cored, seeded, and diced

4 large scallions, trimmed and
   thinly sliced (include some
   green tops)
4 ounces feta cheese, crumbled
4 cups (1-inch pieces) Armenian
   flat bread, toasted pita, bagel
   crisps, or "Crak'ets"
   (see headnote above)

1. For the dressing, whisk together all ingredients and set aside.

2. For the salad, place all ingredients except bread in large salad bowl, add 3/4 cup dressing, toss well, and let stand 10 minutes.

3. Add bread and remaining dressing, toss gently, and serve.

GREEK CHICKPEA SALAD WITH OLIVES, TOMATOES, AND MINT

Makes 4 to 6 servings

A filling salad that puts sunny Mediterranean flavors in a single bowl. The olives I use are the plump purple-black Kalamatas, which can be bought already pitted. I also like to bed the salad on thinly sliced romaine. Packages of trimmed romaine hearts are now sold at most supermarkets and they're terrific time-savers—if they look really crisp, clean, and fresh I don't bother to wash them.

FOR THE DRESSING

5 tablespoons extra-virgin olive oil (the fruitiest you can find)
1 tablespoon fresh lemon juice
1 tablespoon red or white wine vinegar
1 small garlic clove (whole if using mini processor, minced if not)

½ teaspoon dried oregano (preferably Greek), crumbled
½ teaspoon finely grated lemon zest (if using mini processor, use 1-inch strip zest)
1 teaspoon salt
¼ teaspoon freshly ground black pepper

FOR THE SALAD

Two 1-pound 3-ounce cans chickpeas, drained and rinsed
2 Italian plum (Roma) tomatoes, cored, seeded, and diced
One 4-inch Kirby cucumber, peeled, seeded, and diced
2 ounces feta cheese, coarsely crumbled
½ cup coarsely chopped red onion (about 1 medium)

¼ cup coarsely chopped, pitted, oil-packed black olives (preferably Kalamatas)
¼ cup coarsely chopped Italian (flat-leaf) parsley
¼ cup coarsely chopped fresh mint
4 to 6 cups finely sliced romaine lettuce

1. For the dressing, place all ingredients in mini food processor, electric blender, or 2-cup measure and churn or whisk until well blended; set aside.

2. For the salad, place all ingredients except romaine in large bowl. Churn or whisk dressing briskly, drizzle over salad, and toss well to mix. Let stand at room temperature 20 minutes. Taste for salt and pepper and adjust as needed.

3. Arrange 1 cup sliced romaine on each of 4 to 6 salad plates. Toss salad well, mound on romaine, and serve.

VARIATION

Southwestern Red Bean Salad: Prepare dressing as directed, substituting 2 tablespoons vegetable oil blended with 2 tablespoons bacon drippings for olive oil and 2 tablespoons fresh lime juice for lemon juice and vinegar. Also add $1/4$ teaspoon ground cumin. In salad, substitute two 15 $1/2$-ounce drained and rinsed cans red kidney beans for chickpeas; one 10-ounce well-drained can diced tomatoes with green chilies for plum tomatoes; 1 chopped, cored, and seeded small green bell pepper for cucumber; $1/2$ cup finely diced cooked ham or crumbled crisp bacon for feta cheese; and $1/4$ cup chopped fresh cilantro for mint. Omit olives.

TABBOULEH WITH TOASTED WALNUTS AND FETA

Makes 4 to 6 servings

To toast walnuts, spread in pie tin, then set in preheated 325°F. oven for 10 to 12 minutes until they brown lightly and smell irresistible. But watch—nuts burn easily. Shortcut: Measure ½ cup each basil and parsley leaves, then ¼ cup mint leaves (all loosely packed), and pulse together in food processor until coarsely chopped.

¼ cup extra-virgin olive oil (the fruitiest you can find)

5 medium-size scallions, trimmed and coarsely chopped (include some green tops)

1 large garlic clove, finely minced

1¾ cups bulgur

Two 14½-ounce cans chicken broth

½ cup coarsely chopped toasted walnuts (see headnote above)

2 medium-size red-ripe tomatoes, cored, juiced, and coarsely diced

3 ounces feta cheese, coarsely crumbled

½ cup coarsely chopped fresh basil

½ cup coarsely chopped Italian (flat-leaf) parsley

¼ cup coarsely chopped fresh mint

½ teaspoon salt

¼ teaspoon freshly ground black pepper

Juice of 1 lime

1 small bunch arugula or watercress, washed, stemmed, and patted dry (optional)

1. Heat olive oil in large, heavy saucepan over moderate heat for 2 minutes. Add scallions and cook, stirring, until limp and golden, about 3 minutes. Add garlic and cook, stirring, for 1 minute.

2. Add bulgur and stir 1 minute to glaze. Add broth, bring to boiling, then adjust heat so mixture barely bubbles, cover, and cook until all liquid is absorbed, about 15 minutes.

3. Meanwhile, place all remaining ingredients except lime juice and arugula, if using, in large heatproof bowl; do not toss.

4. As soon as bulgur is done, fluff with fork, dump on top of ingredients in bowl, drizzle in lime juice, and toss well. Taste for salt and pepper and adjust as needed. Let stand 15 minutes, then serve, if desired, on beds of arugula.

TACO SALAD

MAKES 6 SERVINGS

Without my refrigerator bank of chopped onion, garlic, and green bell pepper, I'd never attempt this salad: too much last-minute chopping. Whenever I'm in a yank, I even resort to diced canned tomatoes (preferably ones with diced green chilies mixed in) in place of fresh tomatoes. To save even more time, I use packaged shredded jack cheese and ready-to-go romaine hearts—half of one is sufficient. These couldn't be easier to shred: Lay a romaine heart on its side and with a chef's knife, slice crosswise at 1/4-inch intervals.

1/3 cup corn or vegetable oil
Six 6-inch flour tortillas
1 pound lean ground beef chuck
1 teaspoon salt
2 cups fresh or frozen chopped onions (about 2 medium-large yellow onions)
3/4 cup finely diced green bell pepper (about 1 medium)
1 large garlic clove, minced
2 teaspoons chili powder
1 teaspoon dried oregano, crumbled
1/4 teaspoon ground cumin
1/4 teaspoon ground hot red pepper (cayenne)
2 tablespoons ketchup or chili sauce

One 14 1/2-ounce can red kidney beans, drained and rinsed, then half the beans mashed with a potato masher
1/2 cup coarsely chopped fresh cilantro or Italian (flat-leaf) parsley
4 firm-ripe Italian plum (Roma) tomatoes, cored, seeded, and diced (no need to peel), or two 10-ounce cans diced tomatoes with green chilies, well drained
2 cups coarsely shredded romaine (about 1/2 romaine heart; see headnote above)
1 cup finely shredded Monterey jack or sharp Cheddar cheese

1. Preheat oven to its keep-warm setting (150°–200°F.). Line large baking sheet with baking parchment and set aside.

2. Heat oil in large, heavy skillet over high heat 2 minutes. One by one, add tortillas and fry until crisp and lightly browned, 10 to 15

seconds per side. Lift to baking sheet and set uncovered in oven. Pour drippings from skillet, then spoon 2 tablespoons back in.

3. Add beef to skillet, sprinkle with salt, and cook over moderate heat, breaking up large clumps, until no longer pink, about 5 minutes. Add onions, green pepper, garlic, chili powder, oregano, cumin, and cayenne and cook, stirring now and then, for 10 minutes.

4. Mix in ketchup and beans, cover, and simmer over low heat 10 minutes. Stir in cilantro. Taste for salt.

5. To assemble, arrange tortillas on colorful 15- to 18-inch round platter, overlapping as needed. Spoon hot meat mixture on top, then scatter with tomatoes, romaine, and cheese, distributing evenly but letting each layer show around the edge. Serve at once.

TIP

THE MEAT MIXTURE CAN BE MADE A DAY OR TWO AHEAD OF TIME, THEN REHEATED JUST BEFORE SERVING. THIS IS AN ADDITIONAL TIME-SAVER IF YOU PLAN TO SERVE THE SALAD AT A PARTY—A TERRIFIC IDEA BECAUSE THIS ONE'S A SHOW-STOPPER.

THAI BEEF SALAD

MAKES 4 SERVINGS

If you can find fresh lemongrass, by all means use it ___ pe. Otherwise, substitute finely grated lemon zest.

FOR THE SALAD

¾ pound roast beef (from the deli counter), thinly sliced

One 10-ounce bag European salad mix (iceberg, romaine, escarole, endive, and radicchio)

One 14-ounce can bean sprouts, well drained

One 10-ounce can diced tomatoes with green chilies, well drained

½ cup coarsely chopped fresh basil (no substitute; measure loosely packed)

FOR THE DRESSING

2 tablespoons vegetable oil

2 tablespoons Asian roasted sesame oil

2 tablespoons soy sauce

1 large garlic clove, finely minced

1 tablespoon minced fresh lemongrass or 1 teaspoon finely grated lemon zest

1 tablespoon minced fresh ginger

½ cup chicken broth

3 tablespoons fresh lemon juice

¼ teaspoon freshly ground black pepper

Salt to taste

1. Place all salad ingredients in large bowl, toss lightly, and set aside.

2. For the dressing, whisk vegetable and sesame oils, soy sauce, garlic, lemongrass, and ginger briskly in a bowl until creamy. Add broth, lemon juice, and pepper and again whisk until creamy.

3. Drizzle dressing over salad and toss gently. Taste for salt, adjust as needed, and serve.

VARIATION

Thai Shrimp Salad: Prepare as directed, substituting ¾ pound cooked shelled and deveined medium-size shrimp for beef.

SANDY'S MEXICAN PORK SALAD

MAKES 4 SERVINGS

My friend Sandy Gluck, a working mom with a son entering his teens, says this is the kind of jiffy meal Nate loves. Sandy loves it, too, because it can be tossed together out of staples, leftovers, or deli takeout. Also because it takes well to improvisation. Substitute white or black beans for red. Toss in a cup of cooked or canned whole-kernel corn.

⅓ cup bottled mild to medium salsa

2 tablespoons extra-virgin olive oil

1 tablespoon red wine vinegar

½ teaspoon salt

2 cups (½-inch-wide) strips leftover roast pork loin, tenderloin, or shoulder (about 12 ounces)

2 roasted red bell peppers (see Note), cut into ½-inch-wide strips

2 medium-size tomatoes, each cored and cut into 8 wedges

1 cup cooked or canned red beans, drained

1 cup diced cooked sweet potato (about 1 small)

4 cups torn lettuce, washed and spun dry (use packaged shredded romaine, if you like)

1. Whisk together salsa, oil, vinegar, and salt in large bowl.

2. Add pork, peppers, tomatoes, beans, and sweet potato and toss to mix. Taste for salt and fine-tune as needed.

3. Add lettuce and toss well again. Divide evenly among four dinner plates and serve.

NOTE

If you'd like to roast your own peppers for this recipe instead of using the bottled, here's how Sandy does it: Lay peppers on sides on foil-lined baking sheet and broil 4 to 6 inches from heat for 8 to 10 minutes, turning with tongs until evenly charred. Cover with foil and let stand 20 minutes. Slip off skins, core, and seed.

CHICKEN (OR TURKEY) AND RICE SALAD WITH PESTO DRESSING

Makes 6 servings

If you don't have leftover chicken in the fridge, buy a deli or rotisserie chicken. This is also the recipe to make when you have cooked rice on hand (see Al Dente Make-Ahead Rice, page 35).

FOR THE SALAD

2 cups diced cooked chicken or turkey (light meat and dark)

3 cups leftover cooked rice, at room temperature

3 large scallions, trimmed and coarsely chopped (include some green tops)

½ cup pine nuts, lightly toasted (see Note page 47 for how to toast pine nuts)

FOR THE DRESSING

1 cup firmly packed fresh basil leaves

¼ cup extra-virgin olive oil

1 large garlic clove, halved

2 tablespoons pine nuts, lightly toasted

2 tablespoons freshly grated Parmesan cheese

1 teaspoon salt

¼ teaspoon freshly ground black pepper

4 to 5 tablespoons fresh lemon juice

1. Place all salad ingredients in large bowl, toss well, and set aside.

2. Churn all dressing ingredients with 4 tablespoons lemon juice in food processor or electric blender until smooth.

3. Pour dressing over salad, toss, and let stand 20 minutes. Taste, and if bland, add 1 more tablespoon lemon juice. Also add 1 to 2 tablespoons olive oil if salad seems dry. Toss again and serve.

BARBECUED CHICKEN AND WHITE BEAN SALAD

MAKES 6 SERVINGS

A splendid make-ahead. Cover and chill until 1 hour before serving, then let stand at room temperature.

2 tablespoons extra-virgin olive oil

2 tablespoons fresh lemon juice

1 tablespoon Dijon mustard

1 tablespoon ketchup or bottled barbecue sauce

1 teaspoon finely grated lemon zest

1 teaspoon dried oregano, crumbled

½ teaspoon dried thyme, crumbled

½ teaspoon ground cumin

½ teaspoon salt

¼ teaspoon ground hot red pepper (cayenne)

¼ teaspoon freshly ground black pepper

One 3-pound barbecued chicken (from the deli counter), boned and diced

Two 15½-ounce cans white beans, rinsed and drained well

1 medium-size red-ripe tomato, cored, seeded, and diced

4 medium-size scallions, trimmed and thinly sliced (include some green tops)

¼ cup coarsely chopped fresh cilantro

1. Whisk olive oil briskly with lemon juice, mustard, ketchup, lemon zest, oregano, thyme, cumin, salt, and red and black peppers in a large bowl until well blended.

2. Add remaining ingredients and toss well. Let stand 30 minutes at room temperature, toss well again, and serve.

MADRAS-STYLE CHICKEN AND SWEET POTATO SALAD

MAKES 6 SERVINGS

This curried chicken and sweet potato salad is well worth a try as are its four variations. Cut into ½-inch cubes, the potatoes cook in less than 10 minutes. Note that the curry powder is warmed briefly in oil to remove the raw taste.

FOR THE SALAD
2 cups ½-inch cubes peeled
    sweet potato (about 2 small
    sweet potatoes)
3 cups diced cooked chicken
    (leftover or from the deli
    counter) (about 1 pound)

1 ½ cups halved seedless green
    or red grapes or ¾ cup each

FOR THE DRESSING
2 tablespoons peanut or
    vegetable oil
1 tablespoon curry powder
2 tablespoons firmly packed
    light brown sugar
1 teaspoon salt

2 tablespoons fresh lemon juice
1 tablespoon fresh lime juice
½ cup sour cream
½ cup plain yogurt
2 tablespoons finely minced
    drained mango chutney

1. Boil potatoes in lightly salted water to cover in covered medium-size saucepan over moderate heat just until firm-tender, 6 to 8 minutes. Drain well, dump into large bowl, and add chicken and grapes. Toss lightly.

2. For the dressing, heat oil and curry powder in small, heavy skillet over low heat, stirring often, until no raw curry taste lingers, about 3 minutes. Off heat, blend in remaining ingredients.

3. Pour dressing over salad, toss well, and let stand at room temperature 15 to 20 minutes.

4. Toss again and serve.

VARIATIONS

Turkey and Sweet Potato Salad: Prepare as directed, substituting diced cooked turkey for chicken (this is a great way to use up the Thanksgiving bird).

Ham 'n' Yam Salad: Prepare as directed, substituting diced baked or boiled ham for chicken and one 10-ounce package thawed and drained tiny green peas for grapes. Also add 2 tablespoons chopped fresh parsley.

Lamb and Sweet Potato Salad: Prepare Ham 'n' Yam Salad as directed, substituting diced cooked lamb for ham. Also add 2 tablespoons freshly chopped mint along with parsley.

Shrimp and Sweet Potato Salad: Prepare Ham 'n' Yam Salad as directed, substituting 1 pound fresh or thawed, frozen "salad shrimp" (shelled and deveined, cooked small shrimp) for ham. Also add 2 tablespoons chopped fresh cilantro along with parsley. In dressing, sauté 1 teaspoon finely minced ginger and $1/2$ teaspoon chili powder along with curry powder.

PACIFIC RIM CHICKEN SALAD

Makes 4 servings

This salad is best made with leftover roast chicken, but if you have none, substitute deli roast chicken, even canned chicken. Of course roast turkey makes an equally good salad, as does leftover roast pork. Take your pick.

2 ½ cups diced cooked chicken

2 cups finely sliced Napa cabbage or romaine

1 ½ cups bean sprouts, rinsed under hot water and drained well

1 small red bell pepper, cored, seeded, and cut into matchstick strips

One 6-ounce package frozen snow pea pods, thawed and drained

1 ½ tablespoons Asian roasted sesame oil

1 ½ tablespoons vegetable oil

2 tablespoons rice vinegar

1 tablespoon soy sauce

1 tablespoon Chinese plum sauce or orange or ginger marmalade

1 small garlic clove, finely minced

1 teaspoon finely minced fresh ginger

¼ teaspoon ground hot red pepper (cayenne)

1. Place chicken, cabbage, bean sprouts, bell pepper, and snow peas in large salad bowl.

2. Heat sesame and vegetable oils, vinegar, soy and plum sauces, garlic, ginger, and cayenne in butter warmer over high heat just until mixture steams, about 1 minute.

3. Pour hot dressing over salad ingredients and toss well to mix. Let stand 15 minutes, toss lightly, and serve.

TUNA, RICE, AND TOMATO SALAD

Makes 6 servings

This salad's a snap if you have hard-cooked eggs and leftover cooked rice on hand (see Make-Ahead Al Dente Rice, page 35; also directions for perfectly cooked hard-cooked eggs, page 34).

For the salad

One 12-ounce can solid white tuna, drained and flaked

4 cups leftover cooked rice, at room temperature (see headnote above)

2 hard-cooked extra-large eggs, peeled and minced (see headnote above)

2 large Italian plum (Roma) tomatoes, cored, seeded, and diced

½ cup coarsely chopped pitted black olives (preferably oil-packed Kalamatas)

½ cup chopped yellow onion (about 1 medium-small)

¼ cup chopped Italian (flat-leaf) parsley

For the dressing

1 cup mayonnaise (use light, if you like)

3 tablespoons extra-virgin olive oil

¼ cup fresh lemon juice

¼ cup milk

½ teaspoon salt

¼ teaspoon freshly ground black pepper

1. Place all salad ingredients in large salad bowl and toss lightly.

2. Whisk all dressing ingredients together until creamy.

3. Pour dressing over salad and toss well. Let stand at room temperature 15 to 20 minutes, taste for salt and pepper, fine-tune as needed, toss again, and serve.

HOT CHICKEN, BROCCOLI, AND BOW-TIE SALAD WITH SPICY TAHINI DRESSING

Makes 4 to 6 servings

The new fully cooked carved chicken breasts now available in a variety of flavors in nearly every supermarket are huge time-savers because they're ready to pop into soups, salads, casseroles—whatever. The same holds for bagged broccoli florets at the produce counter. I like them both in this Middle Eastern salad.

FOR THE DRESSING

½ cup tahini (sesame seed paste)
2 tablespoons extra-virgin olive oil
¼ cup fresh lemon juice
2 tablespoons balsamic vinegar
1 teaspoon finely grated lemon zest

1 large garlic clove, finely minced
½ teaspoon salt
½ teaspoon hot red pepper sauce
¼ teaspoon freshly ground black pepper
1 cup chicken broth

FOR THE SALAD

2 tablespoons extra-virgin olive oil
3 cups small broccoli florets
One 10-ounce package Italian-flavored fully cooked carved chicken breast
2 large garlic cloves, finely minced

½ teaspoon salt
¼ teaspoon red pepper flakes
6 ounces farfalle (bow-tie pasta), cooked al dente by package directions and drained very well
1 cup coarsely chopped dry-roasted cashews or peanuts

I. For the dressing, whisk together all ingredients, adding only enough chicken broth to give dressing consistency of gravy; set aside.

2. For the salad, heat oil in large, heavy skillet over high heat until it almost smokes, about 2 ½ minutes. Add broccoli, cover, and cook over high heat until brown and crisp, about 2 minutes.

3. Stir in chicken, garlic, salt, and red pepper flakes; reduce heat to moderate, cover, and cook, stirring occasionally, until broccoli is crisp-tender, about 3 minutes.

4. Add hot drained farfalle, cashews, and 1 cup dressing. Toss gently and if mixture seems dry, add a bit more dressing and toss again. Taste for salt and fine-tune as needed. Toss again and serve.

NOTE

You can substitute 2 1/2 to 3 cups diced left-over cooked chicken or turkey for tuna. You can also add a cup or so of leftover cooked vegetables—green peas or beans, whole-kernel corn, even small broccoli florets.

TUNA-VEGETABLE SALAD WITH YOGURT DRESSING

Makes 6 servings

I've taken my favorite tuna salad, cut the mayo with low-fat yogurt and added carrots to make this a more nutritionally balanced meal. To up the carbs, I've tossed in 2 cups of rice—from my make-ahead stash in the fridge.

For the dressing
1 cup low-fat yogurt
3/4 cup low-fat mayonnaise
1 tablespoon Dijon mustard
1 tablespoon ketchup
1 teaspoon dill weed
1 teaspoon dried marjoram, crumbled

1/2 teaspoon finely grated lemon zest
1/2 teaspoon salt
1/2 teaspoon freshly ground black pepper

For the salad
2 medium-size carrots, peeled and finely diced
1 large celery rib, trimmed and finely diced
Two 12-ounce cans water-packed chunk white tuna, drained and coarsely flaked
2 cups Al Dente Make-Ahead Rice (page 35), at room temperature

1 medium-large yellow onion, coarsely chopped
1/4 cup coarsely chopped Italian (flat-leaf) parsley
2 tablespoons well-drained small capers

1. For the dressing, combine all ingredients in large salad bowl; set aside.

2. For the salad, cook carrots in large saucepan of lightly salted boiling water until crisp-tender, about 4 minutes. Add celery and cook 1 minute longer. Drain well.

3. Add carrots and celery to bowl of dressing along with all remaining ingredients. Toss well, let stand at room temperature 20 minutes. Taste for salt and pepper and adjust as needed. If salad seems dry, add a little milk or skim milk. Toss again and serve.

TUNA NIÇOISE

Makes 6 servings

A classic arranged salad from the south of France that contains all the elements of a balanced meal. I've shortcut prep time by using frozen green beans and the washed, chunked, and partially cooked potatoes now available at most good produce counters. Both can be cooked in the same big pot of water and chilled in the same ice bath provided you keep the two separate.

For the dressing
¼ cup red wine vinegar
1 tablespoon Dijon mustard
¼ teaspoon salt
¼ teaspoon freshly ground black pepper
¾ cup extra-virgin olive oil (the fruitiest you can find)

For the salad
Two 9-ounce packages frozen cut green beans (do not thaw)
Half of a 1½-pound package washed, partially cooked Red Bliss potatoes, large pieces halved
1 small romaine heart, trimmed and sliced crosswise at 1-inch intervals
12 cherry tomatoes, halved
Two 6½-ounce jars marinated artichoke hearts, drained
Two 12-ounce cans chunk white tuna, drained (use water-packed, if you like)
12 Niçoise, Picholine, or other oil-cured black olives

1. For the dressing, whisk vinegar, mustard, salt, and pepper in large bowl, then drizzle in olive oil, whisking briskly all the while. Continue whisking until creamy; set aside.

2. For the salad, cook frozen green beans in large saucepan of lightly salted boiling water just until crisp-tender, about 5 minutes. With mesh skimmer or slotted spoon, scoop beans to bowl of ice water.

3. Cook potatoes in same lightly salted boiling water until firm-tender, 10 to 12 minutes, and add to ice water but do not mix with

beans. Let stand 5 minutes. Meanwhile, arrange bed of romaine on large round platter.

4. Quickly whisk dressing, then with mesh skimmer, lift potatoes to large fine-mesh sieve and drain well. Add potatoes to dressing and turn gently to coat; with slotted spoon, lift potatoes from dressing and arrange in three clusters on outer fringe of romaine.

5. Drain greens beans and coat with dressing the same way, then with slotted spoon, lift from dressing and arrange in three clusters between potatoes.

6. Toss cherry tomatoes, then artichoke hearts, with dressing, lifting each with slotted spoon to romaine and clustering in and around beans and potatoes.

7. Add tuna to dressing, breaking into largish chunks, turn to coat, then with slotted spoon, lift from dressing and mound in center of romaine. Add olives here and there to complete the picture and serve. Strain any remaining dressing and pass separately.

NOTE

For a change of pace, try freshly cooked brown rice or wild rice.

SHRIMP, SNOW PEA, AND ORZO SALAD WITH HOT COCONUT MILK DRESSING

Makes 4 to 6 servings

For this recipe, I use "light" (reduced-fat) Thai coconut milk, which many supermarkets sell along with Thai peanut sauce, tamari sauce, and roasted sesame oil. The trick here is to have everything ready to go at the outset because this salad is a stir-fry. Also have the pasta water well salted and bubbling furiously. The orzo should go in just before you start cooking the shrimp—it needs only 4 to 5 minutes to become al dente.

For the salad

One 6-ounce package snow peas, thawed and patted dry on paper toweling

2 tablespoons peanut oil

1 tablespoon Asian roasted sesame oil

1 pound shelled and deveined medium-size raw shrimp

6 large scallions, trimmed and thinly sliced (include some green tops)

1 large garlic clove, minced

1 tablespoon minced fresh ginger

1½ cups orzo, cooked al dente by package directions and drained well

½ cup coarsely chopped fresh cilantro

For the dressing

1 cup Thai coconut milk (use light, if you like)

¼ cup Thai peanut sauce

2 tablespoons tamari sauce

1 tablespoon sugar

1 tablespoon Asian roasted sesame oil

¼ cup fresh lime juice

½ teaspoon salt

¼ teaspoon red pepper flakes

1. For the salad, place snow peas in large heatproof bowl and set aside.

2. Heat peanut and sesame oils in large, heavy skillet over high heat for 2 minutes. Add shrimp, scallions, garlic, and ginger and cook, stirring often, until all shrimp are nicely pink, 3 to 4 minutes.

3. Add shrimp mixture to bowl with snow peas, then add hot drained orzo and cilantro.

4. For the dressing, add the rest of the ingredients to the skillet and boil uncovered, scraping up browned bits on skillet bottom, until mixture thickens slightly and is consistency of thin gravy, about 5 minutes. Taste for salt and red pepper and adjust as needed.

5. Pour hot dressing over salad, toss well, and let stand 5 minutes. Toss again and serve.

VARIATION

Shrimp, Snow Pea, and Rice Salad with Hot Coconut Milk Dressing: Prepare as directed but substitute 3 cups reheated Al Dente Make-Ahead Rice (page 35) for orzo.

WARM SHRIMP AND WILD RICE SALAD WITH CURRY–SOUR CREAM DRESSING

MAKES 4 SERVINGS

It was the late Ruth Buchan, founder of Doubleday's Cookbook Guild, who first served me this stellar salad, then generously shared the recipe. I've reworked it a bit to boost it into the one-dish-dinner category, but all of its unusual flavors and textures remain. If I use frozen green peas, I thaw and drain them well, then toss them into the salad. But if I use frozen cut asparagus, I break up the solidly frozen block, then scatter the asparagus over the wild rice to steam while the rice finishes cooking. Ruth's original recipe calls for hard-cooked eggs. If I have a couple kicking around in the fridge, I'll add them; otherwise, not. The salad's just as good without them.

FOR THE SALAD

2 tablespoons extra-virgin olive oil

One 8-ounce package sliced fresh white mushrooms

½ pound shelled and deveined small raw shrimp

One 10-ounce package frozen baby green peas, thawed and drained, or one 9-ounce package frozen cut asparagus (do not thaw but do break up frozen block)

¾ cup wild rice

2 hard-cooked extra large eggs, peeled and coarsely chopped (optional)

Salt and freshly ground black pepper

FOR THE DRESSING

1 tablespoon extra-virgin olive oil

6 large scallions, trimmed and coarsely chopped (include some green tops)

1 large garlic clove, minced

½ teaspoon dried marjoram, crumbled

¼ teaspoon dried thyme, crumbled

2 teaspoons curry powder

1 cup sour cream (use light, if you like)

1 cup mayonnaise (use light, if you like)

2 tablespoons fresh lemon juice

Salt and freshly ground black pepper

1. For the salad, heat oil in large, heavy saucepan over moderately high heat 2 minutes. Add mushrooms and cook, stirring often, until lightly browned, about 5 minutes. Add shrimp and cook, stirring, just until pink, 3 to 5 minutes. Transfer to large bowl and reserve. If using peas, add to bowl at this point.

2. Cook wild rice in same pan according to package directions. If using frozen cut asparagus, lay pieces on top of rice during last 5 minutes of cooking.

3. Begin to prepare dressing while rice cooks. Heat oil in medium-size heavy skillet over moderately high heat 1 minute. Add scallions, garlic, marjoram, thyme, and curry powder and cook, stirring often, until scallions wilt, about 3 minutes. Off heat, mix in sour cream, mayonnaise, lemon juice, and salt and pepper to taste. Pour half of dressing over shrimp mixture and set rest aside.

4. When rice is done (there should be no water remaining in bottom of pan), fluff with fork and add to shrimp mixture along with asparagus and hard-cooked eggs, if using. Toss well, then season to taste with salt and pepper.

5. If salad seems dry, add a little more dressing and toss again. Mound on dinner plates and top each portion with a hefty spoonful of dressing. Pass any remaining dressing separately.

TWO-POTATO SALAD WITH SHRIMP AND GREEN PEAS

Makes 6 to 8 servings

Potato salad was never easier, thanks to one of the produce counter's newer entries: washed, partially cooked, ready-to-use potatoes. For this salad, I use half a bag of Red Bliss potatoes, the ones with the skins still on. I also use frozen "cocktail" or "salad" shrimp—small shrimp that are cooked, shelled, and deveined. Sometimes the tail shells are left on and must be removed—a quick and easy operation (just pinch and pull). Another time-saver is to processor-chop the scallions and celery together—five to six zaps are all that are needed.

For the dressing
¾ cup light or low-fat
  mayonnaise
½ cup light sour cream
½ cup bottled tartar sauce

1½ tablespoons Dijon mustard
1 teaspoon salt
¼ teaspoon freshly ground
  black pepper

For the salad
1 large sweet potato, peeled and
  cut into ¾-inch cubes (about
  1 pound)
Half of a 1½-pound package
  washed, partially cooked
  Red Bliss potatoes, large
  pieces halved
4 cups frozen cooked cocktail or
  salad shrimp, thawed, drained,
  and tails removed
Half of a 10-ounce package
  frozen tiny green peas,
  thawed and drained

6 medium-size scallions,
  trimmed and coarsely
  chopped (include some green
  tops; see headnote above)
2 large celery ribs, coarsely
  chopped
2 hard-cooked extra-large eggs,
  peeled and coarsely chopped
  (page 34)
½ cup coarsely chopped Italian
  (flat-leaf) parsley
1 small head radicchio, leaves
  separated (optional)

1. For the dressing, combine all ingredients in large serving bowl and set aside.

2. For the salad, boil sweet potato in lightly salted water until firm-tender, 6 to 8 minutes. With mesh skimmer, lift to large bowl of ice water. Boil Red Bliss potatoes in same water until firm-tender, 10 to 12 minutes, and add to bowl of ice water.

3. Add shrimp, peas, scallions, celery, eggs, and parsley to dressing in bowl. Drain potatoes as dry as possible, add to bowl, and toss all well. Let stand at room temperature 20 minutes before serving, or better yet, chill several hours. For a pretty presentation, line clean salad bowl with radicchio leaves, mound salad on top, and serve.

CRAB, ROASTED GREEN BEAN, AND PAPAYA SALAD WITH CAPER-DILL DRESSING

MAKES 4 TO 6 SERVINGS

You can make the dressing a day or two ahead of time. To save time, I use packaged trimmed romaine hearts, and to enjoy the salad out of season, frozen cut green beans and canned diced tomatoes (far better than cardboardy hothouse specimens). The tomato-papaya combo is a refreshing one with the tartness of the tomatoes tempering the sweetness of the papaya.

FOR THE DRESSING

¾ cup mayonnaise (use light, if you like)

2 tablespoons bottled chili sauce

1 large scallion, trimmed and finely minced (include some green tops)

1 tablespoon finely minced green bell pepper

1 tablespoon fresh lemon juice

1 tablespoon small capers, well drained

1 tablespoon freshly snipped dill or ½ teaspoon dill weed

1 teaspoon Worcestershire sauce

¼ teaspoon hot red pepper sauce

FOR THE SALAD

2 cups frozen cut green beans (do not thaw)

1½ tablespoons extra-virgin olive oil

1 small papaya (about 1 pound), peeled, seeded, and cut into ½-inch dice (2 cups diced papaya)

1 pound lump crab meat, bits of shell and cartilage removed

One 14½-ounce can diced tomatoes, drained well and patted dry on paper toweling, or 4 Italian plum (Roma) tomatoes, cored, seeded, and diced but not peeled

One medium-size romaine heart, sliced ½ inch thick

1. Combine all dressing ingredients, cover, and refrigerate until ready to serve.

2. Preheat oven to 425°F. Toss beans with oil in shallow roasting pan, spread evenly, set uncovered in oven, and roast 20 minutes, stirring once at half-time.

3. Dump beans into large heatproof bowl; add papaya, crab, tomatoes, and half the dressing. Toss well. If mixture seems dry, add a bit more dressing and toss again.

4. Bed romaine on large shallow platter, mound salad on top, and serve. Pass any remaining dressing separately.

VARIATION

Crab, Roasted Asparagus, and Papaya Salad with Caper-Dill Dressing: Prepare as directed but omit green beans. Instead, toss $1/2$ pound peeled asparagus spears with the olive oil in shallow roasting pan, spread evenly, and roast 10 to 12 minutes in preheated 450°F. oven until lightly browned, shaking pan well at half-time. Cut asparagus into 1-inch lengths and proceed as directed.

TIPS

PICK OVER THE CRAB AND DICE THE PAPAYA WHILE THE GREEN BEANS ROAST. THE FASTEST WAY TO DICE PAPAYA IS TO HALVE LENGTHWISE, REMOVE SEEDS, SCORE FLESH CRISS-CROSS FASHION, AND SCOOP OUT WITH SPOON.

CURRIED CRAB SALAD

Makes 4 servings

If you can afford lump crab meat, by all means use it. If not, use thawed, frozen snow crab, even canned crab. You'll need a pound of crab meat. Shortcut: To peel and dice avocado quickly, halve, pit, score flesh criss-cross fashion, then scoop out with a spoon.

1 tablespoon vegetable oil
1 tablespoon Asian roasted sesame oil
2 large scallions, trimmed and thinly sliced (include some green tops)
1 small garlic clove, minced
1 tablespoon curry powder
1/4 cup coarsely chopped mango chutney
1/2 cup mayonnaise (use light, if you like)
1/3 cup plain yogurt (use nonfat, if you like)

1/2 teaspoon hot red pepper sauce
1/2 teaspoon salt
1 medium-size Haas avocado, peeled, pitted, and diced
2 tablespoons fresh lemon juice
1 pound lump crab meat, bits of shell and cartilage removed
2 small celery ribs, trimmed and finely diced
2 small hearts of romaine, thinly sliced

1. Heat vegetable and sesame oils in small, heavy skillet over moderate heat 1 minute. Add scallions and garlic and cook, stirring, until limp and golden, about 3 minutes.

2. Blend in curry powder and cook and stir 1 minute. Off heat, blend in chutney, mayonnaise, yogurt, hot red pepper sauce, and salt.

3. Place avocado and lemon juice in large bowl and toss gently to coat avocado. Add crab, celery, and curry mixture and toss lightly to mix. Taste for salt and red pepper sauce and adjust as needed.

4. Nest romaine on dinner plates, dividing amount evenly, top with crab salad, and serve.

Curried Lobster Salad: Prepare as directed, substituting 1 pound diced, cooked lobster meat for crab.

Curried Shrimp Salad: Prepare as directed, substituting 1 pound cooked, shelled, and deveined medium-size shrimp for crab.

Curried Chicken, Turkey, or Ham Salad: Prepare as directed, substituting 2 cups diced, cooked chicken, turkey, or baked ham for crab. Also substitute 1 diced, peeled, pitted mango for avocado, if you like.

CRAB (OR LOBSTER), AVOCADO, AND TOMATO SALAD ON MESCLUN

A Southwestern variation of Crab Louis, an early twentieth-century West Coast classic. Some say it was created at San Francisco's beloved St. Francis Hotel; others believe it originated at Seattle's Olympic Club. Whatever its origin, it's a cool, satisfying meal.

Mesclun, a mix of baby salad greens, can be found binned and/or bagged at most supermarkets. It's also a farmer's market staple. Every good fish market, as well as the fish departments of good supermarkets, sells lump crab and freshly cooked lobster meat. But they're seasonal items unavailable in winter. No matter: this is a summery salad.

FOR THE DRESSING
1 ½ cups mayonnaise (use light, if you like)
½ cup bottled tomato salsa (as mild or hot as you like)
2 tablespoons chili sauce or ketchup
1 small green bell pepper, cored, seeded, and finely chopped
4 large scallions, trimmed and finely chopped (include some green tops)
1 tablespoon fresh lime juice
1 teaspoon Worcestershire sauce
½ teaspoon salt
¼ teaspoon freshly ground black pepper

FOR THE SALAD
½ pound lump crab meat, bits of shell and cartilage removed, or ½ pound cooked lobster meat, cut into ¾-inch cubes
2 firm-ripe Haas avocados, peeled, pitted, finely diced, and gently tossed with 2 tablespoons fresh lime juice
One 10-ounce can diced tomatoes with green chilies, drained very well
⅓ cup coarsely chopped fresh cilantro
4 cups mesclun (mixed baby salad greens)
1 cup coarsely crushed tortilla chips (optional)

1. For the dressing, combine all ingredients, cover, and refrigerate until ready to serve.

2. For the salad, place crab, avocados, tomatoes with chilies, and cilantro in large bowl. Add 1 cup dressing, toss gently, and if mixture seems dry, add more dressing and toss again.

3. Arrange mesclun on large round platter, mound crab mixture on top, sprinkle with crushed tortilla chips if you like, and serve. Pass extra dressing separately, if desired.

NOTE

MAKE THE DRESSING FIRST, EARLY IN THE DAY, IF POSSIBLE, AND REFRIGERATE UNTIL READY TO SERVE. THE RECIPE MAKES MORE THAN YOU WILL NEED TO DRESS THIS SALAD. REFRIGERATE THE BALANCE AND USE TO DRESS CHICKEN, TURKEY, OR SHRIMP SALAD, EVEN LETTUCE HEARTS. OR, IF YOU PREFER, DIVIDE ALL DRESSING INGREDIENTS BY HALF.

SALAD OF BAY SCALLOPS, SWEET GRAPE TOMATOES, AND EMERALD RICE

Makes 4 to 6 servings

This recipe was inspired by one in *Little Meals*, an inventive cookbook written by friend and colleague Rozanne Gold.

FOR THE SALAD

- 2 cups Al Dente Make-Ahead Rice (page 35), at room temperature
- 1 cup loosely packed stemmed parsley sprigs (curly parsley is best)
- 2 large scallions, trimmed and chunked (include some green tops)
- 1 ½ cups loosely packed tender young watercress leaves

- 2 cups water mixed with 2 tablespoons sake (rice wine) or dry vermouth
- 1 pound bay scallops, rinsed
- 20 sweet grape tomatoes, quartered lengthwise, or 10 cherry tomatoes, stemmed and quartered
- 1 cup canned sliced water chestnuts, drained
- 4 cups mesclun (mixed baby greens) (optional)

FOR THE DRESSING

- 6 tablespoons peanut or corn oil
- 2 tablespoons roasted Asian sesame oil
- ¼ cup fresh lime juice
- 1 tablespoon soy sauce
- 1 tablespoon minced fresh ginger

- 1 garlic clove, finely minced
- 1 teaspoon finely grated lime zest
- ½ teaspoon salt
- ½ teaspoon hot red pepper sauce

1. For the salad, place rice in large salad bowl. Pulse parsley four to five times in food processor or electric blender. Add scallions and watercress and pulse until finely chopped. Add to rice and toss well.

2. Bring water mixture to boiling in medium-size nonreactive skillet over high heat. Add scallops, adjust heat so liquid barely trembles, and poach just until scallops turn milky, about 2 minutes. Dump scallops into large fine-mesh sieve and rinse under cool water. Drain well and add to rice along with tomatoes and water chestnuts.

3. For the dressing, whisk together all ingredients, drizzle over salad, and toss well. Let stand at room temperature 20 to 30 minutes. Toss again; serve as is or on bed of mesclun.

NOTE

SWEET GRAPE TOMATOES ARE A RECENT ARRIVAL. IF YOUR SUPERMARKET DOESN'T HAVE THEM, SUBSTITUTE FIRM-RIPE CHERRY TOMATOES. NEXT TIME YOU'RE AT YOUR SUPERMARKET, ASK THE PRODUCE MANAGER TO ORDER SWEET GRAPE TOMATOES FOR YOU. IN MY STORE THEY NOW OUTSELL CHERRY TOMATOES TWELVE TO ONE.

SALMON AND WHITE BEAN SALAD WITH TARRAGON VINAIGRETTE

MAKES 4 SERVINGS

Time permitting, let the salad stand at room temperature 20 to 30 minutes before serving.

3 tablespoons extra-virgin
   olive oil
2 tablespoons tarragon vinegar
1 teaspoon dried tarragon,
   crumbled
1 teaspoon Dijon mustard
½ teaspoon sugar
½ teaspoon salt
¼ teaspoon freshly ground
   black pepper
1 large scallion, trimmed and
   sliced very thin (include some
   green tops)

1 small celery rib, trimmed and
   sliced very thin
1 medium-size red-ripe tomato,
   cored, seeded, and diced
One 15 ½-ounce can navy or
   pea beans, rinsed and drained
   well
One 6-ounce can salmon,
   drained and flaked

1. Combine oil, vinegar, tarragon, mustard, sugar, salt, and pepper in large salad bowl.

2. Add all remaining ingredients and toss well to mix. Serve at room temperature.

VARIATION
Tuna and Chickpea Salad with Dill Vinaigrette: Prepare as directed, substituting 2 teaspoons freshly snipped dill or 1 teaspoon dill weed for tarragon, 2 tablespoons white wine vinegar for tarragon vinegar, one 1-pound can chickpeas for navy beans, and one 6-ounce can solid white tuna for salmon. Also add 1 tablespoon well-drained small capers.

SOUPS AND STEWS

Must soups and stews simmer all day to develop proper flavor? Not at all. Nor, for that matter, should the meats, vegetables, and seasonings take forever to prep.

I jump-start soups and stews by capitalizing on the prepped or partially prepped fresh vegetables now available at supermarket produce counters: peeled baby-cut carrots, for example, sliced fresh mushrooms, coleslaw mixes; also, by taking advantage of frozen bell pepper stir-fry mixes, frozen whole-kernel corn, hash browns, and assorted chopped greens. Equally valuable are canned beets, black beans, roasted sweet red peppers, and crushed or diced tomatoes.

The biggest time-saver, however, is substituting tender ground meat (or frozen meatballs, which I make ahead and freeze) for sinewy "stew" cuts. Or quick-cooking chicken drummettes (even deli-barbecued roasters) for tough old birds. To intensify flavors, I use double-strength canned beef consommé and bottled salsas, barbecue, and marinara sauces with plenty of built-in seasonings. And I pump up the herbs and spices.

I frequently use scallions instead of yellow onions because I find them more flavorful and quicker to prepare, then I caramelize them in drippings or olive oil to make them even tastier.

Prosciutto, I've discovered, is a powerful flavor enhancer, as are duxelles (a rich mushroom paste that I cook ahead and freeze), freshly grated Parmesan, and lemon and orange zests (a strip or two in the pot is all that's needed).

Finally, I use the fruitiest olive oils I can find (or the smokiest bacon drippings) for the initial browning of meat and vegetables (adding herbs at this point enriches their flavor).

These are only a few of my favorite soup-and-stew shortcuts—you'll learn others in the recipes that follow.

SPANISH BLACK BEAN SOUP

MAKES 6 SERVINGS

Canned black beans are a perfectly acceptable shortcut for dried beans, which must be soaked overnight or for an hour if you use the "quick method." This soup is ready to serve in 27 minutes.

2 tablespoons extra-virgin olive oil

2 cups fresh or frozen chopped onions (about 2 medium-large yellow onions)

1 cup coarsely chopped frozen bell pepper stir-fry mix (red, green, and yellow peppers; do not thaw)

1/3 cup finely diced Serrano (Spanish) ham or prosciutto

1 large garlic clove, minced

1 large whole bay leaf

1/2 teaspoon dried thyme, crumbled

1/4 teaspoon ground coriander

Two 1-pound cans black beans, with their liquid

One 14 1/2-ounce can beef broth

3 tablespoons dry sherry

Salt and freshly ground black pepper

3 cups leftover cooked rice, reheated (see Al Dente Make-Ahead Rice, page 35)

2 hard-cooked extra-large eggs (page 34), peeled and chopped

4 tablespoons coarsely chopped Italian (flat-leaf) parsley

1. Heat oil in large, heavy saucepan over high heat 2 minutes. Add onions, stir-fry mix, ham, garlic, bay leaf, thyme, and coriander. Stir well to coat, reduce heat to moderate, cover, and "sweat" 10 minutes. This intensifies flavors.

2. Add beans and their liquid, broth, and sherry; adjust heat so soup barely bubbles, cover, and simmer just until flavors mingle, about 15 minutes. Remove bay leaf and season to taste with salt and black pepper.

3. To serve, mound 1/2 cup rice in each of six heated large soup plates. Ladle in soup, then top with scatterings of hard-cooked egg and parsley.

GREASED LIGHTNING BORSCHT

Makes 6 to 8 servings

True Russian borscht takes hours, sometimes days, to make. This shortcut version makes the most of pre-prepped fresh produce, substitutes quick-cooking ground beef for long-simmering shin bones and makes the most of canned beets, broth, and tomatoes. It's ready to serve in 40 minutes and bubbles unattended most of the time.

3 tablespoons vegetable oil
One 12-ounce package frozen chopped onions (do not thaw)
2 large garlic cloves, minced
1 celery rib, trimmed and coarsely chopped
1 pound ground lean beef chuck
Two 8-ounce packages slaw mix (with carrots)
3 sprigs Italian (flat-leaf) parsley
2 large branches fresh dill or 2 teaspoons dill weed

10 black peppercorns
2 whole bay leaves
Three 14½-ounce cans beef broth
One 1-pound can crushed tomatoes, with their liquid
¼ cup cider vinegar
2 teaspoons sugar
One 15-ounce can sliced beets, with their liquid, coarsely chopped
1 cup sour cream
2 tablespoons freshly snipped dill (no substitute)

1. Heat oil in large, heavy kettle over moderate heat 2 minutes. Add onions and cook, stirring frequently, until nicely browned, 8 to 10 minutes.

2. Add garlic and celery and cook, stirring often, for 1 minute. Add beef and slaw mix and cook, breaking up large beef chunks, until beef is no longer pink, 4 to 5 minutes.

3. Add parsley, dill, peppercorns, bay leaves, broth, tomatoes, vinegar, and sugar and bring to a boil. Adjust heat so mixture bubbles gently, cover, and simmer until flavors meld, about 15 minutes.

4. Add beets and bring just to a simmer. Remove bay leaves, parsley, and dill sprigs.

5. Ladle into heated soup plates, drift each portion with sour cream, and sprinkle with fresh dill.

NOTE

This soup is best served icy cold, so buzz it up early in the day and refrigerate until ready to serve. The add-ons are easy.

HLODNIK (COLD RUSSIAN MEAT, FISH, AND VEGETABLE SOUP)

Makes 4 servings

Begin with a can of beets, buzz them up in a blender or food processor, then set out an array of add-ons: tiny cooked shrimp, diced leftover cooked meat, hard-cooked eggs, sour cream, diced cucumbers, freshly snipped chives. Each person helps himself to whatever he wants and stirs it into his soup. To accompany you need only crusty country bread.

For the soup

One 15 1/4-ounce can whole beets, with their liquid, well chilled

Two 10 1/2-ounce cans beef consommé

1/4 cup fresh lemon juice

1/4 cup red wine vinegar

2 tablespoons freshly snipped dill or 1 teaspoon dill weed

1 large lemon, thinly sliced

Adds-ons

1 cup sour cream (use "light," if you like)

2 medium-size Kirby cucumbers, peeled, seeded, and cut into small dice

2 hard-cooked extra-large eggs (page 34), peeled and coarsely chopped

4 large scallions, trimmed and coarsely chopped (include some green tops)

1/4 cup freshly snipped chives

1/4 pound cooked, shelled, and deveined small shrimp, or one 4-ounce can tiny shrimp, drained

1 cup diced cooked roast beef, chicken, turkey, or baked ham

I. For the soup, puree beets with their liquid in food processor or electric blender. Transfer to small tureen or punch bowl, then mix in consommé, lemon juice, vinegar, and dill; cover and chill several hours.

2. For a knock-out presentation, center tureen on large round platter, float lemon slices on soup, and surround with add-ons, either spooned into separate small bowls or mounded directly on platter. If presentation is not a priority, simply stir all add-ons into soup and serve.

TIP

THE FASTEST WAY TO SNIP CHIVES IS TO HOLD THE BUNDLED CHIVES IN ONE HAND AND WITH SHARP SCISSORS, SNIP ACROSS THE BASE, LETTING THE BITS FALL ONTO WAXED PAPER. FOLD OVER AND REFRIGERATE UNTIL READY TO USE. THE SAME TECHNIQUE WORKS FOR FRESH DILL.

NOTE

If you chill the soup, don't add the dill and parsley until just before serving.

Don't substitute dill weed for fresh dill. Indeed, there's no reason to with the little packets of fresh dill available in nearly every supermarket right around the calendar.

To thaw peas, bang the package against the counter to break up the frozen block, dump the peas into a large fine-mesh sieve, and set under the hot water tap.

FINNISH SUMMER SOUP

Makes 6 servings

Because blistering summers are practically unknown in Finland, this soup is served hot. It's equally delicious cold, however, and the quickest way to chill it is to pour it into a large shallow pan and set it in a sink of crushed ice. Stir often and the soup should be ready to eat in 10 to 15 minutes. To trim prep time, I use bagged shredded carrots, bagged cauliflower florets, and bagged washed baby spinach from the produce counter; I also use frozen baby green peas, which only need to be thawed. Finally, I use freshly cooked shelled and deveined small shrimp, sometimes even frozen "salad shrimp."

3 cups water
2 teaspoons salt
2 medium-size red-skin
   potatoes, peeled and cubed
2 cups small cauliflower florets
1 cup coarsely shredded carrots
½ pound shelled and deveined,
   cooked small shrimp
¼ pound baby spinach, leaves
   stacked and sliced on the bias
   into ribbons ¼ inch wide
One 10-ounce package frozen
   baby green peas, thawed and
   drained well

3 tablespoons all-purpose flour
1½ cups half-and-half cream
1 cup milk or evaporated milk
   (use skim, if you like)
¼ cup freshly snipped dill
   (no substitute)
¼ cup minced parsley
¼ teaspoon freshly ground
   black pepper or, if you prefer,
   white pepper

1. Bring water and salt to a boil in large, heavy saucepan. Add potatoes, cauliflower, and carrots and boil uncovered until almost tender, about 8 minutes. Add shrimp, spinach, and peas and cook 2 minutes.

2. Blend flour with ½ cup half-and-half, then add to soup along with milk and remaining 1 cup half-and-half. Cook and stir until lightly thickened and no raw floury taste remains, about 5 minutes.

3. Stir in dill, parsley, and pepper; taste for salt and pepper and adjust as needed. Ladle into heated soup bowls and serve. Or chill well and serve cold.

SPINACH-BUTTERMILK SOUP WITH MEATBALLS

MAKES 4 SERVINGS

One reason I like to keep a supply of Basic Meatballs in the freezer is so I can rustle up this easy soup. It's the perfect place to use up leftover rice, potatoes, or sweet potatoes.

2 tablespoons extra-virgin
  olive oil
2 cups fresh or frozen chopped
  onions (about 2 medium-large
  yellow onions)
1/4 teaspoon freshly grated
  nutmeg
1 large garlic clove, minced
One 14 1/2-ounce can chicken or
  beef broth
One 10 1/2-ounce can beef
  consommé

16 frozen Basic Meatballs
  (page 29; do not thaw)
One 10-ounce package frozen
  chopped spinach, thawed and
  drained
1 cup buttermilk
1 to 1 1/2 cups leftover rice or
  diced, peeled, cooked Irish
  potato or sweet potato
Salt and freshly ground black
  pepper

1. Heat oil in large, heavy saucepan over moderately high heat 1 minute. Add onions and nutmeg and cook, stirring often, until richly brown, 8 to 10 minutes. Mix in garlic.

2. Add broth and consommé and bring to boil. Add meatballs, return to boil, then adjust heat so mixture bubbles gently. Cover and cook until meatballs are done, 12 to 15 minutes.

3. Add spinach, cover, and cook 5 minutes. Add buttermilk, rice, and salt and pepper to taste; bring just to serving temperature. Do not boil or soup may curdle.

4. Ladle into heated soup bowls and serve.

EASIEST EVER GAZPACHO

Makes 4 to 6 servings

Use your favorite bottled salsa as the foundation of this Spanish cold summer soup. Processor-chop the parsley (for ¼ cup, you'll need about four large sprigs, stemmed). Empty work bowl, add chunks of onion and green pepper, and pulse briskly until coarsely chopped.

2 tablespoons extra-virgin olive oil (the fruitiest you can find)
2 slices firm-textured white bread, torn into 1-inch pieces
One 1-pound can crushed tomatoes, with their liquid
Two 8-ounce jars chunky salsa
2 cups canned vegetable juice
2 tablespoons balsamic or red wine vinegar
1 medium-size Spanish, Vidalia, or Bermuda onion, coarsely chopped (see headnote above)

1 large green bell pepper, cored, seeded, and coarsely chopped
1 large garlic clove, minced
1 small Kirby cucumber, peeled, seeded, and diced
¼ cup coarsely chopped Italian (flat-leaf) parsley
Salt and freshly ground black pepper to taste
8 large fresh basil leaves, stacked and thinly sliced

1. Place oil and bread in large bowl and stir lightly. Add all remaining ingredients except basil, mix well, and let stand at room temperature 20 minutes.

2. Ladle into chilled large soup plates and top each portion with fresh basil.

BUTTERMILK GAZPACHO

MAKES 4 SERVINGS

I've taken an old favorite and added some carbohydrate, leftover rice, if I have it, or croutons that I've made and stuck in the freezer. I try to keep hard-cooked eggs on hand, also chopped bell peppers so everything goes together zip-quick.

2 hard-cooked extra-large eggs (page 34), peeled, then yolks sieved and whites diced
1½ cups canned vegetable juice
1½ cups buttermilk
½ cup diced Vidalia, Bermuda, or Spanish onion
½ cup diced celery
½ cup diced green bell pepper
½ cup diced red bell pepper
1 tablespoon snipped fresh chives

1 tablespoon snipped fresh dill or ½ teaspoon dill weed
Salt and freshly ground black pepper to taste
1⅓ cups Al Dente Make-Ahead Rice (page 35) or 1 cup croutons (page 39), at room temperature
1 lime, cut into slim wedges

1. Place egg yolks, vegetable juice, buttermilk, onion, celery, bell peppers, chives, and dill in large bowl and stir well to mix. Season to taste with salt and pepper.

2. If using rice, mound ⅓ cup in each of four soup plates, ladle in gazpacho, and top with egg whites. If using croutons, sprinkle into gazpacho along with egg whites.

3. Garnish with lime wedges and serve.

CONFETTI CHOWDER

This parti-colored combo of corn, onions, and sweet red, green, and yellow peppers is ready to eat in 30 minutes.

4 strips lean bacon, snipped crosswise into julienne strips

2 medium-size celery ribs, thinly sliced

4 medium-size scallions, trimmed and thinly sliced (include some green tops)

One 1-pound bag frozen bell pepper stir-fry mix (red, green, and yellow peppers; do not thaw)

One 10-ounce package frozen whole-kernel corn (do not thaw)

1 teaspoon chopped fresh rosemary or $\frac{1}{2}$ teaspoon dried rosemary, crumbled

$\frac{1}{2}$ teaspoon chopped fresh lemon thyme or $\frac{1}{2}$ teaspoon dried thyme, crumbled

One 14$\frac{1}{2}$-ounce can chicken broth

$\frac{1}{2}$ cup half-and-half cream blended with 3 tablespoons all-purpose flour

1 cup milk

Salt and freshly ground black pepper to taste

2 tablespoons coarsely chopped parsley

1. Cook bacon in large, heavy saucepan over moderate heat until crisp and brown, 3 to 5 minutes. With slotted spoon, scoop browned bacon to paper toweling to drain.

2. Cook celery and scallions in bacon drippings until limp—about 3 minutes. Raise heat to moderately high; add stir-fry mix, corn, rosemary, and thyme and cook, stirring, until vegetables brown lightly, about 8 minutes.

3. Add chicken broth, adjust heat so mixture barely bubbles, cover, and cook until flavors mingle, about 10 minutes.

4. Reduce heat to low; add half-and-half mixture, milk, salt, and pepper and cook, stirring constantly, until mixture thickens and no raw flour taste remains, about 5 minutes. Do not allow to boil or mixture may curdle. Taste for salt and pepper and adjust as needed.

5. Ladle into heated soup plates and scatter reserved bacon, then parsley, on top of each portion, dividing amounts equally. Serve at once.

MEATBALL SOUP WITH CABBAGE, CARROTS, AND POTATOES

MAKES 6 SERVINGS

With meatballs in the freezer and peeled carrots and shredded cabbage available at the supermarket, this nourishing soup is a snap. To intensify flavors and trim cooking time, I've resorted to an old Portuguese technique called *refogado*, which simply means "sweating" the vegetables in the oil (and in this case the meatballs and a little broth, too) for 15 minutes. I use it for most soups.

2 tablespoons extra-virgin olive oil

1 cup fresh or frozen chopped onion (about 1 medium-large yellow onion)

One 10-ounce package angel hair coleslaw (finely cut green cabbage)

1 large garlic clove, minced

1 cup peeled baby-cut fresh carrots, sliced ½ inch thick

6 golfball-size red-skin potatoes, scrubbed and quartered but not peeled

2 to 3 tablespoons Duxelles (page 33; optional)

1 large whole bay leaf

Two 3-inch sprigs fresh thyme or ½ teaspoon dried thyme, crumbled

½ teaspoon caraway seeds

¼ teaspoon fennel seeds

24 frozen Basic Meatballs (page 29; do not thaw)

Two 14½-ounce cans beef broth

¾ teaspoon salt

¼ teaspoon freshly ground black pepper

¼ cup minced Italian (flat-leaf) parsley

1. Heat oil in medium-size Dutch oven over high heat 2 minutes. Add onion, coleslaw, and garlic and cook, stirring often, until lightly wilted, about 5 minutes.

2. Add carrots, potatoes, duxelles if desired, bay leaf, thyme, caraway and fennel seeds and toss to coat with drippings. Lay meatballs on top and pour in 1 cup broth. Reduce heat to moderate, cover, and "sweat" 15 minutes.

3. Add remaining broth, salt, and pepper; adjust heat so liquid bubbles gently but steadily, cover, and cook until potatoes are tender, about 20 minutes. Taste for salt and pepper and adjust as needed.

4. Remove bay leaf, sprinkle with parsley, and serve.

THE FASTEST WAY TO SLICE
TORTILLAS IS TO STACK
THREE AT A TIME AND SNIP
INTO 1/4-INCH SLICES WITH
SHARP SHEARS. AND THE
EASIEST WAY TO DICE AVO-
CADO IS TO SCORE AROUND
THE MIDLINE (THE LONG WAY)
WITH A SHARP KNIFE, CUT-
TING CLEAR TO THE PIT,
TWIST THE HALVES APART,
TWIST OUT THE SEED, THEN
SCORE THE FLESH IN A
CRISS-CROSS PATTERN,
MAKING THE CUTS 1/2 INCH
APART. TO FREE THE AVO-
CADO DICE, SCOOP OUT
WITH A SPOON.

TORTILLA SOUP WITH AVOCADO, SWEET POTATO, AND BARBECUED PORK

MAKES 6 SERVINGS

Don't be put off by the long ingredients list. My spin on the Mexican classic makes the most of deli barbecued pork, frozen corn, and bottled marinara and barbecue sauces.

Six 6-inch flour tortillas
Butter or olive-oil flavor
    nonstick vegetable cooking
    spray
2 tablespoons corn or
    vegetable oil
1 cup fresh or frozen chopped
    onion (about 1 medium-large
    yellow onion)
1/2 cup diced green bell pepper
    (about 1/2 medium green
    pepper)
1 large garlic clove, minced
1 large whole bay leaf
One 2-inch strip orange zest
1 teaspoon chili powder
1/2 teaspoon ground cumin
Two 14 1/2-ounce cans chicken
    broth
1 teaspoon salt
1/4 teaspoon freshly ground
    black pepper
1 large sweet potato (3/4 to 1
    pound), peeled and cut into
    1/2-inch cubes

2 cups diced boneless deli
    barbecued pork, chicken, or
    turkey (about 1 pound)
One 10-ounce can diced
    tomatoes with green chilies,
    drained
2 cups frozen whole-kernel corn
    (no need to thaw)
1 cup bottled marinara sauce or
    Basic Tomato Sauce
    (page 30) or one 8-ounce
    can tomato sauce
1/3 cup bottled smoky barbecue
    sauce
1/3 cup chopped fresh cilantro or
    parsley (measure loosely
    packed)
1 medium-size firm-ripe Haas
    avocado, peeled, pitted, and
    cut into 1/2-inch dice

1. Preheat oven to 375°F. Coat one side of each tortilla with cooking spray, stack tortillas, three at a time, and with sharp kitchen shears, snip into strands $1/4$ inch wide. Spread on ungreased baking sheet and bake uncovered until crisp and lightly browned, about 10 minutes; stir well at half-time.

2. Meanwhile, heat oil in medium-size Dutch oven over high heat 2 minutes. Reduce heat to moderate; add onion, green pepper, garlic, bay leaf, orange zest, chili powder, and cumin and cook, stirring often, until limp and golden, about 5 minutes.

3. Add broth, salt, black pepper, and sweet potato and bring to boiling. Adjust heat so mixture bubbles gently, cover, and cook until potato is firm-tender, about 10 minutes.

4. Add pork, diced tomatoes with green chilies, corn, and marinara and barbecue sauces; cover and simmer, stirring occasionally, until flavors mingle, about 15 minutes. Remove bay leaf and orange zest. Stir in cilantro, taste for salt and black pepper, and fine-tune as needed.

5. To serve, ladle soup into heated large soup plates, top with diced avocado, then lightly crumble in toasted tortilla strips.

NOTE

INSTEAD OF FRYING THE TORTILLA STRIPS AS AUTHENTIC RECIPES INSTRUCT, I BAKE THEM TO REDUCE FAT.

SHORTCUT CHICKEN-VEGETABLE SOUP

Makes 6 servings

The time-savers here? Chicken drummettes, which cook falling-off-the-bone-tender in no time, packaged peeled baby-cut carrots, frozen hash brown potatoes, and frozen chopped collards. I cut the carrots in thirds, but that goes quickly if I attack three or four of them at a time.

3 tablespoons extra-virgin olive oil or vegetable oil
1 pound chicken drummettes
Half of a 1-pound bag peeled baby-cut fresh carrots, each cut into thirds
1 cup fresh or frozen chopped onion (about 1 medium-large yellow onion)
1 cup diced celery
1 large garlic clove, minced
2 large whole bay leaves
1 teaspoon dried oregano, crumbled

½ teaspoon dried thyme, crumbled
Two 14½-ounce cans chicken broth
1 teaspoon salt
½ teaspoon freshly ground black pepper
2 small turnips, peeled and diced
2 cups frozen hash brown potatoes (do not thaw)
2 cups frozen chopped collards (do not thaw)

1. Heat oil in medium-size Dutch oven over high heat 2 minutes. Add chicken, set lid on askew, and brown well on all sides, 8 to 10 minutes, turning as needed.

2. Add carrots, onion, celery, garlic, bay leaves, oregano, and thyme, stirring well to coat with drippings. Reduce heat to moderate, cover, and "sweat" 10 minutes.

3. Add broth, salt, and pepper; bring to gentle boil, set lid on askew, and cook 20 minutes.

4. Add turnips, potatoes, and collards; set lid on askew and cook just until vegetables are tender and chicken is well done, about 10 minutes. Taste for salt and pepper and fine-tune. Discard bay leaves.

5. Ladle into heated soup bowls and serve.

Shortcut Chicken-Vegetable Soup with Dumplings: Prepare as directed through step 2. In step 3, add 1 additional cup chicken broth (or, if you wish, 1 cup water) and proceed as directed. Meanwhile, quickly fork together 1 cup Dumpling/Biscuit Topping Mix (page 31) and enough milk ($1/4$ to $1/3$ cup) to make soft dough; set aside. In step 4, add turnips and collards to pan but omit potatoes; bring to gentle boil. Discard bay leaves; also taste for salt and pepper and fine-tune. Drop dumpling dough by teaspoonfuls, spacing evenly over top of bubbling soup. Cover tight and cook 15 minutes—no peeking. Ladle into soup bowls and serve.

RUSTIC TUSCAN BREAD AND VEGETABLE SOUP

Makes 4 to 6 servings

To save time, processor-chop the onion, carrot, and celery together. Several zaps should do the job nicely.

1 pound day-old Italian bread
1 quart cold water
⅓ cup extra-virgin olive oil
1 medium-large yellow onion,
   coarsely chopped (1 cup)
1 large carrot, peeled and
   coarsely chopped
1 large celery rib, trimmed and
   coarsely chopped
3 large garlic cloves, minced
½ cup dry white wine

One 28-ounce can Italian plum
   (Roma) tomatoes in puree
Two 8-ounce cans tomato sauce
One 8-ounce can tomato puree
½ cup coarsely chopped Italian
   (flat-leaf) parsley
1 cup freshly grated Parmesan
   cheese
½ cup finely julienned fresh
   basil leaves

1. Coarsely crumble bread into large bowl, add water, toss well, and let stand while you proceed with soup.

2. Heat oil in large, heavy nonreactive skillet until almost smoking, about 2 minutes. Add onion, carrot, and celery and cook and stir until onion is pale golden, about 2 minutes. Reduce heat to moderately low, add garlic, cover, and cook until vegetables are tender, 8 to 10 minutes. Add wine, raise heat, and boil until wine evaporates.

3. Add tomatoes, breaking up large clumps, tomato sauce, and puree. When mixture bubbles, adjust heat so mixture simmers slowly, cover, and cook 15 minutes.

4. Meanwhile, squeeze bread dry. As soon as tomato mixture has cooked 15 minutes, add bread and parsley and cook, stirring often, just until mixture steams.

5. Transfer to large heated bowl (but only if skillet is too messy or ugly to make an appearance at the table), top with grated cheese and basil, and serve.

SHORTCUT CIOPPINO

This classic fish muddle, historians tell us, was created in the early decades of this century by fishermen trolling off the coast of San Francisco. One afternoon, someone aboard ship tossed onions, garlic, and tomatoes into a giant kettle, added some of the day's catch, then let everything simmer until dinner time. Today, there are dozens of variations on the theme. My quick version is ready in less than 40 minutes. Serve with chewy chunks of bread, and, if you like, drizzle each portion with a little intensely fruity olive oil.

¼ cup extra-virgin olive oil
2 cups coarsely chopped fresh or frozen onions (about 2 medium-large yellow onions)
Half of a 1-pound bag frozen bell pepper stir-fry mix (red, green, and yellow peppers; do not thaw)
4 large garlic cloves, minced
2 large whole bay leaves
1 teaspoon dried oregano, crumbled
1 teaspoon dried basil, crumbled
One 28-ounce can crushed tomatoes, with their liquid

Two 1-pound jars chunky salsa (as mild or hot as you like)
Two 8-ounce bottles clam juice
1 cup dry white wine such as a Verdicchio or Soave
1 pound boned and skinned halibut, haddock, or cod
1 pound shelled and deveined medium-size raw shrimp or ½ pound each shrimp and lump crab or sea scallops, these halved if large
Salt and freshly ground black pepper

1. Heat oil in large kettle over moderately high heat 2 minutes. Add onions, stir-fry mix, garlic, bay leaves, oregano, and basil and cook, stirring often, until onions are golden, 8 to 10 minutes.

2. Add tomatoes, salsa, clam juice, and wine; bring to simmering, adjust heat so mixture bubbles gently, and cook uncovered just until flavors meld, about 20 minutes.

3. Add halibut and shrimp and cook uncovered just until shrimp turn pink and fish almost flakes, about 5 minutes.

4. Remove bay leaves, season to taste with salt and pepper, then serve with rough country bread.

MOST SUPERMARKETS CARRY
BOTTLED FISH SAUCE AND
CANNED UNSWEETENED THAI
COCONUT MILK, THE LATTER
IN BOTH REGULAR AND
"LIGHT." FOR TIPS ON USING
LEMONGRASS, SEE HEADNOTE
FOR TOMATO BROTH WITH
SHRIMP, MUSHROOMS AND
LEMONGRASS (PAGE 120).

THAI COCONUT MILK SOUP WITH CHICKEN, LEMONGRASS, AND CILANTRO

MAKES 4 SERVINGS

Ladled over rice, this exquisite Thai soup can become the centerpiece of a light lunch or supper. To save time, I use boned and skinned chicken cutlets instead of whole chicken breasts, which must be cooled until easy to handle after they have poached, then boned, skinned, and cubed.

2 cups Al Dente Make-Ahead
    Rice at room temperature
    (page 35)
1 tablespoon Asian roasted
    sesame oil
1 tablespoon unsalted butter
½ cup chopped onion (about
    1 medium-small yellow onion)
1 stalk lemongrass, trimmed and
    coarsely chopped
1 tablespoon minced fresh
    ginger
½ teaspoon red pepper flakes
Two 14½-ounce cans chicken
    broth

½ cup vegetable broth
1 pound chicken cutlets
1¼ cups Thai coconut milk
    (use light, if you like)
2 tablespoons Asian fish sauce
    (most supermarkets now
    carry it)
1 cup coarsely diced mushrooms
½ cup peeled, seeded, and diced
    firm-ripe tomato
1 large scallion, trimmed and
    thinly sliced (include some
    green tops)
3 tablespoons coarsely chopped
    fresh cilantro

1. Mold rice into 4 small timbales by packing into ½-cup dry measure well coated with vegetable spray. Unmold each timbale in large heated soup plate and set in warm spot.

2. Heat sesame oil and butter in large nonreactive saucepan over high heat 1 minute. Add onion, lemongrass, ginger, and red pepper flakes and cook, stirring often, until onion is limp, about 3 minutes.

3. Add chicken and vegetable broths, bring to boiling, then boil uncovered 10 minutes.

4. Add chicken cutlets, reduce heat to moderate, and simmer gently just until chicken cooks through, about 5 minutes. Remove chicken from pan and strain broth, discarding solids. Cut chicken into $1/2$-inch cubes.

5. Return strained broth to pan; add coconut milk, fish sauce, and mushrooms and simmer, uncovered, 5 minutes.

6. Return chicken to broth, add tomato, scallion, and cilantro, then ladle at once into heated soup plates on top of rice and serve.

CHICKEN AND MUSHROOM SOUP WITH CORNBREAD DUMPLINGS

Makes 4 to 6 servings

Wings, I find, make the best chicken soup—they cook fast and they're full of flavor. They're fatty, of course, but you can significantly trim the fat by using drummettes instead of whole wings. There are shortcuts all round: peeled baby-cut carrots; celery hearts, which can be sliced as a bunch; pre-sliced fresh mushrooms; canned chicken broth; frozen corn kernels; and best of all, cornbread-twist dough from the supermarket refrigerator counter, which I've discovered, can be steamed into supremely light little dumplings.

2 tablespoons olive oil or vegetable oil
2 cups fresh or frozen chopped onions (about 2 medium-large yellow onions)
1 large garlic clove, minced
1 cup thinly sliced celery (include some leaves)
1 cup peeled baby-cut fresh carrots, sliced ½ inch thick
Half of an 8-ounce package sliced fresh white mushrooms
2 tablespoons Duxelles (page 33; optional)
1 large whole bay leaf

Two 3-inch sprigs fresh thyme or ½ teaspoon dried thyme, crumbled
1 pound chicken drummettes
Two 14½-ounce cans chicken broth
1 teaspoon salt
¼ teaspoon freshly ground black pepper
1 cup frozen whole-kernel corn (do not thaw)
Half of an 11½-ounce tube refrigerated cornbread twists
⅓ cup minced parsley

1. Heat oil in medium-size Dutch oven over moderately high heat 2 minutes. Add onions, garlic, celery, carrots, mushrooms, duxelles, if desired, bay leaf, and thyme and turn to coat with oil. Add chicken, reduce heat to moderate, cover, and "sweat" 15 minutes, stirring now and then.

2. Add broth, salt, pepper, and corn; adjust heat so mixture bubbles gently, cover, and cook until flavors marry, 15 to 20 minutes. Skim off excess fat, if any. Taste for salt and pepper and fine-tune as needed.

3. Uncoil strips of cornbread dough and with scissors, snip crosswise at 1 1/4-inch intervals. Bring soup to rapid boil, then drop in pieces of cornbread dough, spacing evenly so they don't touch. Adjust heat so soup bubbles gently, cover, and cook 10 minutes—no peeking!

4. Remove bay leaf, then mix in parsley, taking care not to damage dumplings.

5. Ladle into heated large soup plates and serve.

THE GROVE PARK INN'S WONDERFUL SHRIMP, CORN, AND MUSHROOM SOUP

MAKES 4 TO 6 SERVINGS

I love the Smoky Mountains of North Carolina, and whenever I'm in Asheville, I stay at the Grove Park Inn, a grand old resort built halfway up Sunset Mountain with heart-stopping views of the town. Given the hotel's size (more than 500 rooms), the food is surprisingly good. This is my quick version of the GPI's chowdery classic—a meal in itself.

3 tablespoons extra-virgin olive oil

One 8-ounce package sliced fresh white mushrooms, coarsely chopped

4 large scallions, trimmed and coarsely chopped (include some green tops)

1 small Vidalia or other sweet onion, coarsely chopped

1 large garlic clove, minced

½ teaspoon minced fresh rosemary or ¼ teaspoon dried rosemary, crumbled

2 cups frozen mixed yellow and white whole-kernel corn (do not thaw)

Two 14½-ounce cans chicken broth

¼ teaspoon salt

¼ teaspoon freshly ground black pepper

½ pound shelled and deveined medium-size raw shrimp, halved lengthwise

½ cup half-and-half cream

1. Heat 2 tablespoons olive oil in large, heavy kettle over moderate heat 1 minute. Add mushrooms and cook, stirring often, until juices are released and these evaporate, about 5 minutes. Scoop mushrooms to large plate and reserve.

2. Add remaining 1 tablespoon oil to kettle; also add scallions, onion, garlic, and rosemary. Cook and stir until scallions and onion are golden, about 3 minutes. Add corn, broth, salt, and pep-

per; adjust heat so mixture bubbles gently, cover, and simmer 25 minutes.

3. With slotted spoon, scoop 2 cups soup solids into food processor and puree until smooth. Return to soup, add shrimp, and simmer just until they turn pink, 2 to 3 minutes.

4. Mix in cream and reserved mushrooms and bring to a simmer. Taste for salt and pepper, fine-tune, and serve.

TOMATO BROTH WITH SHRIMP, MUSHROOMS, AND LEMONGRASS

MAKES 4 SERVINGS

This aromatic Thai soup is so quick, so satisfying. Many high-end super-markets now routinely stock lemongrass, as do more and more farmer's markets (if you see potted lemongrass, by all means buy it and set it outside for the summer. It won't winter over in harsh climates, but you can bring the plant indoors and set in a sunny spot). The fleshy ivory-hued stalk is what you want for cooking, not the razor sharp leaves. Remove the tough outer layer of stalk, then coarsely chop the rest. If you're unable to find lemongrass, substitute three 3-inch strips lemon zest (colored part of the rind) and add a thin slice or two of fresh ginger. The flavor won't be the same, but it will be delicious. Don't forget to remove the lemon zest and ginger before serving.

2 cups Al Dente Make-Ahead Rice at room temperature (page 35)

3 cups water

2 stalks lemongrass, trimmed and coarsely chopped

One 10-ounce can diced tomatoes with green chilies, with their liquid

1 pound shelled and deveined medium-size raw shrimp

2 tablespoons Asian fish sauce (most supermarkets now carry it)

3 large scallions, trimmed and thinly sliced (include some green tops)

1 cup finely diced mushrooms

1 teaspoon fresh lime juice

3 tablespoons coarsely chopped fresh cilantro

Finely grated zest of 1 lime

1. Mold rice into 4 small timbales by packing into ½-cup dry mea-sure well coated with nonstick vegetable spray. Unmold each timbale in large heated soup plate and set in warm spot.

2. Bring water to boiling in large nonreactive saucepan over high heat. Add lemongrass, reduce heat to moderate, and boil uncovered 10 minutes. Strain liquid, discarding solids.

3. Return liquid to pan; add tomatoes with green chilies, shrimp, and fish sauce and simmer uncovered 5 minutes.

4. Add remaining ingredients, ladle at once into heated soup bowls, and serve.

CURRIED CARROT SOUP WITH SHRIMP

Makes 4 to 6 servings

To trim prep time, use packaged peeled baby-cut carrots as the foundation of this nourishing soup and, if you're in a yank, 2 cups frozen chopped onions instead of leeks. A quick preliminary roasting caramelizes the carrots, leeks, and garlic and deepens their flavors.

3 tablespoons extra-virgin olive oil

One 1-pound package peeled baby-cut fresh carrots

4 medium-size leeks, trimmed, washed well, and thinly sliced

2 large garlic cloves

One 3-inch sprig fresh rosemary or ½ teaspoon dried rosemary, crumbled

Two 3-inch sprigs fresh lemon thyme or ½ teaspoon dried thyme, crumbled

One 2-inch strip orange zest

2 to 4 teaspoons curry powder (depending on how hot you like things)

1 tablespoon minced mango chutney

One 14½-ounce can each chicken broth and beef broth

One 12-ounce can evaporated skim milk

¾ pound shelled and deveined small raw shrimp

Salt and freshly ground black pepper

¼ cup coarsely chopped Italian (flat-leaf) parsley

1. Preheat oven to 450°F. Place oil, carrots, leeks, garlic, rosemary, thyme, and orange zest in medium-size Dutch oven, turning vegetables to coat. Set uncovered in oven and roast 20 minutes, stirring twice.

2. Transfer to stovetop, set over moderate heat, and mix in curry powder. Add chutney, then chicken and beef broths; bring to a boil, then cover and boil gently until vegetables are soft, about 20 minutes.

3. Remove orange zest and rosemary and thyme sprigs; add milk, then puree soup in batches in food processor or electric blender.

4. Return soup to Dutch oven, add shrimp, bring to serving temperature, and season to taste with salt and pepper.

5. Ladle into heated soup bowls, sprinkle with parsley, and serve with crusty chunks of bread. Or chill and serve cold.

TIP

TO QUICK-CHILL SOUP, POUR INTO 13 X 9 X 2-INCH PAN AND SET IN FREEZER OR IN SINK FULL OF CRUSHED ICE OR ICE CUBES. STIR SOUP OFTEN UNTIL UNIFORMLY COLD.

BUTTERNUT-ROASTED RED PEPPER SOUP WITH CRAB

MAKES 6 SERVINGS

If you can afford fresh lump crab meat, by all means use it.

3 tablespoons extra-virgin olive oil (the fruitiest you can find)
1 large red onion, coarsely chopped
2 large garlic cloves, minced
Two 3-inch sprigs fresh lemon thyme or ½ teaspoon dried thyme, crumbled
Three 3-inch sprigs fresh marjoram or 1 teaspoon dried marjoram, crumbled
One 12-ounce jar roasted red peppers, drained
Two 12-ounce packages frozen cooked winter squash, thawed but not drained

One 14½-ounce can each chicken broth and beef broth
One 3-inch strip lemon zest
½ pound lump crab meat, bits of shell removed, or two 4½-ounce cans white crab meat, drained
Salt and freshly ground black pepper
Six 1-inch-thick slices French or Italian bread, lightly toasted (see Note)
¼ cup freshly snipped chives or minced parsley

1. Heat oil in large, heavy saucepan over moderate heat 1 minute. Add onion, garlic, thyme, and marjoram and cook, stirring often, until golden, 3 to 5 minutes.

2. Add red peppers, squash, chicken and beef broths, and lemon zest; bring to a simmer, cover, and cook about 20 minutes. Cool 5 minutes, remove thyme and marjoram sprigs and lemon zest, then puree in batches in food processor or electric blender.

3. Return to moderate heat, add crab, salt, and pepper to taste, and bring just to serving temperature.

4. Place slice of toast in each of six heated soup plates, ladle in soup, then scatter chives over each portion.

PORTUGUESE POTATO, COLLARD, AND SAUSAGE SOUP

MAKES 6 SERVINGS

The Portuguese call this *caldo verde* (green soup) because it's the color of emeralds. I've shortcut their tedious collard-shaving technique by using chopped frozen collards. I've also increased the amount of sausage to make this a hearty one-dish meal.

3 tablespoons extra-virgin olive
 oil (the fruitiest you can find)
Two 3½-ounce packages sliced
 pepperoni
2 cups fresh or frozen chopped
 onions (2 medium-large
 yellow onions)
2 large garlic cloves, minced
2 large baking potatoes (about
 1½ pounds), peeled and
 diced

6 cups water
One 1-pound package frozen
 chopped collards or turnip
 greens, thawed and drained
Salt and freshly ground black
 pepper

1. Heat 2 tablespoons oil in large, heavy saucepan over moderate heat 1 minute. Add pepperoni and cook, stirring often, until lightly browned, 2 to 3 minutes. Lift pepperoni to paper toweling to drain and pour drippings from pan, reserving 3 tablespoons; return these to pan.

2. Add onions, garlic, and potatoes and cook, stirring often, until onions are glassy, 3 to 5 minutes.

3. Add water, bring to a gentle boil, cover, and cook until potatoes are mushy, 20 to 25 minutes. Remove from heat and with potato masher, mash potatoes right in pan but leave plenty of lumps.

4. Return to moderate heat, add browned pepperoni and collards, and simmer until bright green, 2 to 3 minutes. Stir in remaining 1 tablespoon oil, season with salt and pepper, ladle out, and serve.

SOUP OF SCALLIONS AND BITTER GREENS WITH CHEESE TORTELLINI

Makes 4 to 6 servings

Few soups are faster than this one, or better. Shortcut: While the scallions are still bunched, whack off the root ends and all but two inches of the tops, unband the scallions, wash, and dry on paper toweling. Finally, rebunch the scallions, six at a time, and slice straight across each bunch using a large chef's knife. A couple of minutes is all it takes to slice four bunches.

3 tablespoons extra-virgin olive oil

4 bunches large scallions, trimmed and thinly sliced (include some green tops; about 24 scallions)

2 large whole bay leaves

1 large garlic clove, finely minced

3 cups frozen chopped mustard or turnip greens (no need to thaw)

¼ teaspoon freshly ground black pepper

Two 14½-ounce cans chicken broth

3 tablespoons concentrated chicken broth

One 9-ounce package fresh cheese or mushroom tortellini (from supermarket refrigerator counter)

6 tablespoons freshly grated Parmesan cheese

1. Heat 2 tablespoons oil in large, heavy saucepan over high heat 1 minute. Add scallions and bay leaves, and cook, stirring often, until scallions are lightly browned, about 5 minutes.

2. Add garlic, mustard greens, and pepper and cook, stirring, until limp, about 5 minutes.

3. Add broth and concentrated broth and bring to a boil. Add tortellini, adjust heat so mixture bubbles gently, and cook just until al dente, 4 to 5 minutes.

4. Stir in remaining 1 tablespoon oil, remove bay leaves, taste for salt and pepper, and adjust as needed.

5. Ladle into heated soup plates and top each portion with grated Parmesan.

VARIATION

Green Leek Soup with Potato Gnocchi: Prepare as directed but substitute 6 thinly sliced, well-cleaned medium-size leeks for scallions. Also substitute frozen chopped collards or kale for mustard greens and beef broth for chicken broth (keep the concentrated chicken broth, however). In step 3, omit tortellini, and add 1 1/2 cups dried potato gnocchi (available in every good supermarket) to bubbling broth. Adjust heat so liquid boils gently and cook just until gnocchi float, 3 to 4 minutes. Proceed and serve as directed in steps 4 and 5.

LENTIL SOUP WITH SAUSAGE AND TOMATOES

Makes 6 servings

I've been unorthodox here. I've soaked the lentils to trim cooking time (after two hours in cool water, they're done in ten minutes). I usually soak the lentils early in the day, drain them, then store both the lentils and their soaking water in the refrigerator until needed. To trim time further still, I use canned consommé (richer than broth), a good chunky salsa with plenty of flavor, frozen chopped collards, and gobs of fresh scallions. These, I find, have more flavor than dry onions, they're "tearless," and they can be sliced on the double (see headnote for Soup of Scallions and Bitter Greens with Cheese Tortellini, page 126).

2 tablespoons extra-virgin olive oil

2 fresh sweet Italian sausages (about 4 ounces), casings removed and links sliced ½ inch thick

2 bunches large scallions, trimmed and thinly sliced (include some green tops; about 12 scallions)

2 large garlic cloves, finely minced

Two 10½-ounce cans beef consommé

1 cup brown lentils, soaked 2 hours in 4 cups cold water, drained, and 2 cups soaking water reserved

4 cups frozen chopped collards (no need to thaw)

½ teaspoon salt

½ cup bottled mild to medium chunky tomato-vegetable salsa

One 10½-ounce can diced tomatoes with green chilies, drained

1. Heat 1 tablespoon oil in large, heavy saucepan over high heat 1 minute. Add sausages and cook, breaking up slices, until lightly browned, about 3 minutes.

2. Add scallions and cook, stirring often until limp and golden, about 3 minutes. Add garlic and cook 1 minute.

3. Add 1 can consommé and cook and stir 1 minute, scraping up browned bits on pan bottom. Add remaining consommé, lentils, and soaking water; adjust heat so mixture bubbles gently, and cook uncovered 5 minutes.

4. Add collards and cook uncovered, stirring now and then, 5 minutes. Add salt, salsa, tomatoes with chilies and bring just to serving temperature. Taste for salt and adjust as needed.

5. Smooth in remaining 1 tablespoon olive oil, ladle into heated soup bowls, and serve.

MADEIRA EGG-DROP TOMATO AND ONION SOUP

Makes 6 servings

On the Portuguese island of Madeira, where I fell in love with this meal-in-a-bowl, women cook vine-ripened tomatoes, freshly chopped onions, and garlic down, down, down until they're as thick as marinara sauce. I built this shortcut version around bottled marinara sauce and think it's almost as good as the long-winded original (that one's in my book *The Food of Portugal*).

4 tablespoons extra-virgin olive oil (the fruitiest you can find)
4 cups fresh or frozen chopped onions (4 medium-large yellow onions)
4 large garlic cloves, minced
2 whole bay leaves
Two 10½-ounce cans beef consommé
One 26-ounce bottle marinara sauce or 3¼ cups Basic Tomato Sauce (page 30)
One 14½-ounce can diced tomatoes, drained

¼ cup medium-dry Madeira wine (Verdelho) or dry vermouth
1½ tablespoons sugar (to mellow tartness of tomatoes)
Salt and freshly ground black pepper
6 medium-size eggs
Twelve (½-inch-thick) slices French bread, brushed with olive oil and lightly toasted
¼ cup coarsely chopped Italian (flat-leaf) parsley

1. Heat 3 tablespoons oil in medium-size Dutch oven over moderately high heat 2 minutes. Add onions, garlic, and bay leaves; reduce heat to moderate and cook, stirring often, until lightly browned, 8 to 10 minutes.

2. Add consommé, bring to a gentle boil, cover, and cook until onions are soft, about 10 minutes.

3. Add marinara sauce, tomatoes, wine, and sugar; bring to a gentle boil and cook uncovered until flavors mellow, about 15 minutes.

4. Stir in remaining 1 tablespoon oil, salt, and pepper to taste. Bring soup to rapid boil, then break in eggs, spacing evenly. Adjust heat so mixture bubbles gently, spoon hot soup over eggs, cover, and cook just until yolks are firm, about 10 minutes. Remove bay leaves.

5. Arrange two slices toast in each of six heated soup plates, ladle in soup making sure each person gets an egg, sprinkle with parsley, and serve.

TUSCAN SOUP OF SPRING VEGETABLES

Makes 6 servings

This jiffy soup was inspired by a longer-winded one in Nancy Harmon Jenkins's *Flavors of Tuscany*, a book that brims with irresistible recipes.

3 tablespoons extra-virgin olive oil

4 large scallions, trimmed and coarsely chopped (include some green tops)

1 whole bay leaf

4 ounces sweet Italian sausage, removed from casing

½ pound lean ground beef round

One 9-ounce package frozen baby lima beans (do not thaw)

One 9-ounce package frozen artichoke hearts (do not thaw)

Three 14½-ounce cans chicken broth + enough cold water to total 6 cups

One 9-ounce package frozen cut asparagus (do not thaw)

One 10-ounce package frozen green peas (do not thaw)

Salt and freshly ground black pepper

Six 1-inch-thick slices Italian bread, brushed with olive oil and lightly toasted

6 tablespoons coarsely chopped Italian (flat-leaf) parsley

6 tablespoons freshly grated Parmesan cheese

1. Heat olive oil in large, heavy saucepan over moderate heat 1 minute. Add scallions, bay leaf, sausage, and beef and cook, breaking up clumps of meat, until no longer pink, about 5 minutes.

2. Add limas and artichoke hearts and cook 3 to 5 minutes, turning vegetables to glaze.

3. Add broth, adjust heat so mixture bubbles gently, cover, and simmer 15 minutes.

4. Add asparagus and peas, bring to a boil, cover, and cook 5 minutes, just until asparagus is crisp-tender. Remove bay leaf, then season to taste with salt and pepper.

5. Place a slice of toast in each of six heated large soup plates, ladle in soup, then scatter parsley and Parmesan over each portion, dividing amounts evenly.

SUMMER SQUASH SOUP WITH RED-SKIN POTATOES AND PASTA SHELLS

I'm a huge fan of Deborah Madison's and must confess that her vegetarian minestrone inspired this husky nonvegetarian soup. To make it vegetarian, substitute vegetable broth for chicken. Shortcut: To thaw collards zip-quick, microwave on medium 3 to 5 minutes.

3 tablespoons extra-virgin
   olive oil
6 large scallions, trimmed and
   thinly sliced (include some
   green tops)
3 large garlic cloves, minced
2 whole bay leaves
4 golf-ball-size red-skin
   potatoes, scrubbed and
   quartered but not peeled
Three 14½-ounce cans chicken
   broth
1 cup small pasta shells
½ pound small zucchini,
   trimmed, halved lengthwise,
   then sliced crosswise ½ inch
   thick

½ pound small yellow squash,
   trimmed, halved lengthwise,
   then sliced crosswise ½ inch
   thick
One 1-pound package frozen
   chopped collards, turnip
   greens, or spinach, thawed
   and drained
One 1-pound 3-ounce can
   cannellini (white kidney
   beans), drained and rinsed
1 cup finely sliced fresh basil
   (measure loosely packed)
Salt and freshly ground black
   pepper
½ cup freshly grated Parmesan
   cheese

1. Heat olive oil in large, heavy saucepan over moderate heat 2 minutes. Add scallions, garlic, and bay leaves and cook, stirring often, until limp, 2 to 3 minutes.

2. Add potatoes and broth, bring to a boil, cover, and boil gently until potatoes are barely tender.

3. Add pasta, zucchini, and yellow squash; return to a boil, cover, and boil 8 minutes.

4. Add collards and cannellini, cover, and simmer 3 to 5 minutes until pasta and vegetables are tender and flavors marry.

5. Add basil and salt and pepper to taste. Remove bay leaves.

6. Ladle into heated soup bowls and sprinkle grated Parmesan over each portion.

VARIATION

Winter and Summer Squash Soup: Prepare as directed, omitting pasta shells and adding 1 cup 3/4-inch cubes peeled butternut or acorn squash along with potatoes. Also substitute red kidney beans or chick-peas for cannellini.

MOZZARELLA SOUP WITH VEGETABLES AND BLACK OLIVES

Makes 4 servings

I've always been partial to cheese soups, especially Tillamook, a creamy blend made with Oregon's sharp Cheddar. So, I wondered, why not a lower-calorie mozzarella soup with no stinting on vegetables? To save time, I processor-chop packaged peeled, baby-cut carrots with celery ribs (from packaged, trimmed celery hearts), onion, and potato. I also use pre-pitted black olives. I prefer the plump oil-packed Kalamatas of Greece — and yes, you can buy them pitted.

3 tablespoons extra-virgin olive oil (the fruitiest you can find)
1 large red onion, peeled and very coarsely chopped
Half of a 1-pound package peeled baby-cut fresh carrots, very coarsely chopped
2 small celery ribs, very coarsely chopped
1 large baking potato (about 12 ounces), peeled and diced
1 large garlic clove, minced
1 whole bay leaf
One 3-inch sprig fresh rosemary or ½ teaspoon dried rosemary, crumbled

One 14½-ounce can chicken broth
One 12-ounce can evaporated milk (use skim, if you like)
½ cup fresh whole milk
½ teaspoon hot red pepper sauce
Half of an 8-ounce package finely shredded mozzarella cheese
⅓ cup sliced pitted ripe olives
Salt and freshly ground black pepper

1. Heat oil in large, heavy saucepan over moderate heat 1 minute. Add onion, carrots, celery, potato, garlic, bay leaf, and rosemary; cook, stirring often, 5 minutes. Reduce heat to low, cover, and "sweat" vegetables 10 minutes.

2. Add broth, bring to gentle boil, cover, and cook until potato is tender, about 15 minutes.

3. Add evaporated milk, milk, and red pepper sauce and bring to a simmer. Off heat, add mozzarella and stir until smooth. Stir in olives and salt and pepper to taste.

4. Discard bay leaf and rosemary sprig, ladle into heated soup bowls, and serve.

GARLIC, ONION, AND MUSHROOM BROTH WITH SPINACH RAVIOLI

MAKES 6 SERVINGS

A jiffy cold-day dish that's as delicious as it is quick and easy. No additional salt needed.

2 tablespoons extra-virgin olive oil

2 tablespoons unsalted butter

One 12-ounce package frozen chopped onions (do not thaw)

2 large garlic cloves, minced

1 teaspoon minced fresh lemon thyme or ½ teaspoon dried thyme, crumbled

One 6-ounce package sliced portobello mushrooms, coarsely chopped

¼ cup Duxelles (page 33; optional)

½ teaspoon freshly ground black pepper

Four 14 ½-ounce cans beef broth

Two 13-ounce packages frozen mushroom-spinach ravioli with wild mushroom sauce (do not thaw)

¾ cup freshly grated Parmesan cheese

6 tablespoons freshly snipped chives or dill (optional)

I. Heat oil and butter in large, heavy saucepan over moderate heat 2 minutes. Raise heat to high, add onions, and cook, stirring often, until richly browned, 8 to 10 minutes; reduce heat to moderate.

2. Add garlic, thyme, mushrooms, duxelles if desired, and pepper and cook, stirring often, until mushrooms release their juices and these evaporate, about 5 minutes.

3. Add broth, bring to a boil, then ease in frozen ravioli. Adjust heat so mixture bubbles gently and cook just until ravioli are heated through, about 10 minutes.

4. Ladle into heated soup plates, top each with 2 tablespoons cheese, then, if you like, 1 tablespoon fresh chives. Serve at once.

PANZANELLA

Makes 4 servings

This is nothing more than cold Italian bread and tomato soup. To pump up the protein, I serve it over scoops of ricotta cheese—delicious but highly unorthodox. The dressed-up variation is loosely based on the panzanella served at my favorite New York City Italian restaurant—Follonico on West 24th Street between Fifth and Sixth avenues. Its gifted chef-proprietor is Alan Tardi.

½ loaf French or Italian bread, sliced ½ inch thick (about ½ pound)

2¼ pounds red-ripe Italian plum (Roma) tomatoes, peeled, seeded, and diced; or two 1-pound cans diced tomatoes, drained (reserve liquid)

4 large scallions, trimmed and coarsely chopped (include some green tops)

1 large garlic clove, minced

1 cup finely sliced fresh basil leaves (measure loosely packed)

¼ cup coarsely chopped fresh mint

3 tablespoons extra-virgin olive oil (the fruitiest you can find)

1 tablespoon red wine vinegar

Salt and teaspoon freshly ground black pepper to taste

1⅓ cups ricotta cheese (use part-skim, if you like)

1. Soak bread in enough warm water to cover (about 6 cups) 5 minutes; drain and gently press excess water from bread without crushing it.

2. Place bread in large bowl, add all remaining ingredients except ricotta, and toss gently. If using canned tomatoes, add just enough reserved liquid to moisten bread well. Let mixture stand at room temperature 30 minutes. Taste for salt and pepper and adjust as needed.

3. Place ⅓ cup ricotta in each of four large soup plates. Toss panzanella gently again, spoon over ricotta, and serve.

DRESSED-UP PANZANELLA: PREPARE AS DIRECTED, BUT ADD 1 COARSELY CHOPPED SMALL RED ONION AND 1 CUP DICED BOILED HAM, ROAST PORK, CHICKEN, OR TURKEY, AND 1 CUP FROZEN WHOLE-KERNEL CORN THAT HAS BEEN BLANCHED AND DRAINED. ALSO OMIT RICOTTA CHEESE AND SUBSTITUTE ½ CUP COARSELY CHOPPED FRESH CILANTRO FOR BASIL AND MINT.

45-MINUTE CHILI

MAKES 8 SERVINGS

Championship chilis bubble for hours. This one, thanks to today's gutsy bottled salsas and pasta sauces, rivals their depth of flavor yet is ready to eat in 45 minutes. Best of all, it practically cooks itself and requires little more than an occasional stir. How easy is that?

3 tablespoons bacon drippings or vegetable oil
1¼ pounds lean ground beef chuck
1 tablespoon chili powder
1 teaspoon dried oregano, crumbled
2 large bay leaves
2 cups fresh or frozen chopped onions (2 medium-large yellow onions)
Half of a 1-pound bag frozen bell pepper stir-fry mix (red, green, and yellow peppers; do not thaw)
2 large garlic cloves, minced

One 10-ounce can diced tomatoes with green chilies, drained
One 1-pound jar chunky salsa (as mild or hot as you like)
One 26-ounce jar arrabbiata (spicy red pepper) pasta sauce
4 tablespoons tomato paste
One 12-ounce can beer
1 ounce unsweetened chocolate
One 28-ounce can spicy baked or barbecued beans, drained
Salt

1. Heat bacon drippings in medium-size Dutch oven over high heat 1 minute. Add beef, chili powder, oregano, and bay leaves and brown meat, breaking up clumps, 5 minutes.

2. Add onions, stir-fry mix, and garlic and sauté, stirring often, until onions are golden, about 5 minutes.

3. Reduce heat to moderate, add all remaining ingredients except beans and salt, and boil uncovered—gently—stirring now and then to prevent sticking, until flavors meld and mixture is a good chili consistency—about 30 minutes. Remove bay leaves.

4. Add beans and salt to taste, then heat 2 to 3 minutes longer. Dish up and serve with soda crackers.

NEW MEXICO GREEN CHILI

MAKES 4 TO 6 SERVINGS

Usually an all-day affair, green chili can be made in 30 to 40 minutes if you resort to a few tricks. I've substituted ground pork for chunks of pork shoulder, which take hours to simmer into submission—also, canned pinto beans, frozen chopped onions, and a frozen bell pepper stir-fry mix. Finally, a diced tomato–green chili combo, available by the can, saves many more minutes.

¼ cup bacon drippings or vegetable oil

One 1-pound bag frozen bell pepper stir-fry mix (red, green, and yellow peppers; do not thaw)

1 cup frozen chopped onions (do not thaw)

4 large garlic cloves, crushed

1 pound ground pork shoulder

2 teaspoons dried sage, crumbled

2 teaspoons dried oregano, crumbled

2 whole bay leaves

Four 10-ounce cans diced tomatoes with green chilies, with their liquid

Two 15½-ounce cans pinto or red kidney beans, drained

2 tablespoons tomato paste

½ teaspoon salt

1. Heat drippings in large heavy kettle over moderate heat 2 minutes. Add stir-fry mix and onions and cook, stirring often, until richly browned, 10 to 12 minutes.

2. Add garlic, pork, sage, oregano, and bay leaves and cook, breaking up clumps of pork, until meat is no longer pink, about 5 minutes.

3. Add tomatoes with green chilies, bring to a boil, then adjust heat so mixture bubbles gently, cover, and simmer until flavors get together, about 10 minutes.

4. Add beans, tomato paste, and salt; set kettle lid on askew and simmer 10 minutes more. Remove bay leaves; taste for salt and fine-tune.

5. Ladle into heated soup plates and serve with tortillas or tortilla chips.

SHORTCUT BEEF CATALAN

MAKES 6 SERVINGS

This Spanish beef and bean stew normally cooks long and slow because tough cuts of meat are used. By substituting ground beef, I've pared cooking time to about 50 minutes. I've also significantly trimmed prep time by using packaged, peeled baby-cut carrots, bottled salsa, and canned cannellini.

1 tablespoon extra-virgin olive oil

6 strips lean bacon, snipped crosswise into julienne strips

1 pound lean ground beef chuck

2 cups fresh or frozen chopped onions (2 medium-large yellow onions)

2 large garlic cloves, minced

One 1-pound package peeled baby-cut fresh carrots

2 whole bay leaves

Two 3-inch sprigs fresh thyme or ½ teaspoon dried thyme, crumbled

One 3-inch strip orange zest

One 1-inch piece cinnamon stick

2 whole cloves

One 10 ½-ounce can beef consommé

1 cup dry red wine

One 1-pound jar chunky salsa (not too spicy)

2 tablespoons tomato paste

One 1-pound 3-ounce can cannellini (white kidney beans), drained

3 tablespoons minced Italian (flat-leaf) parsley

Salt and freshly ground black pepper

1. Heat oil in medium-size Dutch oven over moderate heat 1 minute. Add bacon and cook, stirring often, until only browned bits remain, about 5 minutes. Lift browned bits to paper toweling to drain. Raise burner heat to high.

2. Pat ground chuck into large flat patty and brown in drippings, allowing about 3 minutes per side; lift to plate and reserve.

3. Reduce heat to moderate; add onions, garlic, carrots, bay leaves, thyme, orange zest, cinnamon, and cloves to Dutch oven and cook, stirring frequently, 5 minutes until onions are golden.

4. Add consommé and wine, bring to gentle boil, set lid on askew, and cook 15 minutes. Lay meat patty on top of stew, set lid on askew, and cook 15 minutes more.

5. Break meat into 1 1/2-inch clumps, mix in salsa and tomato paste, and cook uncovered 5 minutes. Add cannellini, parsley, and reserved bacon and bring just to serving temperature. Season to taste with salt and pepper.

6. Remove bay leaves, thyme sprigs, and cinnamon stick, ladle into heated soup plates, and serve.

QUICK BEEF CARBONNADE

Makes 6 servings

This Belgian beef and beer stew is such a favorite I wanted to develop a jiffy version. Like Beef Catalan (page 142), the original must simmer for hours. Here, too, I've substituted quick-cooking ground chuck for stew beef without sacrificing flavor. Finally, I cook the potatoes in the stew instead of ladling it over them and add asparagus to make this a true one-dish dinner. Not authentic but definitely delicious.

1 1/4 pounds lean ground beef chuck
1/4 cup all-purpose flour
3 tablespoons unsalted butter or margarine
2 cups fresh or frozen chopped onions (2 medium-large yellow onions)
2 large garlic cloves, minced
Two 3-inch sprigs fresh lemon thyme or 1/2 teaspoon dried thyme, crumbled
1/4 teaspoon freshly grated nutmeg

1 1/2 pounds red-skin potatoes, scrubbed and cut into 1 1/2-inch chunks but not peeled
One 10 1/2-ounce can beef consommé
One 12-ounce can beer blended with 3 tablespoons all-purpose flour
One 9-ounce package frozen asparagus cuts (do not thaw)
Salt and freshly ground black pepper

1. Shape ground chuck into large flat patty and dredge both sides well in flour.

2. Heat butter in medium-size Dutch oven over high heat 1 minute. Add beef patty and brown 3 minutes on each side. Lift to plate and reserve.

3. Lower heat to moderate; add onions, garlic, thyme, and nutmeg to drippings and sauté, stirring often, until onions are golden, about 3 minutes.

4. Add potatoes and consommé, bring to a gentle boil, set lid on askew, and cook 15 minutes. Add beer mixture and cook, stirring often, until liquid thickens slightly, 3 to 5 minutes.

5. Add meat, breaking into largish clumps, cover, and cook 10 minutes. Add asparagus and cook, breaking up frozen clumps, until potatoes are tender and meat shows no signs of pink, 7 to 10 minutes more. Remove thyme sprigs.

6. Season to taste with salt and pepper, ladle into heated soup plates, and serve.

MEATBALL BOURGUIGNON

Makes 4 to 6 servings

Here, too, I substitute quick-cooking ground beef for stew meat, which turns tender only after hours in the pot. And I save additional time by using the prepped fresh vegetables now available in most supermarket produce sections. Don't be daunted by the long ingredients list. This *bourguignon* goes together fast and all but cooks itself.

1 pound lean ground beef chuck
1/4 cup all-purpose flour
6 slices lean bacon, snipped crosswise into julienne strips
2 tablespoons olive oil or vegetable oil
1 cup fresh or frozen chopped onion (1 medium-large yellow onion)
1 garlic clove, minced
2 whole bay leaves
Three 3-inch sprigs fresh lemon thyme or 1/2 teaspoon dried thyme, crumbled
One 8-ounce package sliced fresh white mushrooms

1/4 cup (four 3/4-inch pats) Duxelles (page 33; optional)
Half of a 1-pound package peeled baby-cut fresh carrots
1 cup frozen small whole onions (do not thaw)
One 10 1/2-ounce can beef consommé
1 cup Burgundy or other dry red wine
1/4 cup dry red wine blended with 4 tablespoons all-purpose flour
Salt and freshly ground black pepper
1/4 cup minced parsley

1. Shape beef into 1-inch balls and dredge well in flour; set aside.

2. Sauté bacon in oil in medium-size Dutch oven over moderate heat until crisp and brown, about 5 minutes. With slotted spoon, scoop browned bacon to paper toweling to drain.

3. Brown meatballs well in drippings on all sides; lift to paper toweling to drain.

4. Add chopped onion, garlic, bay leaves, and thyme to pot and cook, stirring often, until onion is limp, about 3 minutes.

5. Add mushrooms, duxelles if desired, carrots, and small whole onions and cook a few minutes, stirring often to glaze. Add consommé, bring to gentle boil, cover, and cook 15 minutes.

6. Return meatballs to pot, add 1 cup red wine, cover, and simmer until meatballs are well done, about 15 minutes.

7. Blend about 1 cup hot pot liquid into wine-flour mixture, stir back into pot, and cook, stirring occasionally, until slightly thickened and no raw flour taste remains, 3 to 5 minutes. Season to taste with salt and pepper. Remove bay leaves and thyme sprigs.

8. Stir in parsley and reserved bacon, ladle into heated soup bowls, and serve with crusty chunks of French bread.

WIENER GOULASH

Wiener, in this case, doesn't mean hot dog. It means Viennese, specifically my quick and easy version of my mother's slow-simmering goulash.

1 pound lean ground beef chuck
⅓ cup all-purpose flour
3 tablespoons unsalted butter
1 tablespoon vegetable oil
2 cups fresh or frozen chopped onions (2 medium-large yellow onions)
Half of a 1-pound bag frozen bell pepper stir-fry mix (red, green, and yellow peppers; do not thaw)
1 garlic clove, minced
Three 3-inch sprigs fresh lemon thyme or ½ teaspoon dried thyme, crumbled

Two 8-ounce packages sliced fresh white mushrooms
3 tablespoons Hungarian sweet rose paprika
Two 10 ½-ounce cans beef consommé
1 cup sour cream (at room temperature)
Salt and freshly ground black pepper
Half of a 12-ounce package medium-wide egg noodles, cooked and drained by package directions

1. Shape beef into large flat patty. Place flour in pie pan and dredge all sides of beef patty well in flour; set aside.

2. Heat 1 tablespoon butter and oil in heavy, deep 12-inch skillet over moderately high heat 1 minute. Add beef and brown 2 minutes on a side; lift to pan of dredging flour and reserve.

3. Add remaining 2 tablespoons butter to skillet and when it melts, reduce heat to moderate; add onions, stir-fry mix, garlic, and thyme and cook, stirring occasionally, until limp, about 5 minutes.

4. Add mushrooms and cook, stirring occasionally, until they release their juices and these evaporate, about 10 minutes.

5. Blend in paprika and all dredging flour, then add consommé and cook, stirring constantly, until mixture boils. Return beef to skillet,

pushing down under liquid, bring to a gentle boil, cover, and cook 15 minutes. Break beef into 1- to 1½-inch chunks and simmer, uncovered and stirring occasionally, until beef is well done, about 10 minutes more.

6. Remove thyme sprigs and stir in sour cream. Season to taste with salt and pepper, add noodles, and toss gently to mix. Ladle into heated soup bowls and serve.

TIP

COOK THE NOODLES WHEN THE STEW IS ALMOST DONE— THEY'LL TAKE 8 TO 10 MINUTES.

EASY IRISH STEW

MAKES 6 SERVINGS

Layer everything into a Dutch oven and let it rip! Dinner's ready in 35 minutes.

2 tablespoons bacon drippings
    or unsalted butter
1 ½ pounds red-skin potatoes,
    scrubbed and cut into 1-inch
    cubes but not peeled
2 large yellow onions, peeled
    and thinly sliced
One 1-pound package peeled
    baby-cut fresh carrots
1 pound lean ground lamb
    shoulder

2 large whole bay leaves
One 10 ½-ounce can beef
    consommé blended with 1 ⅓
    cups water, 2 teaspoons salt,
    and ½ teaspoon freshly
    ground black pepper
⅓ cup all-purpose flour blended
    with ½ cup cold water
½ cup minced parsley

1. Heat bacon drippings in medium-size Dutch oven over moderate heat 1 minute.

2. Layer ingredients into Dutch oven this way: half the potatoes, half the onions, half the carrots, all lamb (break into largish clumps and distribute evenly), remaining onions, carrots, and potatoes. Tuck in bay leaves.

3. Pour in consommé mixture, bring to gentle boil, cover, and cook until potatoes are tender and meat is done, about 30 minutes.

4. Whisk about 1 cup kettle liquid into flour mixture, stir back into pot, and cook, stirring often, until thickened and no raw flour taste remains, about 5 minutes. Discard bay leaves. Taste for salt and pepper and fine-tune.

5. Mix in parsley and serve.

ZIP-QUICK COUNTRY CAPTAIN

Makes 4 to 6 servings

By using deli roast chicken (or turkey) and leftover cooked rice, this slow-simmering Georgia classic is ready to serve in no time.

3 tablespoons bacon drippings
   or vegetable oil
1 large yellow onion, coarsely
   chopped
1 large green bell pepper, cored,
   seeded, and coarsely chopped
1 large red bell pepper, cored,
   seeded, and coarsely chopped
2 large garlic cloves, minced
1 tablespoon curry powder
1 teaspoon dried marjoram,
   crumbled
½ teaspoon dried thyme,
   crumbled
¼ teaspoon ground hot red
   pepper (cayenne)

Three 14½-ounce cans crushed
   tomatoes, with their liquid
One 3-pound rotisserie chicken
   (from deli counter), cut up as
   for frying; or 2 pounds
   boneless cooked turkey
   breast, cubed
½ cup dried currants
Salt and freshly ground black
   pepper to taste
¼ cup minced parsley
3 cups Al Dente Make-Ahead
   Rice (page 35), reheated
¾ cup toasted slivered almonds

1. Heat bacon drippings in large, deep skillet over moderate heat 1 minute. Add onion and bell peppers and cook, stirring often, until onion is limp and golden, 5 to 8 minutes. Mix in garlic, curry powder, marjoram, thyme, and cayenne and cook and stir 2 minutes.

2. Add tomatoes, chicken, currants, salt, and black pepper; adjust heat so mixture bubbles gently, cover, and cook, stirring now and then, until flavors mingle and chicken is heated through—about 15 minutes. Mix in parsley, taste for salt and pepper, and adjust as needed.

3. Mound rice in heated, large, deep platter, ladle chicken mixture on top, sprinkle with almonds, and serve.

SHORTCUT

Processor-chop onion and bell peppers together. Simply chunk each, then pulse quickly to desired texture.

TIPS

Reheat rice in a steamer while sauce and chicken cook. If you don't have a steamer, dump rice into large fine-mesh sieve, balance over large saucepan containing two inches simmering water, cover, and steam about 10 minutes. Fluff with fork before serving. To toast almonds: Spread in pie tin, then set in preheated 325°F. oven for 10 to 12 minutes until lightly browned. Watch closely—nuts burn easily.

RAGOUT OF LAMB, TOMATOES, POTATOES, AND CHICKPEAS

Makes 6 servings

The trick here is to simmer the potatoes before adding the tomato sauce, otherwise they'll never be tender. No problem. Everything's done in the same pot, only in stages.

3 tablespoons extra-virgin olive oil

2 cups fresh or frozen chopped onions (2 medium-large yellow onions)

2 large garlic cloves, minced

Two 3-inch sprigs fresh rosemary or ½ teaspoon dried rosemary, crumbled

2 large whole bay leaves

1 pound red-skin potatoes, scrubbed and cut into ¾-inch chunks but not peeled

Half of a 1-pound package peeled baby-cut fresh carrots

One 10½-ounce can beef consommé + enough water to total 2 cups

1 pound lean ground lamb shoulder or ground beef chuck

One 1-pound 3-ounce can chickpeas, rinsed and drained

One 7-ounce jar sliced pimientos, well drained

2 cups bottled marinara sauce or Basic Tomato Sauce (page 30) mixed with ¼ cup dry vermouth, 1 teaspoon salt, and ½ teaspoon freshly ground black pepper

½ cup minced Italian (flat-leaf) parsley

1. Heat olive oil in medium-size Dutch oven over moderately high heat 2 minutes. Add onions, garlic, rosemary, and bay leaves; reduce heat to moderate and cook, stirring often, until onions are limp, about 5 minutes.

2. Add potatoes, carrots, and consommé mixture; bring to gentle boil, cover, and cook until potatoes are nearly tender, about 15

minutes. Watch closely and if kettle threatens to boil dry, add a little additional water, but not enough to make things soupy.

3. Add lamb, crumbling into large chunks and distributing evenly. Cover and cook 10 minutes.

4. Add chickpeas, pimientos, and marinara mixture; set lid on askew and cook just until flavors meld, about 10 minutes more. Remove bay leaves and rosemary sprigs.

5. Add parsley, ladle into heated soup bowls, and serve.

HAM, GREEN PEAS, AND DUMPLINGS

Makes 4 servings

When I was a child, my mother would make green peas and dumplings whenever I'd been extra-good. I've added ham and carrots (packaged, peeled baby-cut carrots save time) to make this a main dish. Do try to find fresh mint for this recipe (mint flakes are a poor substitute). And do try the variations. They're great ways to recycle leftovers.

1 tablespoon unsalted butter or margarine
½ cup fresh or frozen chopped onion (1 medium-small yellow onion)
Two 2-inch sprigs fresh mint or 1 teaspoon mint flakes
1 tablespoon sugar
1 cup peeled baby-cut fresh carrots, sliced ¼ inch thick
1 cup ¼-inch cubes baked or boiled ham (about 6 ounces)
One 14½-ounce can chicken broth

One 10-ounce package frozen tiny green peas (do not thaw)
1 tablespoon Duxelles (page 33; optional)
1 cup half-and-half or light cream
½ teaspoon salt
¼ teaspoon freshly ground black pepper
1 cup Dumpling/Biscuit Topping Mix (page 31)
¼ to ⅓ cup milk

1. Melt butter in large, heavy saucepan over high heat. Add onion, mint, and sugar and cook, stirring often, until onion is limp, about 3 minutes.

2. Add carrots, ham, and ½ cup broth; reduce heat to moderate, cover, and cook 10 minutes.

3. Add peas, duxelles if using, remaining broth, cream, and salt and pepper to taste. Bring to simmer.

4. Meanwhile, fork together dumpling mix and enough milk to make soft dough. As soon as pea mixture bubbles gently, remove

mint sprigs, then drop in dough by rounded teaspoons, spacing evenly. Cover and simmer undisturbed for 15 minutes.

5. Ladle into heated soup plates and serve.

VARIATIONS

Green Peas, Ham, Mushrooms, and Dumplings: Prepare as directed but omit carrots. Instead, cook half of an 8-ounce package sliced fresh white mushrooms along with onion and increase cooking time to 5 to 6 minutes, long enough for mushrooms to release juices and these to evaporate. In step 3, increase amount of duxelles to 2 tablespoons. Otherwise, proceed as directed.

Green Peas, Chicken (or Turkey), and Dumplings: Prepare as directed, substituting 1½ cups diced cooked chicken or turkey (light meat and/or dark) for ham and two 3-inch sprigs fresh thyme (or ½ teaspoon crumbled dried thyme) for mint. In step 3, increase amount of duxelles to 2 tablespoons. Otherwise, proceed as directed.

Green Peas, Tuna, and Dumplings: Prepare Green Peas, Chicken, and Dumplings as directed but substitute one 6- to 7-ounce drained and flaked can chunk white tuna for chicken. Also substitute one 2-inch sprig fresh rosemary (or ½ teaspoon crumbled dried rosemary) for thyme.

Green Peas, Salmon, and Dumplings with Mint: Prepare Ham, Green Peas, and Dumplings as directed but omit ham and substitute 1½ cups coarsely flaked leftover poached or grilled salmon (or if you must, a 7½-ounce can pink salmon, drained, flaked, and skin removed).

CHICKEN MOLE

This recipe is ridiculously easy—no seeds and nuts to toast, no fiery peppers to seed and core. I don't even bother to puree the sauce as purists would have me do because it cooks down smooth.

2 tablespoons peanut or
  vegetable oil
6 chicken thighs (about
  2 ¼ pounds)
1 cup fresh or frozen chopped
  onion (about 1 medium-large
  yellow onion)
1 large garlic clove, minced
One 1-inch piece cinnamon
  stick
3 whole cloves
4 peppercorns
¼ teaspoon crushed coriander
  seeds
Two 14 ½-ounce jars mild,
  medium, or hot salsa

One 10-ounce can diced
  tomatoes with green chilies,
  drained
½ cup chicken broth or water
1 ounce unsweetened chocolate
3 tablespoons creamy peanut
  butter
1 slice firm-textured white
  bread, torn into small chunks
1 to 2 teaspoons sugar
  (if needed to mellow tartness
  of sauce)
Salt
3 cups Al Dente Make-Ahead
  Rice (page 35), reheated

1. Heat oil in medium-size Dutch oven over high heat 2 minutes. Add chicken, placing skin side down, set lid on askew, and brown 5 to 8 minutes. Lift chicken to plate and reserve. Pour all drippings from Dutch oven, then spoon 2 tablespoons back in. Reduce heat to moderate.

2. Add onion, garlic, and all spices and cook, stirring often, until onion is limp, 2 to 3 minutes.

3. Add salsa, tomatoes with green chilies, broth, chocolate, peanut butter, and bread. Bring to gentle simmer, cover, and cook over low heat 10 minutes. Taste sauce and if too acid, add sugar to temper. Also add salt to taste.

4. Return chicken to Dutch oven, pushing down into sauce, cover, and simmer until chicken is well done, 15 to 20 minutes. Discard cinnamon stick.

5. Bed rice on a heated, large, deep platter, ladle mole on top, and serve.

TUSCAN VEGETABLE RAGOUT ON GRILLED POLENTA

By using frozen bell pepper stir-fry mix, frozen chopped spinach, canned cannellini, and a roll of prepared polenta, you can trim prep time to zilch.

2 tablespoons extra-virgin olive oil

1 medium-size zucchini, diced

1 medium-size carrot, finely diced

4 large scallions, trimmed and thinly sliced (include some green tops)

2 large garlic cloves, minced

2 whole bay leaves

1 teaspoon dried marjoram, crumbled

½ teaspoon crushed fennel seeds

One 1-pound bag frozen bell pepper stir-fry mix (red, green, and yellow peppers; do not thaw)

One 24-ounce roll polenta, sliced ¼ inch thick

One 10-ounce package frozen chopped spinach, thawed and drained

One 19-ounce can cannellini beans, rinsed and drained

One 15 ½-ounce can crushed tomatoes, with their liquid

Salt and freshly ground black pepper

½ cup finely sliced fresh basil

½ cup freshly grated Parmesan cheese

1. Preheat broiler. Lightly coat large, deep flameproof platter with nonstick cooking spray and set aside.

2. Heat oil in large, heavy skillet over moderate heat 2 minutes. Add zucchini, carrot, scallions, garlic, bay leaves, marjoram, fennel, and stir-fry mix and cook, stirring often, 8 to 10 minutes until vegetables are golden brown and excess juices evaporate.

3. Arrange polenta slices, not touching, on platter and broil 5 inches from heat until lightly browned, 3 to 4 minutes. Turn and

brown flip sides 3 to 4 minutes. Remove from broiler and keep warm.

4. Meanwhile, add spinach, beans, and tomatoes to skillet; adjust heat so mixture bubbles gently and simmer uncovered 8 to 10 minutes until flavors mingle. Remove bay leaves and season to taste with salt and pepper.

5. Ladle skillet mixture over polenta on platter, scatter basil and cheese evenly over all, and serve.

VEGETARIAN CHILI WITH BLACK BEANS AND PEPPERS SWEET AND HOT

Makes 6 servings

This is such a good quick chili I make it often. And feel virtuous for doing so because it brims with healthful vegetables. Note: Because of the saltiness of the canned beans and tomatoes, I call for no salt in this recipe. But taste before serving and adjust as needed.

2 tablespoons extra-virgin olive oil

1 cup fresh or frozen chopped onion (about 1 medium-large yellow onion)

1 large celery rib, trimmed and coarsely chopped

Half of a 1-pound bag frozen bell pepper stir-fry mix (red, green, and yellow peppers; do not thaw)

2 large garlic cloves, finely minced

2 teaspoons ground cumin

1 teaspoon dried oregano, crumbled

3 cups cooked or canned black beans, drained

Two 10-ounce cans diced tomatoes with green chilies, with their liquid

2 tablespoons frozen orange juice concentrate

1 tablespoon fresh lemon juice

½ teaspoon hot red pepper sauce

4 cups Al Dente Make-Ahead Rice (page 35), reheated

¼ cup coarsely chopped fresh cilantro

1. Heat oil in medium-size Dutch oven over moderate heat 1 minute. Add onion, celery, stir-fry mix, garlic, cumin, and oregano and cook, stirring often, until vegetables are limp, about 5 minutes.

2. Add 2 ½ cups beans, tomatoes with chilies, orange juice concentrate, lemon juice, and hot pepper sauce. Bring to boiling, adjust heat so mixture bubbles easily, cover, and simmer 10 minutes.

3. Mash remaining $1/2$ cup beans, mix into chili, cover, and simmer slowly until flavors mellow, about 15 minutes. Taste for salt and adjust as needed.

4. Mound rice in heated deep platter, spoon chili on top, sprinkle with cilantro, and serve.

STIR-FRIES AND SKILLET DINNERS

I n these quickest of dinners, choreography is everything. Indeed, if things are to proceed like clockwork, you must have all ingredients, all implements at-the-ready . . . at the outset.

Yet even here there are shortcuts. Newly available, wholly or partially prepared fresh produce eliminates the tedium of peeling, slicing, and shredding. For me, the indispensables are sliced fresh mushrooms, shredded carrots, broccoli and cauliflower florets, washed baby spinach, and slaw mixes (the broccoli as well as the cabbage).

Certain frozen foods are significant time-savers, too—bell pepper stir-fry mixes and snow pea pods, to name two. Bounced in and out of a hissing-hot skillet, these emerge full of color and crunch.

Thanks to supermarket "international" sections, we can at long last be fairly authentic about our Asian stir-fries. Canned *shirataki* noodles are now as available as canned bean sprouts, bamboo shoots, and water chestnuts. Shelves brim with Asian roasted sesame seed oil, mirin (sweet rice wine), Thai coconut milk, and peanut sauce. There are soy sauces galore (including dark double-strength ones), fish sauces, and bean pastes. In addition, many groceries now routinely stock tofu, fresh ginger, lemongrass, and cilantro (also called fresh coriander or Chinese parsley).

When it comes to stir-fries, the biggest time-saver, I find, is having a supply of cooked rice on hand either in fridge or freezer (see page 35). It reheats like a dream—virtually unattended. And it rounds out the meal.

TEXAS BEEF, PEPPERS, AND RICE

Makes 4 to 6 servings

You can serve this colorful skillet dinner over tortillas, but I prefer crisp, finely sliced romaine. To save time, I use packaged, trimmed hearts of romaine.

2 tablespoons vegetable oil
2 cups fresh or frozen chopped onions (2 medium-large yellow onions)
Half of a 1-pound bag frozen bell pepper stir-fry mix (red, green, and yellow peppers; do not thaw)
1 cup frozen whole-kernel corn (do not thaw)
2 large garlic cloves, minced
1½ teaspoons dried oregano, crumbled
½ teaspoon ground cumin
½ teaspoon crushed coriander seeds

¼ teaspoon ground cinnamon
2 whole cloves
Two 3-inch strips orange zest
1 pound lean ground beef chuck
½ cup uncooked converted rice
One 14½-ounce can beef broth
1 teaspoon salt
¼ teaspoon freshly ground black pepper
One 10-ounce can diced tomatoes with green chilies, well drained
½ cup coarsely chopped fresh cilantro or Italian (flat-leaf) parsley, or ¼ cup each

1. Heat oil in large, heavy skillet over moderately high heat for 2 minutes. Add onions, stir-fry mix, corn, garlic, oregano, cumin, coriander seeds, cinnamon, cloves, and orange zest and cook, stirring, until vegetables are limp, 3 to 5 minutes.

2. Add beef and cook, stirring, for 5 minutes.

3. Add rice, broth, salt, and pepper; bring to a gentle boil, cover, and cook 15 minutes. Uncover, raise heat slightly, and boil uncovered until almost all juices evaporate, 5 to 8 minutes. Remove orange zest.

4. Add tomatoes with chilies and bring just to serving temperature. Taste for salt and pepper and fine-tune. Stir in cilantro and serve.

LINE CAMP SKILLET SUPPER

MAKES 4 SERVINGS

This quick scramble of eggs, onions, tomatoes, and crackers was popular among cowhands running fences along boundary lines to keep cattle from wandering the prairie. It was popular, too, around Dodge City, Kansas, especially among crewmen of the old Santa Fe railroad.

6 slices lean bacon, snipped
    crosswise into julienne strips
6 large scallions, trimmed and
    thinly sliced (include some
    green tops)
2 medium-size vine-ripe
    tomatoes, peeled, cored,
    seeded, and coarsely
    chopped; or one 1-pound can
    diced tomatoes, well drained

6 extra-large eggs
3/4 teaspoon salt
1/8 teaspoon freshly ground
    black pepper
6 soda crackers, coarsely
    crumbled

1. Fry bacon in large, heavy skillet over moderate heat until fat renders out and only crisp brown bits remain, about 5 minutes. With slotted spoon, lift bacon to paper toweling to drain. Pour all drippings from skillet, then spoon 2 tablespoons back in.

2. Add scallions to skillet and cook, stirring over moderate heat until soft, 3 to 5 minutes.

3. Add tomatoes and simmer uncovered until as thick as pasta sauce, about 15 minutes.

4. Meanwhile, beat eggs with salt and pepper until frothy. Pour eggs into skillet with tomato mixture and scramble until beginning to set.

5. Scatter in cracker crumbs and reserved bacon and continue scrambling until eggs are softly set.

6. Spoon onto heated plates and serve.

TIP

To peel tomatoes in jig time, spear with a long-handled kitchen fork, plunge into boiling water for 30 to 60 seconds, then quick-dip in ice water. Skins will then slip right off.

THE MEAT WILL SLICE MORE
EASILY IF YOU SET IT IN THE
FREEZER FOR HALF AN HOUR
(USE THIS TIME TO MAKE
THE MARINADE AND PREP
THE VEGETABLES). THE
QUICKEST WAY TO CUT
THE MEAT INTO MATCHSTICK
STRIPS IS TO SLICE 1/4-INCH
THICK, THEN STACK THREE
OR FOUR SLICES AND CUT
THROUGH THEM AT 1/4-INCH
INTERVALS. TO SAVE ADDI-
TIONAL TIME, USE PACKAGED
SHREDDED CARROTS AND
PRE-TRIMMED CELERY
HEARTS FROM THE PRODUCE
SECTION (SLICE STRAIGHT
ACROSS UNTIL YOU HAVE
1 CUP THIN SLICES). AS FOR
THE SCALLIONS, LINE THEM
UP TOGETHER AND SLICE
WITH A SHARP CHEF'S KNIFE.

NOTE

BECAUSE OF THE SALTINESS
OF THE SOY SAUCE, THIS
RECIPE PROBABLY WON'T
NEED SALT. BUT TASTE AND
ADD, IF NEEDED.

SZECHUAN SHREDDED BEEF AND CARROTS

MAKES 4 SERVINGS

The best cut to use for this recipe is beef tenderloin. It's lean, it's tender, and it stir-fries like a dream.

FOR THE MARINADE
1 large garlic clove, minced
1 tablespoon minced fresh
  ginger
1 teaspoon Chinese five-spice
  powder

1/4 teaspoon ground hot red
  pepper (cayenne)
3 tablespoons dry sherry
3 tablespoons soy sauce
1 tablespoon Asian roasted
  sesame oil

FOR THE STIR-FRY
1 pound trimmed beef
  tenderloin, cut into
  matchstick strips
  (see Tips)
3 tablespoons peanut oil
1 1/2 cups coarsely shredded
  fresh carrots (see Tips)
1 cup thinly sliced celery

4 large scallions, trimmed and
  thinly sliced (include some
  green tops)
Salt, if needed
3 cups Al Dente Make-Ahead
  Rice (page 35), reheated

1. For the marinade, combine all marinade ingredients in a bowl.

2. For the stir-fry, add beef to marinade, toss well, and let stand at room temperature for 30 minutes.

3. Heat 2 tablespoons peanut oil in large, heavy skillet over high heat for 2 minutes. Add carrots, celery, and scallions and cook, stirring, for 3 minutes.

4. Add remaining 1 tablespoon oil, beef, and marinade to skillet and stir-fry over high heat until beef is no longer pink, about 3 minutes. Taste for salt and add as needed.

5. Mound rice in heated deep platter, spoon beef mixture on top, and serve.

SUKIYAKI

<small>Makes 4 servings</small>

Like so many Asian recipes, this popular Japanese dish cooks lickety-split. The tedious part is prepping the meat and vegetables. Fortunately, pre-sliced fresh white mushrooms and pre-washed spinach, available by the bag, speed things up.

⅓ cup Japanese soy sauce
⅓ cup mirin (sweet Japanese rice wine) or dry sherry
1 tablespoon sugar
2 tablespoons peanut oil
1 small Spanish or Vidalia onion (about 8 ounces), halved lengthwise and each half thinly sliced
6 large scallions, trimmed and thinly sliced (include some green tops)
One 8-ounce package sliced fresh white mushrooms

4 ounces trimmed and washed baby spinach leaves
One 8-ounce can *shirataki* (cellophane) noodles, drained
One 8-ounce can sliced bamboo shoots, drained
1 pound well-trimmed beef tenderloin, sliced about ⅛ inch thick
4 ounces firm tofu, cut into ½-inch dice
3 cups Al Dente Make-Ahead Rice (page 35), reheated

TIP

<small>Partially freeze the beef and it will slice more quickly and cleanly— about 30 minutes on the freezing surface of a 0°F. freezer should be sufficient. While the meat chills, deal with the onion, scallions, and tofu.</small>

1. Combine soy sauce, mirin, and sugar in small bowl. Set aside.

2. Heat oil in large, heavy skillet over high heat 2 minutes. Add onion, scallions, and mushrooms and stir-fry until mushrooms release juices and most of these evaporate, 5 minutes.

3. Add spinach, *shirataki*, and bamboo shoots and stir-fry until spinach wilts, 3 minutes.

4. Add beef and stir-fry for 2 minutes, then add tofu and reserved soy sauce mixture. Cook and stir just until mixture steams, about 2 minutes longer.

5. Mound rice in heated deep platter, spoon *sukiyaki* on top, and serve.

FLANK STEAK STIR-FRY WITH SNOW PEAS

Makes 4 servings

Flank steak, one of the tougher cuts of beef, can be tenderized by slicing across the grain into thin strips. Overcooking will turn the strips into "shoe leather," but stir-frying's quick blast of heat cooks them without toughening them.

For the marinade

1 tablespoon soy sauce
1 tablespoon Asian oyster sauce (available in high-end groceries and specialty food shops)
1 teaspoon finely minced fresh ginger
1 teaspoon dry sherry
1 teaspoon cornstarch
½ teaspoon Asian roasted sesame oil
½ teaspoon sugar
⅛ teaspoon freshly ground black pepper

For the stir-fry

¾ pound flank steak halved lengthwise, then each half sliced crosswise into strips ¼ inch wide
2 teaspoons cornstarch
½ cup chicken broth
1 tablespoon soy sauce
1 teaspoon Asian oyster sauce
1 teaspoon sugar
1½ tablespoons peanut oil
1 tablespoon Asian roasted sesame oil
1½ teaspoons finely minced fresh ginger
1 garlic clove, finely minced
One 6-ounce package frozen snow peas, thawed and patted dry on paper toweling
3 cups Al Dente Make-Ahead Rice (page 35), reheated

1. For the marinade, combine all ingredients in large bowl.

2. For the stir-fry, add steak to marinade, toss well, and let stand 30 minutes.

3. Meanwhile, mix cornstarch, broth, soy sauce, oyster sauce, and sugar in a small bowl and set aside.

4. When the steak has finished marinating, heat peanut and sesame oils in large, heavy skillet or wok over high heat for 1 minute. Add ginger and garlic and stir-fry for 30 seconds.

5. Add beef and marinade and stir-fry until no longer pink, about 2 minutes.

6. Stir cornstarch mixture, pour into skillet, and cook, stirring, until mixture bubbles and thickens slightly, about 3 minutes.

7. Add snow peas and cook, stirring frequently, until steaming hot, about 1 minute.

8. Mound rice in heated deep platter, spoon skillet mixture on top, and serve.

VARIATIONS

Flank Steak Stir-Fry with Snow Peas and Water Chestnuts: Prepare as directed, but in step 7, add ¹/₂ cup thinly sliced water chestnuts along with snow peas.

Flank Steak Stir-Fry with Broccoli: Prepare as directed, but omit snow peas. In step 7, add 2 cups small broccoli florets that have been blanched in boiling water just until crisp-tender and bright emerald green, about 2 minutes (see Note).

NOTE

FOR THE FLANK STEAK STIR-FRY WITH BROCCOLI VARIATION, THE BROCCOLI CAN BE BLANCHED A DAY OR TWO AHEAD OF TIME, QUICK-CHILLED IN ICE WATER, DRAINED, THEN LAYERED WITH PAPER TOWELING IN A PLASTIC ZIPPER BAG AND STORED IN THE REFRIGERATOR UNTIL READY TO USE.

STIR-FRY OF BEEF, GINGER, CHERRY TOMATOES, AND GREEN PEPPER

MAKES 4 SERVINGS

The only time-consuming part of this recipe is marinating the beef—but this takes only half an hour. Use that time to prepare and measure the other ingredients because this stir-fry, like every other, must move like clockwork.

FOR THE MARINADE
1 tablespoon soy sauce
1 tablespoon Asian fish sauce
1 teaspoon finely minced fresh
  ginger
1 teaspoon dry sherry

1 teaspoon cornstarch
½ teaspoon Asian roasted
  sesame oil
½ teaspoon light brown sugar
⅛ teaspoon ground hot red
  pepper (cayenne)

FOR THE STIR-FRY
1 pound flank steak halved
  lengthwise, then each half
  sliced crosswise into strips
  ¼ inch wide
1½ tablespoons peanut oil
1 tablespoon Asian roasted
  sesame oil
2 teaspoons finely minced fresh
  ginger
2 garlic cloves, finely minced
1 large green bell pepper, cored,
  seeded, and cut lengthwise
  into slivers ¼ inch wide

2 teaspoons cornstarch blended
  with ½ cup beef broth,
  1 tablespoon soy sauce, and
  1 teaspoon each Asian fish
  sauce and light brown sugar
10 firm-ripe cherry tomatoes,
  halved and patted dry on
  paper toweling
3 cups Al Dente Make-Ahead
  Rice (page 35), reheated

1. For the marinade, combine all ingredients in large bowl.

2. For the stir-fry, add steak to marinade, toss well, and let stand 30 minutes.

3. Heat peanut and sesame oils in large, heavy skillet or wok over high heat 1 minute. Add ginger and garlic and stir-fry 30 seconds. Add green pepper and stir-fry 3 minutes. Scoop pepper onto large plate and reserve.

4. Add beef and marinade to skillet and stir-fry until no longer pink, about 2 minutes.

5. Blend in cornstarch mixture and cook and stir until mixture bubbles and thickens slightly, about 3 minutes.

6. Add cherry tomatoes and reserved green pepper and cook, stirring frequently, until steaming hot, about 1 minute.

7. Mound rice in heated deep platter, spoon skillet mixture on top, and serve.

PICADINHO ON RICE AND PEAS

MAKES 6 SERVINGS

Picadinho, a Brazilian spiced beef much like the Mexican *picadillo*, is used to stuff meat pies. I prefer it ladled over rice and peas. To save time, I use rice I've made ahead and reheat it with frozen tiny green peas that have been thawed and drained well. More time-savers are bottled olive salad and that versatile canned combo of diced tomatoes and green chilies.

2 tablespoons extra-virgin olive oil

1 cup fresh or frozen chopped onion (about 1 medium-large yellow onion)

2 large garlic cloves, finely minced

1 pound lean ground beef chuck

½ teaspoon ground coriander

¼ teaspoon ground ginger

Two 10-ounce cans diced tomatoes with green chilies, with their liquid

2 tablespoons minced Italian (flat-leaf) parsley

1 teaspoon light brown sugar

⅓ cup well-drained olive salad (green olives and pimientos)

¼ teaspoon salt

¼ teaspoon freshly ground black pepper

3 cups Al Dente Make-Ahead Rice (page 35), reheated with 1 ½ cups drained, thawed frozen tiny green peas

1. Heat oil in large, heavy skillet over moderate heat 1 minute. Add onion and garlic and cook, stirring often, until very lightly browned, 8 to 10 minutes. Push to one side of skillet.

2. Add beef and brown well, breaking up clumps, 5 to 8 minutes.

3. Add coriander, ginger, tomatoes with chilies, parsley, brown sugar, olive salad, salt, and pepper and cook uncovered, stirring now and then, until liquid has cooked down and mixture is sloppy-joe consistency, about 20 minutes. Taste for salt and pepper and fine-tune as needed.

4. Mound rice and peas in heated deep platter, ladle *picadinho* on top, and serve.

LAMB CHOPS PROVENÇAL

MAKES 6 SERVINGS

The only accompaniment this colorful skillet dinner needs is a loaf of chewy French bread sliced good and thick. To save on cleanup, choose a skillet handsome enough to go to the table.

6 shoulder lamb chops (about 3 pounds)
2 tablespoons extra-virgin olive oil (the fruitiest you can find)
2 large yellow onions, thinly sliced
6 small whole garlic cloves, peeled
Two 3-inch sprigs fresh rosemary or $\frac{1}{2}$ teaspoon dried rosemary, crumbled

One 3-inch sprig fresh lemon thyme or $\frac{1}{4}$ teaspoon dried thyme, crumbled
1 $\frac{1}{2}$ teaspoons salt
$\frac{1}{4}$ teaspoon freshly ground black pepper
2 small zucchini, trimmed and sliced $\frac{1}{4}$ inch thick
6 small cherry tomatoes, stemmed and halved from stem to blossom end

1. Trim lamb chops of excess fat. Heat oil in large, heavy skillet over moderately high heat 2 minutes. Add chops and brown 2 to 3 minutes per side. Lift to plate and reserve.

2. Add onions, garlic, rosemary, and thyme to the skillet and cook, stirring often, until onions are limp and golden, 5 to 8 minutes.

3. Return chops to skillet and sprinkle with half the salt and pepper. Spoon onions on top of chops and sprinkle with remaining salt and pepper. Reduce heat to moderate, cover, and cook 10 minutes.

4. Add zucchini and cook uncovered, stirring gently now and then, until firm-tender, about 5 minutes.

5. Add tomatoes, tossing gently with onions and zucchini, and cook uncovered just long enough to warm through, 2 to 3 minutes. Taste for salt and pepper and fine-tune as needed.

6. Discard garlic and rosemary and thyme sprigs, dish up, and serve.

NOTE

Although this isn't a kosher recipe, I like to use extra-rich kosher egg noodles, which come in short, flat strands and are more suited to skillet cooking than longer or curlier nonkosher brands.

SKILLET BEEF PAPRIKASH

Makes 4 to 6 servings

The noodles cook in the skillet alongside the meat and vegetables.

1 tablespoon unsalted butter or margarine
1 pound lean ground beef chuck
1 cup fresh or frozen chopped onion (about 1 medium-large yellow onion)
Half of a 1-pound bag frozen bell pepper stir-fry mix (red, green, and yellow peppers; do not thaw)
1 large garlic clove, minced
3 tablespoons Hungarian sweet rose paprika
1 teaspoon dried marjoram, crumbled
½ teaspoon dried thyme, crumbled

One 14½-ounce can chicken broth blended with 1 tablespoon all-purpose flour, ½ teaspoon salt, and ¼ teaspoon freshly ground black pepper
One 10½-ounce can beef consommé
½ pound medium egg noodles (4 cups)
One 9-ounce package frozen cut asparagus (do not thaw but do separate into individual pieces)
4 ounces light cream cheese (Neufchâtel), cut into small pieces

1. Melt butter in large, heavy skillet over moderate heat. Add beef and cook, breaking up large clumps, until no longer pink, about 5 minutes.

2. Add onion, stir-fry mix, garlic, paprika, marjoram, and thyme and cook uncovered, stirring often, until mixture is quite dry, 5 to 8 minutes.

3. Add broth mixture and consommé to skillet and bring to boiling. Add noodles, stir well, and return to boil. Adjust heat so liquid bubbles gently but constantly, cover, and cook 5 minutes.

4. Stir well, lay asparagus pieces on top, cover, and cook until noodles are tender, 5 minutes.

5. Off heat, add cream cheese and stir until melted. Taste for salt and pepper, fine-tune as needed, and serve.

Veal and Pork Paprikash: Prepare as directed, but use $1/2$ pound each ground veal shoulder and ground pork shoulder in place of beef. Also substitute one 10-ounce package tiny green peas for asparagus (do not thaw but do break block into small chunks).

Chicken or Turkey Paprikash: Substitute 2 cups diced leftover cooked chicken or turkey for ground beef. Begin with step 2, melting butter in skillet before proceeding. Add chicken or turkey just before proceeding to step 3. Also, if you like, substitute 2 cups parboiled small broccoli or cauliflower florets for asparagus in step 4 and increase cooking time 1 to 2 minutes if needed to make them tender. Take care, however, not to overcook noodles. Finish as directed in step 5.

SKILLET SATÉ WITH BABY CARROTS AND ZUCCHINI

Makes 4 servings

A popular Thai hors d'oeuvre that I've turned into a rib-sticking main dish.

3 tablespoons peanut oil or
  corn oil
Half of a 1-pound package
  peeled baby-cut fresh carrots,
  halved lengthwise
4 small zucchini, trimmed and
  cut into ¼-inch chunks
4 large scallions, trimmed and
  thickly sliced (include some
  green tops)
1 large garlic clove, finely
  minced
2 teaspoons finely minced fresh
  ginger
1 pound flank steak halved
  lengthwise, then each half
  sliced crosswise into strips
  ¼ inch wide
2 teaspoons cornstarch blended
  with ½ cup beef broth and
  1 tablespoon each soy sauce
  and dry sherry

¼ cup Thai peanut sauce
  (available in supermarkets)
2 tablespoons creamy peanut
  butter
1¼ cups Thai coconut milk
  (use light, if you like)
½ teaspoon hot red pepper
  sauce
3 cups Al Dente Make-Ahead
  Rice (page 35), reheated
¼ cup coarsely chopped fresh
  cilantro or Italian (flat-leaf)
  parsley
½ cup coarsely chopped dry-
  roasted peanuts

1. Heat 2 tablespoons oil in large, heavy skillet over high heat 2 minutes. Add carrots and cook, turning in oil, 2 minutes. Cover, reduce heat to moderate, and cook until tender, about 5 minutes.

2. Add zucchini, scallions, garlic, and ginger and cook, stirring often, until zucchini is crisp-tender, 5 to 8 minutes. With slotted spoon, scoop vegetables to large plate and reserve.

3. Add remaining 1 tablespoon oil to skillet and heat over high heat 1 minute. Add flank steak and stir-fry until no longer pink, about 2 minutes.

4. Reduce heat to moderately low, blend in cornstarch mixture, and cook and stir until mixture bubbles and thickens slightly, about 3 minutes. Blend in peanut sauce, peanut butter, coconut milk, and red pepper sauce and cook and stir just until smooth, 1 to 2 minutes.

5. Return carrots and zucchini to skillet and heat 1 minute longer.

6. Mound rice in heated deep platter, spoon skillet mixture on top, sprinkle with cilantro and peanuts, and serve.

GHANIAN GROUNDNUT SKILLET STEW

Makes 4 to 6 servings

Groundnuts are of course peanuts, a staple in Ghana and elsewhere about Africa. They arrived in this country aboard slave ships. "Nuts" is a misnomer because peanuts are legumes like beans and peas—hence our name for them. In Africa, this lusty, rib-sticking stew would most likely be made with a stewing hen and meat from a cow way past its prime. I've substituted frozen diced cooked chicken and beef, now carried by every good supermarket.

2 tablespoons peanut or
   corn oil
2 cups fresh or frozen chopped
   onions (about 2 medium-large
   yellow onions)
1 large green bell pepper, cored,
   seeded, and coarsely chopped
1 large red bell pepper, cored,
   seeded, and coarsely chopped
One 9-ounce package frozen
   cooked, seasoned beef strips
   (do not thaw)
One 9-ounce package frozen
   diced cooked chicken breast
   (do not thaw)
One 10-ounce can diced
   tomatoes with green chilies,
   with their liquid

1 cup beef broth or water
2 tablespoons cider vinegar or
   rice vinegar
1 teaspoon salt
½ cup creamy peanut butter
   (measure firmly packed)
3 cups Al Dente Make-Ahead
   Rice (page 35), reheated
¼ cup coarsely chopped Italian
   (flat-leaf) parsley
¼ cup coarsely chopped dry-
   roasted peanuts

1. Heat oil in large, heavy skillet over moderately high heat 2 minutes. Add onions, and green and red peppers and cook, stirring often, until limp, 5 to 7 minutes.

2. Add beef, chicken, tomatoes with chilies, broth, vinegar, and salt and bring to a simmer. Adjust heat so mixture bubbles gently, cover, and cook until flavors meld, about 20 minutes.

3. Smooth in peanut butter and cook, stirring often, 5 minutes more. Taste for salt and vinegar and fine-tune as needed—stew should be mellow but have a bit of bite, too.

4. Mound rice in a large heated deep platter, ladle stew on top, sprinkle with parsley and peanuts, and serve.

PENNSYLVANIA DUTCH CABBAGE AND NOODLES WITH CORNED BEEF

MAKES 6 SERVINGS

The fastest way to shred cabbage? Use a slaw mix from the produce counter (I prefer a fairly coarse one that's mostly green cabbage, although I won't reject one with a little broccoli and carrot tossed in). The Pennsylvania Dutch would boil corned brisket of beef to serve with the cabbage and noodles. To save time, I use sliced corned beef from the deli (sometimes even canned corned beef) and I don't bother to heat it because smothering it with steaming hot cabbage does the job.

4 slices lean smoky bacon, cut crosswise at ½-inch intervals
2 tablespoons unsalted butter
One 8-ounce bag coleslaw mix
1 cup fresh or frozen chopped onion (about 1 medium-large yellow onion)
1 large golden Delicious apple, peeled, cored, quartered, and each quarter thinly sliced
2 teaspoons light brown sugar
1 teaspoon caraway seeds
¼ cup cider vinegar

1 teaspoon salt
¼ teaspoon freshly ground black pepper
2 cups medium egg noodles, cooked by package directions and drained
1 cup sour cream (use light, if you like)
½ pound thinly sliced corned beef (from the deli counter) or half of a 1-pound can corned beef
¼ cup minced parsley

1. Cook bacon in large, heavy skillet over moderate heat until crisp and brown, 3 to 5 minutes. With slotted spoon, scoop browned bacon to paper toweling to drain.

2. Add butter to skillet and when it melts, add slaw mix, onion, apple, brown sugar, caraway seeds, 2 tablespoons vinegar, salt, and

pepper. Toss well, then cover and cook until cabbage is crisp-tender, 10 to 12 minutes.

3. Mix in noodles and cook uncovered just until steaming hot, about 3 minutes. Mix in sour cream and remaining 2 tablespoons vinegar and heat just until steaming. Do not boil or sour cream may curdle. When steaming hot, set off heat. Taste for salt and pepper and adjust as needed.

4. Arrange corned beef on large platter, slices overlapping. Spoon cabbage and noodles on top, leaving margin of corned beef all round. Sprinkle with parsley and reserved bacon and serve.

MALAY SPICED LAMB AND VEGETABLES

MAKES 6 SERVINGS

On a visit to South Africa, I first tasted spicy Cape Malay cooking. My version of the lamb/cabbage/potato combo I enjoyed in Cape Town gets off to a fast start thanks to bagged coleslaw mix.

The ingredients list may seem long, but these are mostly spices. To keep things moving, I have everything measured before I start cooking. That way dinner's ready in 40 minutes, maybe less.

1 pound lean ground lamb shoulder
¼ cup all-purpose flour
2 tablespoons peanut oil
2 tablespoons Asian roasted sesame oil
2 cups chopped fresh or frozen onions (about 2 medium-large yellow onions)
2 large garlic cloves, minced
1 tablespoon minced fresh ginger
One 2-inch piece cinnamon stick
3 whole cloves
1½ teaspoons curry powder
½ teaspoon ground cumin
½ teaspoon red pepper flakes

One 3-inch strip each lemon and orange zest (see Tip)
One 8-ounce bag coleslaw mix (green and red cabbage plus carrots)
Half of an 8-ounce bag shredded carrots
Half of a 1-pound bag frozen bell pepper stir-fry mix (red, green, and yellow peppers; do not thaw)
1 pound red-skin potatoes, scrubbed and cut into ½-inch cubes but not peeled
1½ cups beef broth
1 cup Thai coconut milk (use light, if you like)
Salt and freshly ground black pepper

1. Shape lamb into large flat patty. Place flour in pie pan and dredge all sides of lamb patty well in flour; set aside.

2. Heat 1 tablespoon each peanut and sesame oil in heavy, deep 12-inch skillet over moderately high heat 1 minute. Add lamb and brown 2 minutes per side; lift to plate and reserve.

3. Add remaining peanut and sesame oils to skillet, reduce heat to moderate, add onions, garlic, ginger, cinnamon, cloves, curry powder, cumin, red pepper flakes, and lemon and orange zests, and cook, stirring, until onions are limp, about 5 minutes.

4. Add coleslaw mix, carrots, stir-fry mix, potatoes, and broth, and bring to gentle boil. Lay meat on top of vegetables, cover, and cook 10 minutes. Break meat into 1-inch chunks, set lid on askew, and cook until potatoes are tender, about 10 minutes more. If mixture seems soupy, boil uncovered, stirring often, until almost all liquid evaporates, about 5 minutes.

5. Add coconut milk and cook uncovered, stirring often, until flavors meld, about 5 minutes. Season to taste with salt and black pepper, discard cinnamon stick and lemon and orange zests, and serve.

TIP

THE EASIEST WAY TO OBTAIN 3-INCH STRIPS OF LEMON AND ORANGE ZEST IS TO PULL A SWIVEL-BLADED VEGETABLE PEELER THE LENGTH OF THE FRUIT. IT REMOVES THE ZEST (THE COLORED PART OF THE RIND) ONLY, LEAVING BEHIND THE BITTER WHITE PITH.

30-MINUTE SKILLET DINNER OF PORK (OR TURKEY) AND BOWS

MAKES 4 SERVINGS

This recipe, "a childhood favorite," comes from my good friend and colleague Joanne Lamb Hayes. Her mother would have made the recipe with homemade pork or turkey broth and if you should have any on hand, use it. If not, substitute a good canned chicken or vegetable broth. You can also substitute leftover roast chicken for pork or turkey.

1 cup fresh or frozen chopped onion (about 1 medium-large yellow onion)

1 tablespoon unsalted butter

3 cups chicken or vegetable broth

1 large red-skinned potato, scrubbed (but not peeled) and cut into ½-inch cubes (about ½ pound)

2½ cups pasta bow-ties (about one-third 16-ounce package)

½ cup milk or evaporated skim milk blended with 2 tablespoons all-purpose flour

2 cups 1-inch cubes cooked pork or turkey

1 cup frozen peas and carrots, thawed and drained

¼ teaspoon salt

⅛ teaspoon freshly ground black pepper

¼ cup minced parsley (optional)

1. Cook onion in butter in large, heavy skillet over moderate heat, stirring frequently, until edges brown, 5 to 8 minutes.

2. Add broth, potato, and bow-ties. Bring to boiling, cover, and cook over moderate heat 10 minutes.

3. Stir in milk-flour mixture along with pork, peas, carrots, and salt and pepper. Cook, stirring occasionally, until mixture thickens and potato and bow-ties are tender, 8 to 10 minutes. Taste for salt and pepper and fine-tune as needed.

4. Sprinkle with parsley, if desired. Serve directly from skillet or transfer to heated serving bowl or tureen.

SPICY PORK STIR-FRY WITH BROCCOLI, RED AND YELLOW PEPPERS

MAKES 4 SERVINGS

Once the pork has marinated, this recipe cooks in about 10 minutes. Shortcut: Use packaged, washed broccoli florets from the produce counter.

FOR THE MARINADE
1 tablespoon soy sauce
1 tablespoon dry sherry
1 teaspoon finely minced fresh
  ginger
1 teaspoon cornstarch
½ teaspoon Asian roasted
  sesame oil

½ teaspoon honey
½ teaspoon ground hot red
  pepper (cayenne)
½ teaspoon Chinese five-spice
  powder

FOR THE STIR-FRY
1 pound boneless pork loin,
  sliced ½ inch thick, then each
  slice cut into strips ½ inch
  wide
2 tablespoons peanut oil
1 tablespoon Asian roasted
  sesame oil
2 teaspoons finely minced fresh
  ginger
2 garlic cloves, finely minced
2 cups small broccoli florets
1 large red bell pepper, cored,
  seeded, and cut lengthwise
  into slivers ½ inch wide

1 large yellow bell pepper,
  cored, seeded, and cut
  lengthwise into slivers ½ inch
  wide
2 teaspoons cornstarch blended
  with ½ cup chicken broth,
  1 tablespoon soy sauce, and
  1 teaspoon each Asian oyster
  sauce and sugar
3 cups Al Dente Make-Ahead
  Rice (page 35), reheated

continued

TIP

THE PORK WILL BE EASIER TO SLICE IF YOU SET IN THE FREEZER FOR ABOUT 30 MINUTES.

1. For the marinade, combine all ingredients in large bowl.

2. For the stir-fry, add pork to marinade, toss well, and let stand 30 minutes.

3. Heat peanut and sesame oils in large, heavy skillet or wok over high heat 1 minute. Add ginger and garlic and stir-fry 30 seconds. Add broccoli and red and yellow peppers and stir-fry 4 minutes. Scoop vegetables onto large plate and reserve.

4. Add pork and marinade to skillet and stir-fry until no longer pink, about 3 minutes.

5. Blend in cornstarch mixture and cook and stir until mixture bubbles and thickens slightly, about 3 minutes.

6. Return vegetables to skillet and cook, stirring frequently, until steaming hot, about 1 minute.

7. Mound rice in heated deep platter, spoon skillet mixture on top, and serve.

SKILLET TOSS OF CARAMELIZED ONIONS, ITALIAN SAUSAGE, SNOW PEAS, PORCINI, AND BOW-TIES

MAKES 4 SERVINGS

Dried porcini, or cèpes as the French call these meaty European mushrooms, add tons of flavor to this easy skillet dinner. Look for little packets of them in the supermarket produce section and in Italian markets. Shortcut: Soak the porcini overnight in the refrigerator so you can move right ahead with the recipe. My friend Michele Urvater, author of the *Monday to Friday* cookbook series and as such, the busy cook's guru, keeps soaked porcini at the ready. See page 11 in "Getting Set" for directions on how Michele does it.

One ½-ounce package dried
   porcini mushrooms
1 ½ cups hot water
1 tablespoon extra-virgin
   olive oil
2 fresh sweet Italian sausages
   (about 4 ounces) or 1 sweet
   Italian sausage and 1 hot,
   casings removed and meat
   coarsely crumbled
1 tablespoon unsalted butter
1 medium-size red onion (8 to
   10 ounces), halved
   lengthwise, then each half
   thinly sliced

2 bunches medium-size scallions
   (about 12 scallions), trimmed
   and sliced ¼ inch thick
1 large garlic clove, finely
   minced
One 6-ounce package frozen
   snow peas, thawed, drained,
   and patted dry on paper
   toweling
Half of a 1-pound package bow-
   tie pasta (farfalle), cooked al
   dente by package directions
   and drained well
Salt and freshly ground black
   pepper

continued

1. Rinse porcini, place in small bowl, add hot water, and let stand 1 hour. Line small fine-mesh sieve with coffee filter, set over bowl, pour in porcini, and soaking liquid and let water drip through. Set porcini aside. Filter soaking water once more and reserve.

2. Heat oil in very large, heavy skillet over high heat 1 minute. Add sausages and cook, breaking up clumps, until lightly browned, about 3 minutes. Add $1/2$ cup reserved porcini soaking water and boil uncovered 2 minutes. Scrape skillet mixture onto plate and reserve.

3. Add butter to skillet and melt over moderately high heat. Add onion and scallions and cook, stirring now and then, until soft and lightly browned, about 8 minutes. Add garlic and cook, stirring, 1 minute.

4. Return sausages to skillet, then add reserved porcini and another $1/4$ cup soaking water. Turn heat to lowest point, cover, and mellow 10 to 12 minutes.

5. Add snow peas to skillet, then hot drained pasta and toss well. If mixture seems dry, add a little more porcini soaking water.

6. Season to taste with salt and pepper and serve.

CHINESE PORK AND PEPPERS

MAKES 4 SERVINGS

Boneless pork loin is best for this recipe. Trim well, slice ¼-inch thick, spread slices on a baking sheet, and set in a 0°F. freezer for half an hour. Then make matchstick strips by stacking partially frozen slices, three or four at a time, and cutting through them at ¼-inch intervals.

¼ cup soy sauce
3 tablespoons dry sherry
1 tablespoon light brown sugar
2 teaspoons cornstarch
3 tablespoons peanut oil
1 pound well-trimmed boneless
  pork loin, cut into matchstick
  strips (see headnote above)
1 medium-size Spanish onion
  (about ¾ pound), quartered
  lengthwise and each quarter
  thinly sliced
1 large garlic clove, finely
  minced

1 tablespoon finely minced fresh
  ginger
⅛ to ¼ teaspoon red pepper
  flakes (depending on how hot
  you like things)
1 large green bell pepper, cored,
  seeded, and cut lengthwise
  into slivers ¼ inch wide
1 large red bell pepper, cored,
  seeded, and cut lengthwise
  into slivers ¼ inch wide
3 cups Al Dente Make-Ahead
  Rice (page 35), reheated

1. Combine soy sauce, sherry, brown sugar, and cornstarch in small bowl and set aside.

2. Heat oil in large, heavy skillet or wok over high heat 2 minutes. Add pork and stir-fry until lightly browned, 4 to 5 minutes. With slotted spoon, lift pork to large bowl and reserve.

3. Add onion, garlic, ginger, red pepper flakes, and green and red bell peppers to skillet and stir-fry over high heat until onion begins to turn translucent, about 3 minutes.

continued

4. Return pork to skillet, add soy mixture, and cook and stir just until mixture bubbles, thickens slightly, and turns clear, 3 to 4 minutes.

5. Mound rice in heated deep platter, spoon pork mixture on top, and serve.

VARIATIONS

Chinese Beef and Peppers: Prepare as directed but substitute 1 pound beef tenderloin, cut into matchstick strips, for pork. Also reduce stir-fry time for beef to 3 minutes.

Chinese Chicken (or Turkey) and Peppers: Prepare as directed but substitute 1 pound chicken (or turkey) cutlets (breast meat), cut into matchstick strips, for pork. Also reduce stir-fry time for chicken (or turkey) to 3 minutes.

SARA'S CRISPY SKILLET BROCCOLI IN BROTH WITH CAPELLINI, PROSCIUTTO, AND PARMESAN

MAKES 2 SERVINGS

My best bud Sara Moulton wears four hats: she's executive chef at *Gourmet* magazine, she's food editor at ABC-TV's *Good Morning America,* she hosts two weekday hour-long call-in cooking shows on the Food Network. And if that weren't enough, she's a wife and mother of two active children. Quick dishes, needless to say, are her forte. At least at home. This one's a particular favorite, something she serves husband Bill Adler when Ruthie and Sammy are off visiting their chums. "The trick to this dish," Sara says, "is getting the oil hot enough to make the broccoli crisp—literally brown around the edges."

3 tablespoons extra-virgin olive oil
4 cups (2-inch-long) broccoli florets
½ teaspoon salt
One 14½-ounce can chicken broth (or 2 cups homemade)
¼ to ½ teaspoon red pepper flakes

½ cup finely slivered prosciutto ham (about 2 ounces)
6 ounces capellini (angel hair pasta), cooked al dente by package directions and drained well
½ cup freshly grated Parmesan cheese
Freshly ground black pepper

1. Heat oil in large, heavy skillet over high heat until it just smokes, 2½ to 3 minutes.

2. Add broccoli, sprinkle with salt, cover, and cook over high heat for 2 minutes. Stir, reduce heat to moderate, cover, and cook, stirring occasionally, until broccoli is crisp-tender, about 3 minutes.

continued

NOTE

CHOREOGRAPHY IS EVERYTHING HERE. SARA PUTS THE PASTA WATER, A BIG POT OF IT, ON TO BOIL WITH 1 TABLESPOON SALT JUST BEFORE SHE BEGINS FRYING THE BROCCOLI (THE PASTA ITSELF COOKS FOR 2 MINUTES ONLY). SHE KEEPS ½ INCH OF STEM ON THE BROCCOLI FLORETS AND TRIMS THEM TO A THICKNESS OF ¼ INCH. THAT WAY STEMS AND FRAGILE TOPS ARE DONE AT THE SAME TIME. FOR THIS AMOUNT OF BROCCOLI SARA SAYS YOU'LL NEED ABOUT ONE LARGE BUNCH.

3. Add chicken broth and red pepper flakes and bring to simmering over low heat.

4. Add prosciutto, hot drained capellini, and 6 tablespoons Parmesan. Toss well. Taste for salt and fine-tune as needed; also add freshly ground black pepper to taste. Toss well again.

5. Ladle into heated soup plates and sprinkle remaining Parmesan on top.

HAM, RICE, AND CORN SKILLET SCRAMBLE

MAKES 6 SERVINGS

Try this recipe when you have plenty of leftover ham. As for the leftover rice, I cook it ahead for just such last-minute dishes.

4 tablespoons bacon drippings, butter, or vegetable oil

2 large scallions, trimmed and thinly sliced (include some green tops)

One 1-pound bag frozen bell pepper stir-fry mix (red, green, and yellow peppers; do not thaw)

1 teaspoon dried marjoram, crumbled

½ teaspoon dried thyme, crumbled

One 10-ounce package frozen whole-kernel corn (do not thaw)

2 cups diced baked or boiled ham

3 cups Al Dente Make-Ahead Rice (page 35)

One 12-ounce can evaporated milk (use skim, if you like)

½ teaspoon salt

¼ teaspoon freshly ground black pepper

½ cup coarsely chopped parsley

1 ½ cups shredded sharp Cheddar or jack cheese

1. Heat drippings in large, heavy skillet over moderate heat for 1 minute. Add scallions and stir-fry until limp and lightly browned, about 3 minutes.

2. Add stir-fry mix, marjoram, and thyme and stir-fry until limp, about 5 minutes.

3. Add corn, ham, and rice and heat 5 minutes, breaking up clumps of rice. Add milk, salt, and pepper and cook and stir 5 minutes more.

4. Off heat, mix in parsley and cheese. As soon as cheese melts, taste for salt and pepper, adjust as needed, and serve.

continued

Shrimp, Corn, and Rice Creole: Prepare as directed through step 2. In step 3, add corn and 1 pound shelled and deveined medium-size raw shrimp (fresh or frozen) instead of ham; cook and stir 5 minutes. Omit milk and black pepper; add rice and two 10-ounce well-drained cans diced tomatoes with green chilies. Cook and stir just until heated through, 3 to 5 minutes. Proceed as directed in step 4.

CUBAN CHICKEN AND YELLOW RICE

Makes 4 servings

This recipe comes from my good friend Jeanne Voltz, formerly food editor of *Woman's Day* and before that, food editor of the *Miami Herald*, then the *Los Angeles Times*. It was during her Miami days that Jeanne became acquainted with Cuban Chicken and Yellow Rice and began making it as a hurry-up family dinner. "My kids loved it," she says. She adds that asparagus (a 9-ounce package frozen asparagus cuts, broken up but not thawed) could be substituted for peas. And she thinks tiny broccoli florets (perhaps 1 cup) would be good, too, though not authentic.

2 tablespoons canola or olive oil
4 boned chicken thighs (about ¾ pound)
½ teaspoon salt
¼ teaspoon freshly ground black pepper
3½ cups hot water (faucet hot)
1 medium-size garlic clove, minced

One 10-ounce package yellow (saffron) rice mix
Half of a 1-pound package frozen green peas (do not thaw)
2 roasted red bell peppers (from a jar), halved or quartered lengthwise

1. Heat oil in large, deep, heavy skillet over moderately high heat 2 minutes. Add chicken and brown lightly on both sides, 5 to 8 minutes. Lift to plate, sprinkle with salt and black pepper, and reserve.

2. Pour water into the skillet, add garlic, and bring to boiling. Add rice, then stir or tilt skillet to spread rice. Lay chicken on top, bring to gentle boil, cover, and cook until liquid is absorbed and rice is tender, about 20 minutes.

3. Spoon peas on top, in piles or random pattern, then add red peppers. Cover and cook just until peas are heated through, 3 to 5 minutes.

4. Taste for salt and pepper, adjust as needed, and serve.

CHICKEN ALFREDO WITH MUSHROOMS AND ASPARAGUS

Makes 4 servings

This zip-quick dinner takes advantage of the carved, fully cooked chicken breasts now available at nearly every supermarket (for this particular recipe, I prefer the original roasted chicken instead of a flavored one). I also make the most of packaged sliced mushrooms, prepared alfredo sauce, and frozen cut asparagus. Result? Dinner in less than 30 minutes.

2 tablespoons extra-virgin olive oil

One 8-ounce package sliced fresh white mushrooms

1 cup fresh or frozen chopped onion (about 1 medium-large yellow onion)

1 small garlic clove, minced

½ teaspoon dried marjoram, crumbled

¼ teaspoon dried thyme, crumbled

¼ teaspoon freshly ground black pepper

One 10-ounce package carved, fully cooked chicken breast (see headnote above)

One 10-ounce package prepared alfredo sauce (from the refrigerator counter; use light or "reduced fat," if you like)

¼ cup dry Marsala, sherry, or white wine

One 9-ounce package frozen asparagus cuts (do not thaw but do separate into individual pieces)

3 cups Al Dente Make-Ahead Rice (page 35), reheated

1. Heat oil in large, heavy skillet over moderate heat 2 minutes. Add mushrooms, onion, garlic, marjoram, thyme, and pepper and cook, stirring often, until mushrooms release their juices and these evaporate, about 5 minutes.

2. Add chicken, alfredo sauce, and wine; adjust heat so mixture bubbles gently, then cook, stirring frequently and breaking up chicken, until steaming, about 3 minutes.

3. Add asparagus, distributing evenly over surface of mixture, cover, and cook just until crisp-tender, 2 to 3 minutes—no longer or asparagus will become mushy.

4. Bed rice on heated deep platter, spoon chicken mixture on top, and serve.

POULET BASQUAIS (BASQUE-STYLE CHICKEN)

Makes 6 servings

Basque cooks would bubble this stew in a big pot for the better part of a day. They would also begin with a tough old bird. The point of a skillet is to trim cooking time to less than an hour. And the point of using chicken thighs is to inject a lot of flavor fairly fast. I've further shortcut the prep by substituting bottled marinara sauce for half a dozen different ingredients. The perfect catch-all for this colorful stew: boiled rice or buttered noodles. I favor rice because I usually have some in the refrigerator.

3 tablespoons extra-virgin olive oil

6 chicken thighs (about 2 pounds)

2 cups fresh or frozen chopped onions (about 2 medium-large yellow onions)

½ cup diced red bell pepper (½ medium-size)

½ cup diced green bell pepper (½ medium-size)

2 large garlic cloves, minced

2 large whole bay leaves

1 teaspoon dried marjoram, crumbled

½ teaspoon dried thyme, crumbled

One 8-ounce package sliced fresh white mushrooms

4 ounces baked or boiled ham, diced

1½ cups bottled marinara sauce or 1½ cups Basic Tomato Sauce (page 30)

¼ cup dry red or white wine

¼ teaspoon freshly ground black pepper

¼ cup minced Italian (flat-leaf) parsley

4 cups Al Dente Make-Ahead Rice (page 35), reheated; or ½ pound medium egg noodles cooked and drained by package directions, then tossed with 1 tablespoon melted unsalted butter or margarine

1. Heat oil in large, heavy skillet over high heat 2 minutes. Add chicken skin side down, cover, and fry until nicely brown, about 10 minutes; loosen chicken at half-time so it doesn't stick to pan but do not turn. Lift chicken to large plate and reserve. Pour all drippings from skillet, then spoon 3 tablespoons back in.

2. Add onions, red and green peppers, garlic, bay leaves, marjoram, and thyme and turn to coat with drippings. Reduce heat to moderate, cover, and "sweat" vegetables 10 minutes, stirring once or twice. Mix in mushrooms and ham, cover, and "sweat" 5 minutes.

3. Combine marinara sauce, wine, and black pepper and add to skillet. Return chicken to skillet skin side up, and spoon sauce on top. Adjust heat so mixture bubbles gently, cover, and cook until chicken is done, about ½ hour. If mixture seems soupy, simmer uncovered 3 to 5 minutes.

4. Mix in parsley, taste for salt and black pepper, and adjust as needed. Bed rice on heated deep platter, ladle chicken mixture on top, and serve.

CHICKEN AND MANGO STIR-FRY

Makes 4 servings

This recipe was inspired by one in Eileen Yin-Fei Lo's *New Cantonese Cooking*, a book and a cook for whom I have great respect.

FOR THE MARINADE
1 tablespoon soy sauce
1 tablespoon Chinese oyster sauce
1 teaspoon dry sherry or vermouth
1 teaspoon cornstarch

½ teaspoon Asian roasted sesame oil
½ teaspoon sugar
½ teaspoon finely minced fresh ginger
½ teaspoon salt
Pinch white pepper

FOR THE STIR-FRY
¾ pound thin chicken cutlets, cut crosswise into strips ½ inch wide
3 tablespoons peanut oil
1 tablespoon finely minced fresh ginger
1 small mango (10 to 12 ounces), peeled, pitted, and cut into matchstick strips (see Tip)
4 medium-size scallions, trimmed and cut on the bias into ½-inch chunks

1 small green bell pepper, cored, seeded, cut into wedges ½ inch wide, then each wedge cut crosswise and on the bias into ½-inch lengths
One 8-ounce can thinly sliced water chestnuts, drained well
1 garlic clove, finely minced
2 teaspoons cornstarch blended with ½ cup chicken broth
3 cups Al Dente Make-Ahead Rice (page 35), reheated

1. For the marinade, combine all marinade ingredients in large bowl.

2. For the stir-fry, add chicken to marinade, toss well, and let stand 30 minutes.

3. Heat 1½ tablespoons oil in large, heavy skillet or wok over high heat for 1 minute. Add ginger and stir-fry for 30 seconds. Add mango, scallions, green pepper, water chestnuts, and garlic and stir-fry just until pepper turns bright emerald, 2 to 2½ minutes. With slotted spoon, lift skillet mixture to large plate and reserve.

4. Wipe skillet dry, add remaining 1½ tablespoons oil, and heat over high heat for 1 minute. Spread chicken and marinade in thin layer in skillet and cook 1 minute without stirring. With spatula, flip chicken over, spread, and cook until lightly browned, 1 to 1½ minutes.

5. Return mango mixture to skillet and stir-fry 1½ minutes. Blend in cornstarch mixture and cook and stir until mixture bubbles and thickens slightly, 2 to 3 minutes.

6. Mound rice in heated deep platter, spoon skillet mixture on top, and serve.

TIP

CUTTING CHICKEN CUTLETS INTO THIN STRIPS WILL BE EASIER IF YOU PARTIALLY FREEZE THEM; ½ HOUR IN THE FREEZER SHOULD DO IT.

JAPANESE STIR-FRY OF CHICKEN, BROCCOLI, AND PEPPERS OVER SOBA

MAKES 4 SERVINGS

Soba (Japanese buckwheat noodles), stocked by most good supermarkets, and failing that, any Asian grocery or specialty food store, add distinctive nutty flavor to this stir-fry. (The soba at Asian groceries will be fresher than that at supermarkets because there's faster turnover. Stale soba may cook up "sticky" and clump). To save time, I use packaged broccoli florets from the produce counter. I prefer them to frozen stir-fry vegetables because they don't lose their crunch. I also use a relatively new supermarket staple: carved, fully cooked chicken breasts, available in several flavors (I like the "honey-roasted" here).

2 tablespoons peanut or corn oil

1 tablespoon Asian roasted sesame oil

2 cups small broccoli florets (see headnote)

1 medium-size red bell pepper, cored, seeded, and cut lengthwise into strips ½ inch wide

½ teaspoon red pepper flakes

2 large scallions, trimmed and thinly sliced (include some green tops)

1 large garlic clove, finely minced

1 tablespoon finely minced fresh ginger

One 10-ounce package carved, fully cooked chicken breast (see headnote above)

2 tablespoons teriyaki sauce

2 tablespoons Asian fish or oyster sauce

½ pound soba, cooked and drained by package directions (see headnote above)

1. Heat peanut and sesame oils in large, heavy skillet over moderately high heat until nearly smoking, about 2 minutes.

2. Add broccoli and bell pepper and stir-fry 2 minutes. Reduce heat to moderate; mix in red pepper flakes, scallions, garlic, ginger, and chicken. Cover and cook just until broccoli is crisp-tender, 2 to 3 minutes.

3. Mix in teriyaki and fish sauces and heat until steaming, about 2 minutes.

4. Bed soba on heated deep platter, spoon skillet mixture on top, and serve.

CHICKEN STIR-FRY WITH BEAN SPROUTS, MUSHROOMS, AND SUN-DRIED TOMATOES

A cross-cultural recipe that gets dinner into single dish—on the double.

FOR THE MARINADE
2 teaspoons soy sauce
2 teaspoons Asian oyster
   sauce
1 teaspoon finely minced fresh
   ginger

1 teaspoon finely minced garlic
1 teaspoon cornstarch
1/2 teaspoon Asian roasted
   sesame oil
1/2 teaspoon sugar

FOR THE STIR-FRY
1 pound chicken cutlets, cut
   crosswise into strips
   1/2 inch wide
3 tablespoons peanut oil
2 garlic cloves, finely minced
2 teaspoons finely minced fresh
   ginger
4 medium-size scallions,
   trimmed and cut on the
   diagonal in 2-inch lengths
   (include some green tops)
One 8-ounce package sliced
   fresh white mushrooms

2 teaspoons cornstarch blended
   with 1/2 cup chicken broth, 1
   tablespoon soy sauce, and 1
   teaspoon each Asian oyster
   sauce and sugar
1/2 cup thinly slivered oil-packed
   sun-dried tomatoes, drained
2 cups fresh bean sprouts,
   washed well and drained
   very dry
3 cups Al Dente Make-Ahead
   Rice (page 35), reheated

1. For the marinade, combine all ingredients in large bowl.

2. For the stir-fry, add chicken to marinade, toss well, and let stand 20 minutes.

3. Heat peanut oil in large, heavy skillet or wok over high heat 1 minute. Add garlic, ginger, and scallions and stir-fry until scallions are limp, about 2 minutes. Add mushrooms and stir-fry until juices are released and these evaporate, about 5 minutes.

4. Add chicken and marinade and stir-fry just until no longer pink, about 3 minutes.

5. Blend in cornstarch mixture and cook and stir until mixture bubbles and thickens slightly, about 3 minutes.

6. Add sun-dried tomatoes and bean sprouts and cook, stirring and turning frequently, until steaming hot, about 2 minutes.

7. Mound rice in heated deep platter, spoon skillet mixture on top, and serve.

SKILLET RUMAKI WITH BITTER GREENS AND RICE

Makes 4 servings

I've always loved rumaki, those sweet-sour, bacon-wrapped chicken livers that were once such a popular hors d'oeuvre. I've turned them into a skillet dinner, served with rice, and wreathed with arugula wilted with the pan drippings.

8 slices lean smoky bacon, cut crosswise at ½-inch intervals

1 pound chicken livers, washed, trimmed of fat, halved at the natural separation, and lightly dusted with flour

1 large garlic clove, finely minced

1 teaspoon finely minced fresh ginger

One 8-ounce can thinly sliced water chestnuts, drained well

2 teaspoons cornstarch blended with ½ cup chicken broth, ¼ cup soy sauce, and 1 tablespoon light brown sugar

2 cups Al Dente Make-Ahead Rice (page 35), reheated

3 tablespoons balsamic vinegar

5 cups tender young arugula leaves, washed and spun dry

1. Cook bacon in large, heavy skillet over moderate heat until crisp and brown, 7 to 8 minutes. With slotted spoon, scoop browned bacon to paper toweling to drain.

2. Raise heat to high; add chicken livers, garlic, and ginger and stir-fry until livers are lightly browned, 3 to 4 minutes.

3. Add water chestnuts, then blend in cornstarch mixture and cook and stir until mixture bubbles and thickens slightly, about 3 minutes.

4. Mound rice in heated deep platter, then with slotted spoon, ladle chicken livers on top and keep warm.

5. Add vinegar to liquid in skillet, bring quickly to boiling, add arugula, and turn to coat. Using slotted spoon, wreathe arugula around rice and chicken livers. Pour remaining skillet liquid over all, sprinkle with reserved bacon, and serve.

CANTONESE-STYLE SHRIMP STIR-FRY WITH SNOW PEAS

MAKES 4 SERVINGS

Many of us have become so fond of the heat of Szechuan and Hunan cooking that we've forgotten the cool delicacy of Cantonese. This fast stir-fry is reason enough to reacquaint ourselves with it.

FOR THE MARINADE
2 teaspoons soy sauce
2 teaspoons Chinese oyster
    sauce
1 teaspoon finely minced fresh
    ginger

1 teaspoon finely minced garlic
1 teaspoon cornstarch
½ teaspoon Asian roasted
    sesame oil
½ teaspoon sugar

FOR THE STIR-FRY
1 pound shelled and deveined
    medium-size raw shrimp,
    halved lengthwise
3 tablespoons peanut oil
4 medium-size scallions,
    trimmed and cut on the
    diagonal in 2-inch lengths
    (include some green tops)
One 8-ounce can thinly sliced
    water chestnuts, drained well

2 teaspoons cornstarch blended
    with ½ cup chicken broth,
    1 tablespoon soy sauce, and
    1 teaspoon each Chinese
    oyster sauce and sugar
One 6-ounce package frozen
    snow peas, thawed and patted
    dry on paper toweling
3 cups Al Dente Make-Ahead
    Rice (page 35), reheated

1. For the marinade, combine all ingredients in large bowl.

2. For the stir-fry, add shrimp to marinade, toss well, and let stand 20 minutes.

continued

3. Heat peanut oil in large, heavy skillet or wok over high heat 1 minute. Add scallions and water chestnuts and stir-fry until scallions are limp, about 2 minutes.

4. Add shrimp and marinade and stir-fry just until shrimp turn pink, about 3 minutes.

5. Blend in cornstarch mixture and cook and stir until mixture bubbles and thickens slightly, about 3 minutes.

6. Add snow peas and cook, stirring frequently, until steaming hot, about 1 minute.

7. Mound rice in heated deep platter, spoon skillet mixture on top, and serve.

SHRIMP MOQUECA

Makes 4 servings

Dendê, a reddish palm oil so saturated that it's sludgy at room temperature, is what Brazilian cooks would use to make this classic dish. I've substituted olive oil because *dendê* is rarely available here and if it is, it is usually rancid. *Dendê,* moreover, is an artery-clogger. A good fruity olive oil combined with sweet paprika approximates the flavor and color of *dendê* and is actually heart-healthy. The best shrimp to use for this recipe are fresh medium-size ones—have your fishmonger shell and devein them, raw. In a pinch, I've substituted frozen "salad" or "cocktail" shrimp, which are already cooked, shelled, and deveined (they should be thawed and any tail-end shells pinched off). To save time, I use rice I've made ahead, add a package of thawed and drained frozen green peas, and heat the two together. If you have all ingredients measured and ready to go at the outset, this recipe will be ready to serve in less than 20 minutes.

2 tablespoons extra-virgin olive oil (the fruitiest you can find)

6 medium-size scallions, trimmed and thinly sliced (include some green tops)

2 large garlic cloves, minced

1 tablespoon sweet paprika

One 10-ounce can diced tomatoes with green chilies, drained well

One 14-ounce can Thai coconut milk (use light, if you like)

1 tablespoon tomato ketchup

½ teaspoon salt

⅛ teaspoon freshly ground black pepper

1 pound shelled and deveined medium-size raw shrimp; or 1 pound bite-size pieces cooked lobster meat; or 1 pound lump crab, bits of shell and cartilage removed

Half of an 8-ounce package light cream cheese (Neufchâtel), cubed

1 tablespoon fresh lime juice

⅓ cup coarsely chopped fresh cilantro

3 cups Al Dente Make-Ahead Rice (page 35), reheated with one 10-ounce package frozen tiny green peas that have been thawed and drained well

continued

1. Heat oil in large, heavy skillet over moderate heat 1 minute. Add scallions, garlic, and paprika and cook, stirring often, until scallions are limp, about 3 minutes.

2. Add tomatoes with chilies, coconut milk, ketchup, salt, and pepper and boil, uncovered, until reduced by about half, 4 to 5 minutes.

3. Add shrimp and cook, turning often, just until pink, about 3 minutes.

4. Remove from heat, mix in cheese, and when it melts, stir in lime juice and cilantro. Taste for salt and pepper and adjust as needed.

5. Mound rice and peas in heated deep platter, ladle shrimp moqueca on top, and serve.

SHRIMP GUMBO

Makes 6 servings

Some years ago I interviewed a serious Cajun cook who told me that a properly made gumbo is an all-day affair. She further told me that a roux should be worked over slow heat for at least 45 minutes—preferably longer—until it is as red as rust. Finally, she told me that a true Cajun gumbo contains okra or gumbo filé (powdered sassafras leaves), never both. She, of course, uses a giant kettle for making gumbo. I use a skillet—a shallow mixture cooks ten times as fast as a deep one.

3 tablespoons bacon drippings, lard, or vegetable oil

5 tablespoons all-purpose flour

2 cups fresh or frozen chopped onions (about 2 medium-large yellow onions)

2 large garlic cloves, minced

Half of a 1-pound bag frozen bell pepper stir-fry mix (red, green, and yellow peppers; do not thaw)

2 medium-size celery ribs, trimmed and diced

One 10-ounce package frozen cut okra, thawed but not drained

One 8-ounce can tomato sauce or 1 cup Basic Tomato Sauce (page 30)

4 cups chicken or vegetable broth

1 teaspoon salt

½ teaspoon freshly ground black pepper

½ teaspoon hot red pepper sauce

1 pound shelled and deveined medium-size raw shrimp

⅓ cup minced parsley

4 cups Al Dente Make-Ahead Rice (page 35), reheated

1. Heat drippings for 2 minutes in large, heavy skillet over moderately high heat. Add flour and cook and stir until color of pale caramel, 5 to 8 minutes.

2. Add onions, garlic, stir-fry mix, and celery and cook, stirring often, for 5 minutes. Mix in okra and its liquid, cover, and "sweat" 10 minutes, stirring occasionally.

continued

3. Add tomato sauce, broth, salt, black pepper, and red pepper sauce and cook uncovered, stirring often, until slightly thickened, 5 to 8 minutes.

4. Add shrimp and cook uncovered just until pink, 3 to 5 minutes. Mix in parsley, taste for salt and pepper, and fine-tune.

5. Mound ⅔ cup rice in each of six heated large soup plates, ladle in gumbo, and serve.

CASSEROLES, PIES, AND POT PIES

Casseroles may seem totally retro, a throwback to the days when our mothers tossed bits of meat and vegetables into an earthenware dish, mixed in a can of creamy soup, topped the lot with crumbs, potato chips, or canned French-fried onions, then baked it until bubbling and brown.

The truth is, casseroles are the quintessential dinners in a dish. The hurried—*harried*—cook's best friend. They are supremely forgiving, virtually failsafe even when refrigerator odds and ends are added to the mix.

Casseroles appear to be an early twentieth-century phenomenon, created, it's believed, when American potteries began mass-producing economical bakeware. World War I, the Depression, and World War II all popularized casserole cookery because it enabled frugal cooks to stretch precious meat (with noodles, rice, or bread crumbs) and at the same time to recycle leftovers.

My goal here was to create a modern repertoire of quicker-cooking casseroles. And toward that end, I call for somewhat higher oven temperatures and use larger than usual baking dishes so that ingredients can be spread thinner. Faster still, I sometimes cook casseroles on top of the stove.

To pare prep times, I keep frozen deep-dish pie crusts on hand (choosing those that show no signs of drying or cracking). I also stock a variety of toppers: frozen puff pastry (the fastest way to dress up a pot pie), homemade bread crumbs, and croutons. And for almost instant biscuit toppings, I've concocted a handy mix that also makes light-as-air dumplings (see page 31).

I don't use canned soups to bind my casseroles, but I do rely upon a huge roster of "acceptable" canned, frozen, and prepped-ahead fresh produce. All of them save time.

AMERICAN CHOP SUEY

To save time, use a richly seasoned bottled marinara sauce. You're not likely to need additional salt, but taste before baking and add if needed.

2 tablespoons extra-virgin olive oil
One 1-pound bag frozen bell pepper stir-fry mix (red, green, and yellow peppers; do not thaw)
2 large garlic cloves, minced
⅓ teaspoon freshly ground black pepper
1 pound ground lean beef chuck

One 26-ounce bottle marinara sauce or 3¼ cups Basic Tomato Sauce (page 30)
One 8-ounce can tomato sauce
8 ounces fusilli or penne pasta, cooked al dente by package directions and drained well
⅓ cup freshly grated Parmesan cheese

1. Preheat oven to 375°F. Coat 2½- to 3-quart casserole with non-stick vegetable spray and set aside.

2. Heat oil in large, heavy skillet over moderate heat 2 minutes. Add stir-fry mix, garlic, and black pepper and cook, stirring often, until vegetables brown lightly, 8 to 10 minutes.

3. Add meat and cook, breaking up clumps, until no longer pink, about 5 minutes. Add marinara and tomato sauces and bring just to a simmer. Taste for salt and add as needed.

4. Arrange fusilli in bottom of prepared casserole, top with skillet mixture, then scatter with cheese.

5. Bake uncovered until bubbling and browned, 20 to 25 minutes, and serve.

UPSIDE-DOWN TAMALE PIE

Makes 6 servings

I've used a chunky salsa with plenty of built-in seasonings as the basis of the meat filling. I could have used a corn bread mix for the topping, but I find them too sweet. Besides, it's easy to do a from-scratch corn bread if you assemble the components while the meat filling cooks.

For meat filling

- 2 tablespoons extra-virgin olive oil or vegetable oil
- 1 ½ cups chopped fresh or frozen onions (2 medium yellow onions)
- 1 large garlic clove, minced
- Half of a 1-pound bag frozen bell pepper stir-fry mix (red, green, and yellow peppers; do not thaw)
- 2 teaspoons chili powder
- 1 teaspoon dried oregano, crumbled
- 1 pound lean ground beef chuck
- 3 tablespoons all-purpose flour
- One 1-pound jar chunky salsa (as mild or hot as you like)
- 2 tablespoons tomato paste
- One 9-ounce package frozen whole-kernel corn (do not thaw)
- Salt and freshly ground black pepper
- 2 tablespoons coarsely chopped fresh cilantro or parsley

For corn bread topping

- 1 cup all-purpose flour
- ¾ cup yellow cornmeal
- 2 tablespoons freshly grated Parmesan cheese
- 2 teaspoons baking powder
- 1 teaspoon baking soda
- 1 teaspoon salt
- 1 teaspoon chili powder
- 1 teaspoon dried oregano, crumbled
- ¼ teaspoon freshly ground black pepper
- 1 cup buttermilk
- ¼ cup extra-virgin olive oil or vegetable oil
- 1 extra-large egg

1. Preheat oven to 400°F.

2. To prepare meat filling, heat oil in 11- to 12-inch, deep, oven-proof skillet over moderate heat 1 minute. Add onions, garlic, and stir-fry mix and cook, stirring, until onions are limp and golden, 5 to 8 minutes. Add chili powder, oregano, and beef, breaking up clumps. Cover and cook 10 minutes. Blend in flour, add salsa and tomato paste, stirring well to incorporate, then add corn and simmer uncovered 5 to 10 minutes, stirring often, until meat shows no signs of pink. Season to taste with salt and pepper, mix in cilantro, and set off heat.

3. To prepare corn bread topping, combine flour, cornmeal, and all remaining dry ingredients in bowl and make well in center. Combine buttermilk, oil, and egg in 1-quart measure, dump into well in dry ingredients, and mix briskly just until dough holds together. Spread on top of meat filling, leaving 1- to 1 1/2-inch margin all round.

4. Bake uncovered until bubbly and brown, 15 to 20 minutes. Serve at once.

STROGANOFF CASSEROLE WITH SPINACH

MAKES 6 SERVINGS

I've made a meal of this '70s party pleaser by adding a package of frozen chopped spinach and pre-sliced fresh mushrooms (most supermarkets now carry them). I've also lightened things up by substituting part-skim ricotta for cream-style cottage cheese, low-fat cream cheese (Neufchâtel) for the "fully loaded," and freshly grated Parmesan for Cheddar (although I still offer this as an option).

2 tablespoons unsalted butter or margarine
1 pound lean ground beef chuck
One 8-ounce package sliced fresh white mushrooms
1 cup fresh or frozen chopped onion (about 1 medium-large yellow onion)
1 small garlic clove, minced
1/2 teaspoon dried marjoram, crumbled
1/4 teaspoon dried thyme, crumbled
1/2 cup tomato sauce or Basic Tomato Sauce (page 30)
1/2 cup part-skim ricotta cheese

Half of an 8-ounce package light cream cheese (Neufchâtel), cut into small pieces
1 1/4 teaspoons salt
1/4 teaspoon freshly ground black pepper
One 10-ounce package frozen chopped spinach, thawed and drained very dry
6 ounces medium egg noodles, cooked al dente by package directions and drained
1/2 cup freshly grated Parmesan cheese or coarsely shredded sharp Cheddar

1. Preheat oven to 350°F. Butter shallow 2 1/2-quart casserole and set aside.

2. Melt 2 tablespoons butter in large, heavy skillet over moderately high heat; add beef, mushrooms, onion, garlic, marjoram, and thyme

and cook, stirring and breaking up chunks of meat, until meat is no longer pink, about 10 minutes.

3. Reduce heat to low, add tomato sauce, and cook and stir 1 to 2 minutes. Add all remaining ingredients except noodles and Parmesan and cook, stirring, just until cream cheese melts. Taste for salt and pepper and adjust as needed. Fold in noodles.

4. Turn into casserole, spreading evenly, top with grated Parmesan and bake uncovered until bubbly and tipped with brown, about 20 minutes. Serve at once.

TIP

Buy thinly sliced corned beef rather than one big piece—it's easier to chop. Make a series of vertical cuts through the stacked slices at 1/8-inch intervals, then an identical series of cuts at right angles to them.

REUBEN PIE

Makes 6 servings

If you like Reuben sandwiches, you'll love this quiche-like pie of corned beef, rye bread crumbs, sauerkraut, and Swiss cheese. Use fresh sauerkraut, if possible, or a mild Bavarian-style canned one with caraway seeds.

1 frozen 9-inch deep-dish pie shell, thawed and recrimped to form high fluted edge
1/2 cup mayonnaise-relish sandwich spread
1/3 cup half-and-half cream or evaporated milk (use skim, if you like)
1/4 cup thawed frozen egg product or 1 extra-large egg, well beaten
1 tablespoon chili sauce
1 teaspoon Dijon mustard

1/4 cup finely diced green bell pepper
1/4 cup finely diced scallions
1/2 teaspoon freshly ground black pepper
12 ounces corned beef, trimmed of excess fat and coarsely chopped
1 1/2 cups sauerkraut, drained well
3/4 cup soft rye bread crumbs
1 cup coarsely shredded Gruyère or Swiss cheese (about 4 ounces)

1. Preheat oven to 400°F. Set pie shell (still in foil pan) in standard 9-inch pie tin (it provides extra support for heavy Reuben filling); set aside.

2. Whisk together sandwich spread, half-and-half, egg product, chili sauce, mustard, green pepper, scallions, and black pepper in large bowl. Add corned beef, sauerkraut, and bread crumbs and mix.

3. Spread half corned beef mixture over bottom of pie shell and scatter with 1/2 cup shredded cheese. Top with remaining corned beef mixture, spreading evenly.

4. Bake uncovered 15 minutes. Scatter remaining cheese on top, reduce oven temperature to 350°F., and bake just until cheese melts and filling is softly set, 15 to 20 minutes.

5. Let stand 15 minutes at room temperature, cut into wedges and serve.

PORK AND SPANISH RICE BAKE

MAKES 6 SERVINGS

A wholly accommodating recipe. Substitute leftover roast beef or lamb for pork, baked or boiled ham, even leftover roast chicken or turkey. I often use frozen chopped onions and frozen bell pepper stir-fry mix. And I nearly always opt for the pre-sliced fresh mushrooms now widely available.

¼ cup extra-virgin olive oil
2 cups fresh or frozen chopped onions (about 2 medium-large yellow onions)
1 cup frozen bell pepper stir-fry mix (red, green, and yellow peppers; do not thaw)
2 large garlic cloves, minced
1 teaspoon finely grated orange zest
One 8-ounce package sliced fresh white mushrooms
2 cups diced leftover roast pork (or beef, lamb, ham, chicken, or turkey)

1 ¼ cups uncooked converted rice
2 ½ cups chicken broth blended with 1 teaspoon salt, ¼ teaspoon each paprika and freshly ground black pepper, and ⅛ teaspoon powdered saffron
½ cup Basic Tomato Sauce (page 30), tomato sauce, or marinara sauce
1 ½ cups frozen tiny green peas (do not thaw)

1. Preheat oven to 350°F.

2. Heat oil in 2-quart flameproof casserole over moderate heat for 2 minutes. Add onions, stir-fry mix, garlic, and orange zest and cook, stirring often, until limp and most juices have evaporated, 5 to 8 minutes. Add mushrooms and cook, stirring, 5 minutes longer.

3. Mix in all remaining ingredients except peas, and bring to a boil. Cover, transfer to oven, and bake 30 minutes.

4. Break up chunks of frozen peas and mix peas into casserole. Cover and bake until peas are tender and rice has absorbed almost all liquid, 10 to 15 minutes. Serve at once.

NOTE

Resist the temptation to substitute mint and parsley flakes for the fresh. They lack the delicacy this recipe needs.

PERSIAN LAMB PILAF BAKED WITH MINT, LEMON, AND ZUCCHINI

Makes 4 to 6 servings

This easy layered casserole is reminiscent of one I once enjoyed in the Middle East. Lamb is the preferred meat in that part of the world, but if lean ground lamb shoulder is unavailable (or you're not partial to lamb), substitute ground beef.

2 tablespoons extra-virgin olive oil

1 pound lean ground lamb shoulder or beef chuck

1 cup fresh or frozen chopped onion (about 1 medium-large yellow onion)

1 large garlic clove, finely minced

$\frac{1}{3}$ cup uncooked converted rice

$\frac{1}{4}$ cup coarsely chopped fresh mint

$\frac{1}{4}$ cup coarsely chopped Italian (flat-leaf) parsley

1 teaspoon finely grated lemon zest

1 $\frac{1}{2}$ teaspoons salt

$\frac{1}{2}$ teaspoon freshly ground black pepper

4 medium-size zucchini, trimmed and thinly sliced

1 cup chicken broth

1 cup Soft White Bread Crumbs (page 36) mixed with 1 tablespoon fruity olive oil

1. Preheat oven to 375°F. Coat shallow 2- to 2$\frac{1}{2}$-quart casserole with nonstick vegetable cooking spray and set aside.

2. Heat olive oil in large, heavy skillet over moderately high heat 1 minute. Add lamb, breaking up clumps, and cook, stirring often, until no longer pink, 3 to 5 minutes.

3. Mix in onion and garlic and cook, stirring often, until onion is glassy, about 3 minutes.

4. Stir in rice, mint, parsley, lemon zest, $\frac{3}{4}$ teaspoon salt, and $\frac{1}{4}$ teaspoon pepper. Cook, stirring, 3 minutes.

5. Layer half the zucchini in bottom of casserole; sprinkle with half the remaining salt and pepper. Ladle lamb mixture on top, cover with remaining zucchini, and sprinkle with remaining salt and pepper. Pour broth evenly over all.

6. Scatter crumbs on top and bake uncovered until bubbling and brown, about 30 minutes. Accompany, if you like, with a tartly dressed green salad.

PISSALADIÈRE (PROVENÇAL PIZZA)

MAKES 6 SERVINGS

What a tour de force this used to be. Today, with frozen bell pepper stir-fry mixes and pitted black olives as near as the nearest supermarket, not to mention bottled puttanesca sauce, shredded mozzarella, and refrigerated pizza crust dough, there's no excuse not to make it. Unlike Italian pizza, this one's best eaten with a fork. Add a crisp green salad and the meal's complete.

One 10-ounce package refrigerated pizza dough
1 tablespoon extra-virgin olive oil
1 medium-size red onion, halved lengthwise, then each half thinly sliced
Half of a 1-pound bag frozen bell pepper stir-fry mix (red, green, and yellow peppers; do not thaw)
1 large garlic clove, minced
¼ teaspoon dried thyme, crumbled
¼ teaspoon dried rosemary, crumbled

½ cup freshly grated Parmesan cheese
Half of an 8-ounce package coarsely shredded mozzarella cheese
1 ½ cups bottled puttanesca sauce (olive and anchovy sauce for pasta)
Two 2-ounce tins flat anchovy fillets, drained, rinsed, and patted dry on paper towels
14 pitted black olives (preferably oil-packed), halved lengthwise

1. Preheat oven to 425°F. Coat baking sheet with nonstick vegetable cooking spray. Unwrap pizza dough and pat into 10 × 14-inch rectangle on baking sheet. Bake uncovered until pale golden, 7 to 8 minutes. Remove from oven and set aside; leave oven on.

2. Heat oil in large, heavy skillet over high heat 2 minutes. Add onion, stir-fry mix, garlic, thyme, and rosemary and cook, stirring often, until limp and quite dry, 7 to 8 minutes.

3. Sprinkle Parmesan over crust, leaving 1-inch margin all round. Then add in this order, each time distributing evenly and leaving 1-inch margin: skillet mixture, mozzarella, puttanesca.

4. Using anchovies, make decorative crisscross design over surface of *pissaladière*, then stud with olives.

5. Return to oven and bake uncovered until bubbly, about 10 minutes.

6. Cool 10 minutes, cut into large squares, and serve.

STOVE-TOP PORK CHOP CASSEROLE

Makes 4 servings

I've souped up this old favorite, not with a can of soup but by adding a hefty dose of seasonings. I also cook the casserole on top of the stove because simmering is faster than baking.

One 14 ½-ounce can chicken
    broth
1 tablespoon mango chutney or
    orange or ginger marmalade
1 teaspoon Dijon mustard
½ teaspoon salt
¼ teaspoon hot red pepper
    sauce
⅛ teaspoon dried thyme,
    crumbled
1 ½ tablespoons vegetable oil
Four ¾-inch-thick boneless
    center-cut pork loin chops
    (1 ⅓ to 1 ½ pounds)
1 cup fresh or frozen chopped
    onion (about 1 medium-large
    yellow onion)

1 large whole bay leaf
¼ teaspoon poultry seasoning
1 cup uncooked converted rice
4 slices unpeeled ripe tomato
    about ⅜ inch thick and
    3 ½ to 4 inches across
4 green bell pepper rings, sliced
    about ⅜ inch thick and
    3 ½ to 4 inches across
4 slices peeled Vidalia or yellow
    onion about ⅜ inch thick and
    3 ½ to 4 inches across

1. Combine broth, chutney, mustard, salt, red pepper sauce, and thyme in food processor or electric blender or by hand; set aside.

2. Heat oil in small Dutch oven over high heat for 2 minutes. Add pork chops, cover, and brown for 3 minutes; turn, cover, and brown flip sides for 3 minutes. Lift to plate and reserve.

3. Add chopped onion, bay leaf, and poultry seasoning to drippings in Dutch oven and cook and stir for 3 minutes, scraping up browned bits on pan bottom.

4. Add rice and turn to coat with drippings. Add reserved broth mixture, bring to boiling, adjust heat so mixture bubbles gently but steadily, cover, and cook 10 minutes.

5. Reduce heat to low, return pork chops and any accumulated juices to Dutch oven, then top each with tomato slice, bell pepper ring, and onion slice. Cover and cook until chops are done and rice has absorbed all liquid, 20 to 25 minutes.

6. Remove bay leaf and serve.

VARIATIONS

Chicken Stove-Top Casserole: Prepare as directed, but substitute 4 small skinned and boned chicken half-breasts (5 to 6 ounces each) for pork chops. Also, if you like, increase chutney in broth mixture to 2 tablespoons, omit mustard, and add 2 teaspoons curry powder.

Chili Chops: Prepare as directed but omit chutney and mustard and add 1 teaspoon chili powder and ½ teaspoon ground cumin to broth mixture. Also omit tomato slices, bell pepper rings, and onion slices in step 5. Instead, top each chop with ½ cup bottled tomato salsa. Proceed as directed. Sprinkle with ¼ cup chopped fresh cilantro or parsley before serving.

Cod and Rice Casserole with Fresh Dill: Prepare as directed, but substitute four 1-inch-thick boned cod slices (or haddock, salmon, or tuna) for pork chops. In step 4, cook rice mixture 15 minutes instead of 10. In step 5, omit tomato slices, bell pepper rings, and onion slices. Instead, top each cod slice with ½ cup bottled tomato salsa. Proceed as directed, but cook only long enough for rice to absorb all liquid, 10 to 15 minutes. Sprinkle with ¼ cup freshly snipped dill or 2 tablespoons freshly minced tarragon or parsley before serving.

TIP

To save time, use broccoli slaw mix from the fresh produce counter.

SCALLOPED POTATOES WITH BROCCOLI AND HAM

MAKES 4 SERVINGS

In going through a family recipe file, my friend Joanne Hayes, a first-rate food editor/cookbook author, says, "I think the only thing we ate was pork and ham." That's understandable, given the fact that her mother's people were Pennsylvania Dutch. This particular recipe is one Joanne remembers fondly from her childhood. It contained no broccoli, but Joanne's added it to boost this easy casserole into the one-dish-dinner category.

1 cup fresh or frozen chopped onion (about 1 medium-large yellow onion)
1 tablespoon extra-virgin olive oil
2 ½ cups milk
¼ cup all-purpose flour
¼ teaspoon salt
⅛ teaspoon freshly ground black pepper

4 cups sliced, peeled all-purpose potatoes (4 to 5 medium-size) or 4 cups thawed frozen hash brown potatoes
3 cups broccoli slaw mix or coarsely chopped fresh broccoli
1 pound boiled or baked ham, cut into 1-inch cubes
1 tablespoon Dijon mustard

1. Preheat oven to 400°F. Coat shallow 2-quart casserole with non-stick vegetable cooking spray and set aside.

2. Cook onion in oil in heavy medium-size saucepan over moderate heat until golden, about 5 minutes.

3. Combine milk, flour, salt, and pepper in 1-quart measure, add to onion, and cook and stir until thickened, about 3 minutes.

4. Layer half the potatoes into prepared casserole then top with the broccoli and half the sauce. Arrange ham on top, dot with mustard, then cover with remaining potatoes and sauce.

5. Cover tightly with aluminum foil and bake until potatoes are just tender, 40 to 45 minutes.

6. Remove foil and bake until lightly browned, about 15 minutes longer. Serve at once.

SHORTCUT

TO BROWN CASSEROLE MORE QUICKLY (IT MUST BE IN A FLAMEPROOF CASSEROLE DISH), SLIDE INTO BROILER SETTING 4 TO 5 INCHES FROM HEAT AND BROIL JUST UNTIL BUBBLY AND BROWN, ABOUT 2 MINUTES.

NOTE

IF YOU HAVE BREAD CRUMBS IN THE FREEZER (PAGE 36), YOU'RE AHEAD OF THE GAME. SET THE FROZEN CORN IN THE FRIDGE IN THE MORNING AND IT'LL BE THAWED BY DINNER.

SCALLOPED CORN, HAM, AND SWEET PEPPERS

MAKES 4 SERVINGS

This casserole can be stirred up in a jiff, shoved in the oven, and forgotten till it smells irresistible.

3 tablespoons unsalted butter or margarine
1 cup fresh or frozen chopped onion (about 1 medium-large yellow onion)
½ cup chopped green bell pepper (about 1 small)
2 tablespoons all-purpose flour
1 cup evaporated milk or half-and-half cream blended with ¾ teaspoon salt and ¼ teaspoon each freshly ground black pepper and freshly grated nutmeg

1 extra-large egg, lightly beaten
¼ cup canned diced pimientos, drained
2 cups frozen whole-kernel corn, thawed and drained
1 cup diced baked or boiled ham
¾ cup Buttered Bread Crumbs (page 36)

1. Preheat oven to 350°F. Lightly butter shallow 6-cup casserole and set aside.

2. Melt 3 tablespoons butter in large, heavy skillet over moderate heat, add onion and green pepper, and cook, stirring, until limp, about 3 minutes.

3. Blend in flour. Quickly combine milk mixture and egg, add to skillet, and cook, stirring constantly, until thickened, about 3 minutes. Do not boil or mixture may curdle.

4. Mix in pimientos, corn, and ham; turn into casserole and top with buttered crumbs.

5. Bake uncovered until bubbling and browned, 35 to 40 minutes, then serve.

Scalloped Corn with Chicken or Turkey: Prepare as directed, but substitute 1 cup diced cooked chicken or turkey for ham. Also add 2 tablespoons each freshly grated Parmesan cheese and dry sherry to skillet after milk-egg mixture has thickened.

Scalloped Corn and Crab: Prepare Scalloped Corn with Chicken or Turkey as directed, but substitute $\frac{1}{2}$ pound flaked lump crab meat for chicken or turkey. Also stir in 2 tablespoons each minced parsley and freshly snipped dill (or $\frac{1}{2}$ teaspoon dill weed) along with crab.

Scalloped Corn and Shrimp: Prepare Scalloped Corn and Crab as directed, but substitute $\frac{1}{2}$ pound cooked, shelled, and deveined small shrimp for crab. Also blend 1 tablespoon each Dijon mustard and ketchup with milk mixture and omit sherry.

SANTA FE HOMINY AND SAUSAGE CASSEROLE

This recipe was inspired by a dish I once enjoyed at Cafe Pasqual's, to my mind, Santa Fe's consistently best restaurant because chef-proprietress Katharine Kagel cares passionately about food and is forever dreaming up new flavor combinations. This one merges Old Mexico and New. Kathy would prepare everything from scratch, even making her own sausages. To shortcut this long-winded recipe, I use supermarket sausages, prepared produce, bottled salsa, and pre-shredded cheese.

4 fully-cooked Southwestern-style gourmet turkey or chicken sausages, cut into 1-inch chunks (13 to 16 ounces)

2 cups chopped thawed frozen mixed onions and red and green bell peppers

3 cups cooked or canned hominy, well drained

2 tablespoons coarsely chopped fresh cilantro or parsley

¼ teaspoon salt

One 11½-ounce jar medium-hot salsa

1½ cups shredded Monterey jack or mixed Mexican-style cheeses (about 6 ounces)

1. Preheat oven to 375°F.

2. Cook sausages with onion-pepper mixture in large, heavy oven-proof skillet or shallow 2-quart flameproof casserole over moderate heat until vegetables begin to brown, 5 to 6 minutes. Mix in hominy, cilantro, and salt.

3. Top with salsa and cheese and bake uncovered until bubbling and brown, 15 to 20 minutes. Serve at once.

COQ AU VIN

MAKES 4 TO 6 SERVINGS

Given the speed with which this cooks, I think it's a pretty good approximation of the real thing.

It's imperative that you trim as much excess fat from the chicken as possible, otherwise the vegetables will be greasy. It's also important that you choose small red-skin potatoes of uniform size, preferably ones a little smaller than Ping-Pong balls. They must cook whole, in their skins, so the red wine doesn't discolor their white flesh. For this recipe, I like to use a heavy baking dish that measures $14 \times 11\frac{1}{2} \times 2\frac{1}{4}$ inches but a heavy-gauge roasting pan of similar size will also work well.

4 slices lean bacon, snipped
   crosswise into julienne strips
6 chicken thighs (about 2
   pounds), trimmed of
   excess fat
Half of a 1-pound package
   peeled baby-cut fresh carrots
1 pound uniformly small red-
   skin potatoes, scrubbed but
   not peeled
1 cup frozen small whole onions
   (do not thaw)
4 large garlic cloves, peeled
$\frac{3}{4}$ pound button mushrooms,
   trimmed of coarse stems and
   wiped clean

4 large parsley sprigs
Three 3-inch sprigs fresh thyme
   or $\frac{3}{4}$ teaspoon dried thyme,
   crumbled
2 large whole bay leaves
$1\frac{1}{2}$ cups Burgundy or other
   dry red wine blended with
   3 tablespoons all-purpose
   flour, 1 teaspoon salt, and
   $\frac{1}{2}$ teaspoon freshly ground
   black pepper

1. Preheat oven to 450°F.

2. Wreathe bacon pieces around edge of ungreased $14 \times 11\frac{1}{2} \times 2\frac{1}{4}$-inch baking dish. Arrange chicken thighs, skin side up and not touching, in center of dish. Add carrots, potatoes, onions, and garlic, distributing evenly but not covering chicken. Roast uncovered for 15 minutes.

continued

3. Add mushrooms, stir with other vegetables to coat with pan drippings, again distributing evenly but not covering chicken. Tuck in parsley, thyme, and bay leaves and roast uncovered for 10 minutes.

4. Quickly whisk wine mixture, then add slowly, distributing evenly and stirring constantly. Cover baking dish with foil and bake until potatoes and chicken are done, about 10 minutes more.

5. Discard bay leaves, parsley, and thyme sprigs, and serve.

DEEP SOUTH BAKED CHICKEN SALAD

Makes 6 to 8 servings

To save time, wait till you have leftover chicken (or turkey) before preparing this casserole — a good choice, by the way, for a party buffet. Or use deli roast chicken or frozen, diced, cooked chicken. Also, processor-chop the celery, scallions, and parsley together by pulsing briskly.

4 cups diced cooked chicken or turkey

4 extra-large hard-cooked eggs, peeled and diced

2 cups coarsely chopped celery

2 large scallions, trimmed and coarsely chopped (include some green tops)

½ cup minced parsley

One 5-ounce can sliced water chestnuts, drained well

¼ cup canned diced pimientos, drained

¼ cup freshly grated Parmesan cheese

1 tablespoon fresh lemon juice

1 teaspoon finely grated lemon zest

One 12-ounce can evaporated milk blended with 3 tablespoons all-purpose flour

1 cup mayonnaise (use low-fat, if you like)

1 teaspoon salt

½ teaspoon freshly ground black pepper

1 teaspoon poultry seasoning

1½ cups Soft White Bread Crumbs (page 36) tossed with 2 tablespoons melted unsalted butter

1. Preheat oven to 375°F. Coat 13 × 9 × 2-inch baking pan with nonstick cooking spray and set aside.

2. Combine all ingredients except bread crumbs in large bowl, then turn into prepared pan, spreading to corners. Scatter bread crumbs evenly on top.

3. Bake, uncovered, until bubbling and browned, about 30 minutes, then serve.

continued

Hard-cooked eggs are good to have in the refrigerator. Unshelled, they will keep about a week.

Deep South Baked Chicken Salad with Biscuit Topping: Prepare as directed through step 2, but preheat oven to 425°F. and omit crumb mixture. Instead, fork enough milk (about ¾ to 1 cup) into 2 cups Dumpling/Biscuit Topping Mix (page 31) to make soft dough. Drop from rounded tablespoon on top of casserole ingredients, spacing evenly, then bake uncovered until puffed and tipped with brown, about 15 minutes.

Deep South Baked Ham Salad: Prepare as directed, substituting 4 cups diced baked or boiled ham for chicken. Also omit poultry seasoning, reduce salt to ½ teaspoon, and blend 2 tablespoons Dijon mustard with mayonnaise. If you like, omit crumb topping and cover with biscuits as directed in Deep South Baked Chicken Salad with Biscuit Topping (above).

Deep South Baked Shrimp Salad: Prepare Deep South Baked Ham Salad as directed, but substitute 1 pound cooked, shelled, and deveined medium-size shrimp for ham. Increase lemon juice to 2 tablespoons, omit mustard, and substitute relish-style sandwich spread for mayonnaise. Also mix in 2 tablespoons well-drained small capers.

Baked Curried Shrimp Salad: Prepare Deep South Baked Shrimp Salad as directed, but use mayonnaise in place of sandwich spread and omit capers. Also blend 1 tablespoon curry powder, ⅓ cup finely chopped mango chutney, and ½ teaspoon hot red pepper sauce with mayonnaise.

Deep South Baked Crab Salad: Prepare Deep South Baked Shrimp Salad as directed, but omit shrimp and substitute 1 pound flaked lump crab meat (bits of shell and cartilage removed). Also add 2 tablespoons Dijon mustard to sandwich spread along with capers.

CHICKEN POT PIE

Makes 6 servings

By using frozen small whole onions, green peas, and puff pastry, I eliminate the tedium of peeling and shelling plus the eternal rolling and turning required to make puff pastry from scratch. I also use packaged, peeled, baby-cut fresh carrots. To speed-slice, I line them up four abreast and cut with a large chef's knife. Finally, I dip into my refrigerator bank of chopped onions and parsley.

3 tablespoons unsalted butter or margarine

1 cup chopped fresh or frozen onion (about 1 medium-large yellow onion)

1 garlic clove, minced

1 large celery rib, trimmed and thinly sliced

Half of a 1-pound package peeled baby-cut fresh carrots, sliced ½ inch thick

1 cup frozen small whole onions (do not thaw)

2 whole bay leaves

Two 3-inch sprigs fresh lemon thyme or ½ teaspoon dried thyme, crumbled

¼ teaspoon freshly grated nutmeg

2 skinned and boned chicken half-breasts (about 1 pound)

One 14 ½-ounce can chicken broth

1 cup frozen tiny green peas (do not thaw)

One 12-ounce can evaporated milk blended with ⅓ cup all-purpose flour

¼ cup minced parsley

Salt and freshly ground black pepper

1 sheet frozen puff pastry (from a 17 ¼-ounce package), thawed and unfolded by package directions, then cut into twelve rounds with a floured 3-inch biscuit cutter

1. Preheat oven to 400°F.

2. Melt butter in 12 ¼ × 10 ¼ × 2 ¼-inch range-to-oven casserole over moderate heat. Add chopped onion, garlic, celery, carrots, whole onions, bay leaves, thyme, and nutmeg and cook, stirring often, until chopped onion is limp, about 5 minutes.

continued

3. Add chicken and broth, bring to gentle boil, cover, and cook 15 minutes, turning chicken at half-time. Cut chicken into $1/2$-inch cubes—carefully—right in casserole.

4. Add peas and milk mixture and cook, stirring often, 5 minutes until thickened. Mix in parsley and salt and pepper to taste. Discard bay leaves and thyme sprigs.

5. Space puff pastry rounds evenly on top of chicken mixture, bake uncovered until puffed and nicely browned, 15 to 20 minutes, then serve.

VARIATIONS

Chicken Pot Pie with Biscuit Topping: Prepare as directed through step 4, but preheat oven to 425°F. In step 5, omit frozen puff pastry. Instead, fork enough milk (about $3/4$ to 1 cup) into 2 cups Dumpling/Biscuit Topping Mix (page 31) to make soft dough. Drop from rounded tablespoon on top of casserole ingredients, spacing evenly, then bake uncovered until puffed and tipped with brown, about 15 minutes.

Turkey and Corn Pot Pie: Prepare as directed, substituting 1 pound turkey cutlets for chicken and 1 cup frozen whole-kernel corn for green peas. Also substitute one 3-inch sprig fresh rosemary (or $1/4$ teaspoon crumbled dried rosemary) for thyme. If you like, omit puff pastry topping and cover with biscuits as directed in Chicken Pot Pie with Biscuit Topping (above).

Shrimp Pot Pie: Prepare Chicken Pot Pie through step 2, substituting 2 tablespoons snipped fresh dill (or $1/2$ teaspoon dill weed) for thyme. In step 3, omit chicken; add broth plus $1/4$ cup dry vermouth, cover, and simmer 12 minutes. Add 1 pound shelled and deveined medium-size raw shrimp, cover, and cook just until shrimp turn pink, 2 to 3 minutes. Proceed as directed in steps 4 and 5.

Deviled Crab Pie: Prepare Shrimp Pot Pie as directed, omitting vermouth and blending $1^{1}/2$ tablespoons Dijon mustard and $1/2$ teaspoon hot red pepper sauce with broth. Cover and cook until vegetables are tender, 15 minutes. Omit shrimp and fold in 1 pound lump crab meat (bits of shell and cartilage removed); proceed as directed in steps 4 and 5.

Tuna Pot Pie: Prepare Shrimp Pot Pie as directed, omitting vermouth. Cover and cook until vegetables are tender, 15 minutes. Omit shrimp and fold in one 12-ounce can solid white tuna, well drained and flaked, and 2 tablespoons well-drained small capers. Proceed as directed in steps 4 and 5.

Ham Pot Pie: Prepare Shrimp Pot Pie as directed, omitting vermouth but blending 1 tablespoon each Dijon mustard and India relish with broth. In step 3 cover and cook until vegetables are tender, 15 minutes. Omit shrimp and fold in 2 cups diced boiled or baked ham and 2 tablespoons well-drained small capers. Proceed as directed in steps 4 and 5.

TUNA TETRAZZINI

The original *Tetrazzini*, created in honor of the Italian coloratura soprano Luisa Tetrazzini, is made with turkey and contains no vegetables other than mushrooms, scallions, and pimiento. I've used chunk white tuna and added peas to make it a meal. Also try the turkey and chicken variations.

3 tablespoons unsalted butter

One 8-ounce package sliced fresh white mushrooms

2 medium-size scallions, trimmed and coarsely chopped (include some green tops)

¼ teaspoon dried thyme, crumbled

1 cup chicken broth

½ cup evaporated milk (use skim, if you like) blended with 2 tablespoons all-purpose flour

1 tablespoon dry white wine or dry vermouth

½ pound No. 9 spaghetti, broken in half, then cooked al dente by package directions and drained well

½ cup freshly grated Parmesan cheese

One 10-ounce package frozen baby green peas, thawed and drained

One 12-ounce can chunk white tuna, drained and coarsely flaked

¼ cup canned diced pimientos, drained

Salt and freshly ground black pepper to taste

1. Preheat oven to 375°F. Coat shallow 2-quart casserole with non-stick vegetable cooking spray and set aside.

2. Melt butter in very large, heavy skillet over moderately high heat; add mushrooms, scallions, and thyme and cook, stirring often, until mushrooms are limp and juices evaporate, about 5 minutes.

3. Add broth, milk mixture, and wine and cook, stirring often, until sauce thickens, about 3 minutes. Add spaghetti, ¼ cup grated cheese, and all remaining ingredients. Toss gently but thoroughly.

4. Turn into prepared casserole, top with remaining ¼ cup grated cheese and bake uncovered until bubbly and brown, about 20 minutes.

VARIATIONS

Turkey Tetrazzini: Prepare as directed, substituting 2 cups diced cooked turkey for tuna and dry sherry for white wine. Also, if you like, substitute one 9-ounce package thawed and drained, frozen cut asparagus for peas.

Chicken Tetrazzini: Prepare as directed, substituting 2 cups diced, cooked chicken for tuna and dry sherry for white wine. Also, if you like, substitute one 10-ounce package thawed and drained, frozen peas and carrots for peas.

SCALLOPED TUNA WITH GREEN PEAS AND TOASTED ALMONDS

This is one easy tuna casserole that doesn't depend upon a can of soup. There is a white sauce to make, but it's ready in six minutes. The recipe calls for two cups of croutons. I prefer to use those I've made myself (see Homemade Croutons, page 39), but in a pinch I'll use the store-bought, steering clear of those with ersatz cheese, garlic, or Italian seasonings.

3 tablespoons unsalted butter
½ cup finely minced yellow onion (about 1 medium-small)
1 large celery rib, trimmed and finely diced
½ teaspoon dried rosemary, crumbled
¼ cup all-purpose flour
One 12-ounce can evaporated milk (use skim, if you like)
½ cup fresh whole milk
1 tablespoon Dijon mustard
½ teaspoon salt

½ teaspoon hot red pepper sauce
½ cup freshly grated Parmesan cheese
One 12-ounce can chunk white tuna, drained and coarsely flaked
1 cup frozen baby green peas, thawed and drained well
2 cups croutons (see headnote above)
¼ cup minced parsley
1 tablespoon fresh lemon juice
½ cup sliced almonds

1. Preheat oven to 375°F. Coat 2 ½-quart casserole with nonstick vegetable cooking spray and set aside.

2. Melt butter in large, heavy skillet over moderate heat, add onion, celery, and rosemary and cook, stirring often, until limp, about 3 minutes. Blend in flour, then add evaporated milk and whole milk and cook, stirring constantly, until thickened, about 3 minutes. Mix in mustard, salt, red pepper sauce, and cheese and stir until cheese melts.

3. Add tuna, peas, croutons, parsley, and lemon juice and toss gently to mix.

4. Turn into prepared casserole, top with almonds, and bake uncovered until bubbling and almonds are lightly toasted, about 25 minutes. Serve at once.

MUSHROOM-BAKED FLOUNDER WITH RICE AND PEAS

Few casseroles are more accommodating than this one, thanks to duxelles (mushroom paste), a freezer staple I couldn't cook without, at least when I'm rushed. Frozen green peas save time, too.

¾ cup low-fat milk or
   evaporated skim milk
2 tablespoons all-purpose flour
¼ cup (four ¾-inch pats)
   Duxelles (page 33)
¼ teaspoon salt
2 cups Al Dente Make-Ahead
   Rice (page 35)

1 cup frozen baby green peas,
   thawed and drained well
4 fresh or thawed frozen
   flounder or sole fillets
   (1 to 1 ¼ pounds)
¾ teaspoon freshly snipped dill
   or ¼ teaspoon dill weed
¼ teaspoon sweet paprika

1. Preheat oven to 375°F. Butter shallow 2-quart casserole lightly and set aside.

2. Combine milk and flour in small saucepan, beating until smooth. Bring to boiling over moderate heat, stirring constantly until thickened, about 3 minutes. Stir in 2 tablespoons duxelles and ⅛ teaspoon salt.

3. Mix rice and peas in prepared casserole and pour duxelles sauce evenly over all. Arrange flounder on top, spooning about ½ tablespoon remaining duxelles at bottom center of each fillet. Overlap fillets slightly to cover most of duxelles. Sprinkle fillets with dill, paprika, and remaining ⅛ teaspoon salt.

4. Cover and bake until fish almost flakes and mixture bubbles, 18 to 22 minutes. Serve immediately.

RICE, SALMON, AND ASPARAGUS CASSEROLE

Makes 4 to 6 servings

Once the white sauce is made, this meal-in-one goes together lickety-split. The white sauce, moreover, takes very little time and I think makes a better casserole binder than a can of soup.

3 tablespoons unsalted butter
¼ cup finely minced yellow onion (about 1 small)
¼ cup all-purpose flour
One 12-ounce can evaporated milk (use skim, if you like) + ½ cup fresh whole milk
1 teaspoon salt
½ teaspoon hot red pepper sauce
½ cup freshly grated Parmesan cheese
¼ cup freshly snipped dill or 1 teaspoon dill weed
¼ cup minced parsley

1 tablespoon fresh lemon juice
1 teaspoon finely grated lemon zest
Two 6-ounce cans pink salmon, drained, coarsely flaked, and bits of skin removed
One 9-ounce package frozen asparagus cuts, thawed and drained well
2 cups Al Dente Make-Ahead Rice (page 35)
⅓ cup coarsely shredded Monterey jack or sharp Cheddar cheese

1. Preheat oven to 375°F. Coat 2- to 2 ½-quart casserole with non-stick vegetable cooking spray and set aside.

2. Melt butter in large, heavy skillet over moderate heat, add onion, and cook, stirring often, until limp, about 3 minutes. Blend in flour, then add evaporated milk and whole milk and cook, stirring constantly, until thickened, about 3 minutes. Mix in salt, red pepper sauce, and Parmesan cheese and stir until cheese melts. Stir in dill, parsley, lemon juice, and zest.

3. Add salmon, asparagus, and rice and toss gently to mix.

4. Turn into prepared casserole, top with Monterey jack, and bake uncovered until bubbling and lightly browned, 25 to 30 minutes. Serve at once.

JOANNE'S CATFISH CASSEROLE WITH HUSH PUPPY TOPPING

Makes 4 servings

My friend Joanne Lamb Hayes, formerly the Food Editor of *Country Living* magazine, came up with this ingenious one-dish dinner. She says that you can further trim prep time by substituting thawed frozen onion and bell pepper stir-fry mix for fresh onion and bell pepper. "Add 2 cups to the potatoes," she instructs, "and finely chop ¼ cup for the hushpuppy batter."

½ teaspoon salt
½ teaspoon sweet paprika
¼ teaspoon freshly ground black pepper
2 teaspoons unsalted butter, margarine, or vegetable oil
2 cups coarsely chopped, peeled baking potatoes or 2 cups frozen hash brown potatoes, thawed

1 cup coarsely chopped yellow onion (about 1 medium-large)
1 cup coarsely chopped red or green bell pepper (about 1 medium-large)
1 ¼ pounds fresh or thawed, frozen catfish fillets
1 cup water
2 tablespoons all-purpose flour

For hush puppy topping
¾ cup white or yellow cornmeal
¼ cup all-purpose flour
1 teaspoon baking powder
1 teaspoon sugar

¼ teaspoon salt
½ cup milk
1 extra-large egg
¼ cup finely chopped yellow onion

I. Preheat oven to 375°F. Lightly butter 2 ½-quart casserole and set aside. Combine salt, paprika, and black pepper and reserve.

2. Melt butter in large, heavy skillet over moderate heat. Add potatoes, onion, and bell pepper. Cook uncovered, stirring often, until potatoes are just tender and onion has started to brown, 8 to 10 minutes.

3. Meanwhile, to make the hush puppy topping, mix cornmeal, flour, baking powder, sugar, and salt in medium-size bowl. Add milk, egg, and onion; stir only enough to combine and set aside.

4. Stir half of reserved salt mixture into hot skillet mixture, then spoon into casserole and arrange catfish fillets on top.

5. Combine water, flour, and remaining salt mixture in skillet and cook, stirring constantly, until thick and bubbly, about 3 minutes. Pour into casserole.

6. Top with hush puppy batter, spreading to edge, and bake uncovered until topping springs back when gently touched in center, 25 to 30 minutes. Serve at once.

ELAINE HANNA'S SAVANNAH SHRIMP AND RICE

Makes 4 to 6 servings

Elaine Hanna, my co-author of *The New Doubleday Cookbook*, is a superlative cook and an endlessly inventive one. "Here's a recipe," she says, "I often fix for Sunday supper with friends after golf. I make it as far as ready to bake, then refrigerate until one hour before serving." If you follow Elaine's lead, making the casserole ahead and refrigerating it, increase the initial baking time to 45 minutes or, as she instructs, "until most of the liquid is absorbed and rice is tender." Then proceed as recipe directs. Elaine adds that she sometimes substitutes boneless chicken breasts for shrimp or 1/2 pound each shrimp, lump crab, and bay scallops.

1 cup fresh or frozen chopped onion (about 1 medium-large yellow onion)
2 garlic cloves, finely minced
1/3 cup extra-virgin olive oil
One 8-ounce package sliced fresh white mushrooms
1 1/2 pounds shelled and deveined medium-size raw shrimp
1 1/4 cups uncooked converted rice
1 1/4 teaspoons salt
Pinch ground hot red pepper (cayenne)

1/8 teaspoon sweet paprika
1/8 teaspoon powdered saffron
3 tablespoons tomato paste
Two 10 1/2-ounce cans chicken broth
1 cup frozen green peas, thawed and drained
1/2 cup thawed and drained frozen, canned, or leftover cooked whole-kernel white corn
2 tablespoons minced parsley

1. Preheat oven to 350°F.

2. Cook onion and garlic in oil in shallow 2-quart flameproof casserole over moderate heat, stirring now and then, until golden,

about 5 minutes. Add mushrooms and cook, stirring occasionally, until lightly browned, about 5 minutes.

3. Add shrimp and cook and stir just until pink, 3 to 5 minutes. Mix in rice, salt, cayenne, paprika, saffron, tomato paste, and broth.

4. Bring to a simmer, cover, and transfer to oven. Bake until all liquid is absorbed and rice is tender, about 25 minutes.

5. Use fork to mix in peas, corn, and parsley; cover, bake 10 minutes more, then serve.

MOST FISHMONGERS AND
HIGH-END SUPERMARKETS
SELL FRESHLY COOKED
SHELLED AND DEVEINED
SHRIMP. IF THEY'RE
UNAVAILABLE IN YOUR
AREA, USE FROZEN
COOKED SHELLED AND
DEVEINED SHRIMP. BUT
THAW AND DRAIN BEFORE
USING.

LOW COUNTRY SHRIMP PUDDING

Makes 4 to 6 servings

The classic Low Country shrimp pudding, a breakfast/brunch favorite in and around Charleston, South Carolina, contains no vegetables. I've added thawed and drained frozen tiny green peas to make this a one-dish dinner. The pudding bakes for 50 minutes—but it requires no "baby-sitting," so you can put your feet up and relax. As for the prep, that's a breeze.

6 slices stale firm-textured white bread

3 tablespoons unsalted butter or margarine, at room temperature

½ pound shelled, deveined, and cooked shrimp, coarsely chopped

1 ½ cups frozen tiny green peas, thawed and drained

1 ½ cups shredded Cheddar, Gruyère, or Monterey jack cheese (about 6 ounces)

3 extra-large eggs, lightly beaten

One 12-ounce can evaporated milk + ½ cup fresh whole milk

¾ teaspoon salt

¼ teaspoon freshly grated nutmeg

½ teaspoon hot red pepper sauce

1. Preheat oven to 350°F. Coat a 2-quart casserole with nonstick vegetable cooking spray and set aside.

2. Spread bread slices on one side with butter, then cut into ½-inch cubes (see Tip). Dump bread cubes into casserole along with shrimp, peas, and cheese. Toss well.

3. Quickly whisk together eggs, milk, salt, nutmeg, and red pepper sauce and pour evenly over shrimp mixture.

4. Set casserole in larger shallow baking pan and pour hot water into pan to depth of 1 ½ inches.

5. Bake uncovered until silver knife inserted midway between rim and center of pudding comes out clean, about 50 minutes. Serve straightaway.

VARIATIONS

Shrimp and Corn Pudding: Prepare as directed, but substitute 1 ½ cups cream-style corn (canned or thawed, frozen) for green peas and ½ teaspoon freshly ground black pepper for hot red pepper sauce. Also add ½ teaspoon crumbled dried rosemary and ¼ teaspoon crumbled dried thyme.

Santa Fe Shrimp and Corn Pudding: Prepare Shrimp and Corn Pudding as directed, but use ¼ teaspoon each freshly ground black pepper and hot red pepper sauce. Also substitute finely diced jalapeño jack cheese for Cheddar. Omit rosemary and thyme and add 3 tablespoons each finely grated yellow onion, freshly minced cilantro, and parsley.

Shrimp and Spinach Pudding: Prepare Santa Fe Shrimp and Corn Pudding as directed, substituting one 10-ounce package thawed, very well-drained frozen chopped spinach for corn and one diced 6-ounce roll garlic cheese for jalapeño jack. Omit cilantro and parsley.

TIP

THE EASIEST WAY TO CUBE BREAD IS TO STACK THE SLICES, THREE AT A TIME, AND WITH A SHARP SERRATED KNIFE, MAKE A SERIES OF LENGTHWISE CUTS, SPACING ½ INCH APART, THEN A SERIES OF CROSSWISE CUTS, AGAIN ½ INCH APART.

CASSEROLE OF ARTICHOKE HEARTS AND SHRIMP

Makes 4 to 6 servings

This all-in-one dinner, inspired by a recipe in Marcella Hazan's *Marcella Cucina*, needs only crusty bread to accompany it. Be sure to use a skillet with an oven-proof handle so this is truly "a dinner in a dish or a dash."

2 tablespoons extra-virgin olive oil

2 large garlic cloves, slivered lengthwise

2 large whole bay leaves

Two 9-ounce packages frozen artichoke hearts, thawed, drained, and sliced crosswise very thin

1 pound shelled and deveined medium-size raw shrimp (if using frozen shrimp, thaw and drain)

2 tablespoons fresh lemon juice

¼ teaspoon salt

¼ teaspoon freshly ground black pepper

4 ounces Fontina cheese, coarsely shredded

4 ounces mozzarella cheese, coarsely shredded

3 tablespoons freshly grated Parmesan cheese

1. Preheat oven to 425°F. Heat olive oil in heavy overproof 12-inch skillet over moderate heat for 2 minutes. Add garlic and bay leaves and cook, stirring, until garlic is color of amber, 2 to 3 minutes; remove and discard garlic and bay leaves.

2. Add artichoke hearts to skillet and cook, stirring, until beginning to brown, 2 to 3 minutes. Add shrimp and cook, stirring often, until no longer pink, 3 to 5 minutes.

3. Remove from heat; add lemon juice, salt, and pepper. Combine the three cheeses, add half to skillet mixture, and toss well.

4. Scatter remaining combined cheeses evenly on top and bake uncovered until bubbling and lightly browned, about 20 minutes. Serve hot with chunks of crusty bread.

SHRIMP, MUSHROOM, AND RICE BAKE

NOTE

I COULDN'T COOK ON FAST-FORWARD WITHOUT A STASH OF LEFTOVER RICE.

Makes 4 servings

The ingredients list is long, it's true, yet most items are quickly measured seasonings and pre-prepped foods. Assemble everything at the outset and you'll work like the wind. If you can get fresh shelled and deveined shrimp, by all means use them, adding in step 3 after the mushrooms are limp and cooking them just until pink, 3 to 4 minutes.

3 tablespoons unsalted butter
1 cup Soft White Bread Crumbs
  (page 36)
1 medium-size yellow onion,
  coarsely chopped
1 small green bell pepper, cored,
  seeded, and coarsely chopped
1 medium-size celery rib,
  trimmed and diced
1 cup sliced fresh white
  mushrooms (from an 8-ounce
  package)
1 small garlic clove, minced
½ teaspoon dried marjoram,
  crumbled
¼ teaspoon dried thyme,
  crumbled
½ pound "salad shrimp"
  (frozen, cooked, shelled, and
  deveined shrimp; do not
  thaw) or two
  4-ounce cans medium-size
  shrimp, drained well

1 cup frozen tiny green peas
  (do not thaw)
¼ cup canned diced pimientos,
  drained
2 cups Al Dente Make-Ahead
  Rice (page 35)
¾ cup evaporated milk (use
  skim, if you like)
½ cup mayonnaise (use "light,"
  if you like)
1 tablespoon dry white wine or
  dry sherry
1 ½ teaspoons Worcestershire
  sauce
½ teaspoon salt
¼ teaspoon hot red pepper
  sauce
⅛ teaspoon freshly ground
  black pepper

1. Preheat oven to 400°F. Butter a shallow 2-quart casserole well and set aside.

continued

2. Melt 3 tablespoons butter in large, heavy skillet over moderate heat. Spoon out 1 tablespoon melted butter, drizzle over bread crumbs, toss lightly, and reserve.

3. Add onion, green pepper, celery, mushrooms, garlic, marjoram, and thyme to butter in skillet and cook, stirring often, until mushrooms are limp, about 5 minutes.

4. Add shrimp, peas, pimientos, and rice; toss lightly and turn into casserole. Quickly whisk together remaining ingredients and pour evenly over all. Top with reserved crumbs.

5. Bake uncovered just until bubbling and browned, about 20 minutes.

TOMATO COBBLER

MAKES 4 SERVINGS

My mother used to make scalloped tomatoes—no stinting on bread—and serve it as the centerpiece of a simple family supper. Although I liked the flavor, I didn't like the texture or appearance. No "A" for visuals here. What I've done is separate the layers and put a cornmeal cobbler topping on a ragout of three tomatoes: fresh roasted sweet grape tomatoes (everyone's new favorite), sun-dried tomatoes, and chopped canned tomatoes with plenty of Italian seasonings.

1 pint sweet grape tomatoes, halved lengthwise, or 1 pint cherry tomatoes, quartered

½ cup boiling water

¼ cup sun-dried tomatoes, cut into strips ¼ inch wide

6 slices lean smoky bacon, cut crosswise at 1-inch intervals

1 small yellow onion, coarsely chopped

1 tablespoon all-purpose flour

One 14 ½-ounce can chopped tomatoes with basil, garlic, and oregano

¾ teaspoon minced fresh thyme or ¼ teaspoon dried thyme, crumbled

1 ½ cups Dumpling/Biscuit Topping Mix (page 31)

½ cup white or yellow cornmeal

¼ cup freshly grated Parmesan cheese

1 teaspoon sugar

⅓ cup milk

1 extra-large egg

1. Preheat oven to 450°F. Line rimmed baking sheet with foil; lightly oil foil. Arrange grape tomatoes in a single layer on foil, cut sides up. Roast until edges begin to brown, about 15 minutes. Meanwhile, combine boiling water and sun-dried tomatoes in small bowl; set aside.

2. Fry bacon in large, heavy ovenproof skillet or shallow flameproof 6- to 7-cup casserole over low heat until crisp, 6 to 8 minutes. With slotted spoon, lift bacon to paper toweling to drain. Spoon all but 1 tablespoon drippings from skillet.

continued

3. Cook onion in bacon drippings, stirring, until golden, 2 to 3 minutes. Sprinkle flour over onion and stir until evenly coated. Stir chopped tomatoes, sun-dried tomatoes with their liquid, and thyme into onion mixture. Heat just to boiling over moderate heat, stirring constantly; set aside.

4. About 5 minutes before grape tomatoes finish roasting, prepare cobbler topping. Use fork to combine topping mix, cornmeal, reserved bacon, 2 tablespoons Parmesan cheese, and sugar in medium-size bowl. Stir in milk and egg.

5. When tomatoes have finished roasting, reduce oven temperature to 375°F. Stir roasted tomatoes into chopped tomato mixture. Spoon cobbler topping over tomato mixture; sprinkle with remaining 2 tablespoons Parmesan cheese.

6. Bake uncovered 20 to 25 minutes or until topping is lightly browned and springs back when gently touched in center. Serve immediately.

BAKED POT OF SQUASH, CORN, AND SAUSAGE

MAKES 4 SERVINGS

If you have a 2- to 2½-quart casserole that can take burner heat, by all means use it. You'll avoid having to wash a skillet. I like to use a half-and-half mix of zucchini and yellow squash for this particular casserole, although I'll occasionally use all of one or the other.

½ pound bulk sausage

1 cup fresh or frozen chopped onion (about 1 medium-large yellow onion)

1 medium-size green bell pepper, cored, seeded, and coarsely chopped

1 large garlic clove, finely minced

2 slim young zucchini, trimmed and cut into ½-inch cubes

2 slim young yellow squash, trimmed and cut into ½-inch cubes

One 10-ounce package frozen whole-kernel corn, thawed and drained well

1 cup moderately hot bottled salsa

1 cup mayonnaise (use light, if you like)

2 extra-large eggs beaten well with 2 tablespoons all-purpose flour, ½ teaspoon salt, and ¼ teaspoon freshly ground black pepper

1 cup Soft White Bread Crumbs (page 36) mixed with ¼ cup freshly grated Parmesan cheese and 2 tablespoons melted butter

1. Preheat oven to 375°F. Coat 2- to 2½-quart casserole with non-stick vegetable cooking spray, preferably a stovetop-to-oven casserole.

2. Set casserole (if it can take burner heat) or large, heavy skillet over moderately high heat, add sausage, breaking up clumps, and brown well, 7 to 8 minutes.

continued

TIP

TO SAVE TIME, THAW THE CORN BY MICROWAVE; 3 TO 5 MINUTES ON HIGH SHOULD DO IT. OR PLACE IN A LARGE SIEVE AND RUN HOT TAP WATER OVER IT. EITHER WAY, DRAIN THE CORN AS DRY AS POSSIBLE.

3. Add onion, green pepper, and garlic and cook, stirring often, until onion is limp and golden, about 5 minutes.

4. Add zucchini, yellow squash, and corn and cook, stirring often, until squash is crisp-tender, about 5 minutes.

5. Set off heat and mix in salsa, mayonnaise, and egg mixture. If using skillet, turn mixture into casserole.

6. Scatter crumb mixture evenly on top and bake uncovered until bubbly and brown, about 30 minutes. Serve at once.

BARBECUED CHICKEN PIZZA WITH COLESLAW TOPPING

Makes 6 servings

I must confess that the idea for this particular pizza surfaced one night while I was watching Sara Moulton on the TV Food Network's popular *Cooking Live* program. The subject that evening? Twenty-minute dinners. Sara, a friend from way back (see her Crispy Skillet Broccoli in Broth with Capellini, Prosciutto, and Parmesan, page 191), was demonstrating how to make an instant—well, almost instant—pizza using leftover chicken and bottled barbecue sauce. Mid-recipe, a viewer phoned in to say that one of her favorite pizza toppings was deli slaw. So there you have it. In the South where I grew up, coleslaw (or "sweet slaw" as they call it in these parts) is the traditional accompaniment for barbecue. My adaptation of Sara's on-camera recipe is the perfect way to recycle any meat leftovers—beef, pork, chicken, turkey, even lamb. The meat will be juicier and more tender if you pull it apart rather than cut it into cubes. Try it!

One 10-ounce package
   refrigerated pizza dough
1 ¼ cups bottled barbecue
   sauce (mild or hot)
3 cups leftover roast chicken
   (use deli rotisserie chicken,
   if you like), pulled apart
   into bite-size chunks

4 large scallions, trimmed and
   thinly sliced (include some
   green tops)
1 ½ cups coarsely shredded
   Monterey jack or sharp
   Cheddar cheese
1 ½ cups deli coleslaw, very
   well drained

1. Preheat oven to 425°F. Coat baking sheet with nonstick vegetable cooking spray. Unwrap pizza dough and pat into 10 × 14-inch rectangle on baking sheet. Bake uncovered until pale golden, 7 to 8 minutes. Remove from oven and set aside; leave oven on.

continued

NOTE

FOR HER BARBECUED CHICKEN PIZZA, SARA USED A READY-MADE PIZZA CRUST (EVERY SUPERMARKET CARRIES THEM). I LIKE TO BAKE MY OWN, BUT I DO USE PACKAGED PIZZA DOUGH (LOOK IN THE STORE'S REFRIGERATED ROLL AND BISCUIT SECTION) BECAUSE THE CRUST IS CRISPER. SUIT YOURSELF.

2. Spread ¼ cup barbecue sauce over crust, leaving 1-inch margin all round. Mix remaining 1 cup barbecue sauce with chicken, then spoon evenly over crust, again leaving a 1-inch margin. Scatter scallions and cheese on top.

3. Return to oven and bake uncovered until bubbly, about 10 minutes.

4. Spoon slaw on top of pizza, distributing evenly, cut into large squares, and serve.

BACON, CLAM, AND ONION PIZZA

MAKES 6 SERVINGS

This jiffy pizza captures all the flavors of a good Yankee clam chowder and for that reason, I prefer a chewier crust than I do for my Barbecued Chicken Pizza with Coleslaw Topping (page 259). Pre-baked pizza crusts, now sold at every supermarket, work perfectly. Just be sure they are good and fresh, not hard and dry. An additional shortcut? The newly available crisp bacon bits, sold both by the plastic package at the meat counter and by the bottle among the cupboard staples. This is *real* bacon, *not* imitation.

One 1-pound package baked
   pizza crust
½ cup bottled alfredo sauce
   (use "light," if you like)
1 cup coarsely shredded Fontina
   or other mild white cheese
Two 6 ½-ounce cans diced
   clams, well drained
1 medium-size yellow onion,
   halved lengthwise, then each
   half thinly sliced

One 2-ounce bottle crisp bacon
   bits (about ¾ cup)
½ cup freshly grated Parmesan
   cheese
⅓ cup coarsely chopped parsley
¼ teaspoon freshly ground
   black pepper

1. Preheat oven to 400°F. Coat 10- or 12-inch pizza pan or baking sheet with nonstick vegetable cooking spray and set aside.

2. Spread pizza crust evenly with alfredo sauce, leaving 1-inch margin all round. Scatter fontina cheese evenly on top, then diced clams, onion slices, bacon bits, Parmesan cheese, parsley, and pepper.

3. Slide pizza onto prepared pizza pan and bake uncovered until bubbly and tipped with brown, 16 to 18 minutes. Serve at once.

EGGS, CHEESE, PASTA, AND GRAINS

Eggs, pasta, and grains share much in common. Their blandness makes them the perfect backdrop for punchy fillings and sauces. Their versatility means they can be dressed up or down. As for cheese, it's the perfect add-on. Take your pick: mild, medium or sharp, soft or hard. All can be mixed into countless egg, pasta, and grain dishes. All can be sprinkled on top.

Before the vegetarian movement began revolutionizing our lives in the 1960s, our use of grains was pretty much confined to polished white rice. Wild rice we knew, but few of us could afford it. In big-city ethnic enclaves, however, bulgur, couscous, and kasha were staples, as were brown rice, basmati, and Arborio. Yet only within the last ten to fifteen years have these made it into supermarkets in deepest heartland.

The pasta story is similar. What most of us ate before the '60s were macaroni and cheese, tuna-noodle casserole, and spaghetti with meatballs. Today every supermarket worth its salt stocks aisle-long assortments of pastas fresh and dry, plain and fancy, of bottled and refrigerated sauces.

Even with eggs, we've only recently come of age. Quiches were probably the breakthrough, thanks to Julia Child, who introduced them to us in the early '60s. Next we discovered frittatas, those flat Italian omelets that are as adaptable as they are filling, fast, and cheap.

For me, eggs, grains, and pastas will forever be invitations to improv. Are there better ways to get dinner on the table in a dash? Not likely!

GARDEN FRITTATA

MAKES 2 SERVINGS

If you're in a tearing hurry, substitute 1 cup frozen bell pepper stir-fry mix (red, green, and yellow peppers) for the red bell pepper and 1 cup frozen chopped onion for the scallions, but don't expect your frittata to be as flavorful. Finally, you can add snippets of leftovers to the skillet after the vegetables have "sweated" 10 minutes. Particularly good are cooked small broccoli or cauliflower florets, sliced or diced zucchini and/or yellow squash, spinach, or other dark leafy green.

2 tablespoons extra-virgin olive oil

4 large scallions, trimmed and sliced very thin (include some green tops)

1 medium-size red bell pepper, cored, seeded, and cut into matchstick strips

1 medium-size yellow squash or zucchini, halved lengthwise and sliced very thin

$\frac{1}{2}$ teaspoon dried marjoram, crumbled

$\frac{1}{4}$ teaspoon dried rosemary, crumbled

5 extra-large eggs, well beaten

$\frac{1}{4}$ cup freshly grated Parmesan cheese

$\frac{1}{4}$ cup coarsely chopped fresh basil

$\frac{1}{4}$ cup coarsely chopped fresh Italian (flat-leaf) parsley

$\frac{1}{2}$ teaspoon salt

$\frac{1}{4}$ teaspoon freshly ground black pepper

1. Heat olive oil in large, heavy skillet with flameproof handle (not cast iron) over moderate heat 1 minute. Add scallions, bell pepper, and squash and cook, stirring, 5 minutes until limp.

2. Reduce heat to lowest setting, mix in marjoram and rosemary, cover skillet, and allow vegetables to "sweat" 15 minutes, until soft and lightly browned. Transfer to bowl.

3. Beat eggs with cheese, basil, parsley, salt, and black pepper until foamy; preheat broiler.

4. Spray skillet bottom and sides with nonstick cooking spray and heat 1 minute over moderately low heat. Return vegetables to skillet,

add egg mixture, and when it begins to set around edges, after about 5 minutes, loosen with rubber spatula, encouraging unset eggs to run underneath. Continue cooking slowly without stirring until frittata is nearly set, about 10 minutes.

5. Slide skillet into broiler and broil frittata 5 inches from heat until top is set and lightly browned, 1 to 1 $\frac{1}{2}$ minutes.

6. Halve frittata and serve warm or at room temperature.

Ham and Spinach Strata:
Prepare as directed,
substituting one 10-ounce
package thawed and
drained frozen chopped
spinach for broccoli.
Also add ¼ teaspoon
freshly grated nutmeg to
egg mixture before pour-
ing into casserole.

Ham and Asparagus Strata:
Prepare Ham and Spinach
Strata as directed, but
substitute one 9-ounce
package thawed and
drained frozen asparagus
cuts for spinach.

HAM AND BROCCOLI STRATA

Makes 6 to 8 servings

No need to cook the broccoli. Just thaw and drain well. Shortcut: To cube bread quickly, stack 4 slices and cut lengthwise into strips ½ inch wide, then cut strips crosswise at ½-inch intervals.

8 slices firm-textured white bread, cut into ½-inch cubes
One 10-ounce package frozen chopped broccoli, thawed and drained
1 cup finely diced cooked ham
6 extra-large eggs, lightly beaten
One 12-ounce can evaporated milk (use skim, if you like) + enough whole milk to total 3½ cups

2 tablespoons finely grated yellow onion
1 tablespoon Dijon mustard
1 teaspoon dill weed
1 teaspoon salt
½ teaspoon freshly ground black pepper
2 cups coarsely shredded sharp Cheddar cheese
½ cup freshly grated Parmesan cheese

1. Preheat oven to 375°F. Butter shallow 3-quart casserole.

2. Cover bottom of casserole with bread cubes; top with broccoli, then ham.

3. Combine all remaining ingredients in large bowl, pour into casserole, and stir well. Let stand at room temperature 10 minutes.

4. Bake uncovered until bubbly and touched with brown, 25 to 30 minutes, then serve.

TOMATO, SCALLION, AND POTATO FRITTATA

Makes 4 servings

For this recipe you will need a skillet with an ovenproof handle so that you can move the frittata from stovetop to broiler.

3 tablespoons extra-virgin olive oil

2 bunches large scallions, trimmed and sliced about ¼ inch thick (see Tip)

2 large garlic cloves, finely minced

1½ teaspoons chopped fresh lemon thyme or ½ teaspoon dried thyme, crumbled

1 pound golfball-size red-skin potatoes, scrubbed and sliced ¼ inch thick but not peeled

1 teaspoon salt

½ teaspoon freshly ground black pepper

6 extra-large eggs

2 tablespoons minced Italian (flat-leaf) parsley or fresh basil

2 tablespoons freshly snipped chives

1 large firm-ripe tomato, cored, seeded, and finely diced

½ cup bottled mild or medium tomato salsa

1. Heat 2 tablespoons olive oil in heavy 10-inch skillet (not cast iron) over moderate heat 2 minutes. Add scallions, garlic, and thyme and brown lightly, stirring often, about 3 minutes.

2. Spread scallion mixture over bottom of skillet, then layer potatoes on top, brushing with remaining 1 tablespoon olive oil as you go and sprinkling with half the salt and pepper. Cover and cook until potatoes are tender, about 20 minutes. Meanwhile, preheat broiler.

3. Beat eggs until frothy with parsley, chives, and remaining salt and pepper and pour over potatoes in skillet. Cook without stirring until nearly set, about 10 minutes.

4. Combine tomato and salsa and spoon evenly on top of frittata. Slide skillet into broiler, setting 4 to 5 inches from heat, and broil just until tomato is touched with brown, 3 to 5 minutes. Using heavy-duty pot holder, remove from broiler, cut into wedges, and serve.

TIP

THE MOST EFFICIENT WAY TO SLICE SCALLIONS IS TO REBUNCH THEM ONCE THEY'VE BEEN TRIMMED AND WASHED, THEN WITH A LARGE, SHARP CHEF'S KNIFE, CUT STRAIGHT THROUGH THE BUNCH, MAKING THE SLICES AS THICK OR THIN AS YOU LIKE.

NOTE

To be safe, the eggs must be thoroughly cooked (160°F.), but that doesn't mean they'll be rubbery. Tend them with care and keep the heat moderately low.

PIPERADE (BASQUE OMELET OF ONIONS, PEPPERS, AND TOMATOES)

Makes 4 servings

An easy, inexpensive, all-in-one-skillet meal from the Pyrenees. The skillet you use should be large and heavy, preferably an enameled cast-iron one pretty enough to go from stovetop to table. By no means use an old-fashioned iron skillet, the one that fries chicken perfectly. You'll discolor the eggs.

3 tablespoons extra-virgin olive oil (the fruitiest you can find)
2 cups fresh or frozen chopped onions (about 2 medium-large yellow onions)
Half a 16-ounce bag frozen bell pepper stir-fry mix (red, green, and yellow bell peppers; do not thaw)
One 14½-ounce can diced tomatoes, drained very dry
1 teaspoon dried marjoram, crumbled
¼ teaspoon dried thyme, crumbled
8 extra-large eggs
1 teaspoon salt
¼ teaspoon freshly ground black pepper

1. Heat oil in heavy 12-inch skillet over moderately high heat 2 minutes. Add onions, stir-fry mix, tomatoes, and half the marjoram and thyme. Reduce heat to moderate and cook, stirring occasionally, until juices evaporate and mixture is consistency of puree, 12 to 15 minutes.

2. Whisk eggs until frothy with salt, pepper, and remaining marjoram and thyme.

3. Pour into skillet, reduce heat to moderately low, and cook slowly, pulling "set" eggs from edges in toward center and tilting skillet so uncooked portions run underneath.

4. As soon as eggs are uniformly set but not hard, dish up and serve.

EGGS, ASPARAGUS, AND SHRIMP DONE THE BELGIAN WAY

Makes 4 servings

Belgium is famous for its plump white asparagus and that's what Belgian cooks would use for this recipe. To shortcut the prep time, I use frozen green asparagus, the color most Americans prefer. If you want to try white asparagus and can find it fresh, trim it, cut into 1-inch chunks, and parboil just until crisp-tender, 2 to 3 minutes. I don't recommend canned white asparagus. I find it mushy and don't like its "tinny" taste. Two additional time-savers: I dip into my refrigerator bank of hard-cooked eggs and I buy freshly shelled and deveined cooked shrimp from my fishmonger (many supermarkets also sell these). In a pinch, you could use packaged frozen "salad" or "cocktail" shrimp, but thaw and drain them well and pinch off any shells that may have been left on the tips of the tails.

½ pound shelled and deveined, cooked medium-size shrimp, halved lengthwise

One 9-ounce package frozen asparagus cuts, thawed and drained well

6 hard-cooked eggs (see page 34), peeled and sliced

2 tablespoons all-purpose flour

1 tablespoon Dijon mustard

1 teaspoon salt

¼ teaspoon white pepper

1 cup half-and-half cream

½ cup milk or evaporated milk (use skim, if you like)

¾ cup coarsely shredded Gruyère or Emmentaler cheese

⅓ cup minced parsley

1½ cups Soft White Bread Crumbs (page 36) tossed with 2 tablespoons melted unsalted butter

1. Preheat oven to 425°F. Coat shallow 2- to 2½-quart casserole with nonstick vegetable cooking spray.

2. Place shrimp, asparagus, and hard-cooked eggs in casserole and toss gently; set aside.

continued

3. Blend flour, mustard, salt, pepper, and $1/4$ cup half-and-half in small, heavy saucepan. Stir in remaining $3/4$ cup half-and-half and milk, set over moderate heat, and cook, whisking constantly, until thickened and smooth, about 3 minutes.

4. Add cheese, set off heat, and stir until melted. Mix in parsley, pour into casserole, and stir gently.

5. Scatter crumbs evenly on top and bake uncovered until bubbling and richly browned, about 20 minutes. Serve at once.

ITALIAN SAUSAGE RAVIOLI WITH THREE-PEPPER RAGU

Makes 4 servings

TIP

For the most efficient way to chiffonade fresh basil, see the headnote for Linguine with Three-Tomato Sauce, page 273.

For this recipe, I like to use refrigerated, prepared ravioli, especially the Italian Sausage Ravioli with Green Bell Pepper Pasta. But you could substitute Chicken-Herb Parmigiana Ravioli, a four-cheese one, or any flavor you fancy. The only time-consuming part of this recipe is cutting the bell peppers into strips—but that job's done in ten minutes or less. And even that job can be finessed by substituting half of a 1-pound bag frozen bell pepper stir-fry mix (red, green, and yellow peppers). This can go into the skillet solidly frozen.

2 tablespoons extra-virgin olive oil

1 small green bell pepper, cored, seeded, and cut lengthwise into ½-inch-wide strips

1 small red bell pepper, cored, seeded, and cut lengthwise into ½-inch-wide strips

1 small yellow bell pepper, cored, seeded, and cut lengthwise into ½-inch-wide strips

1 teaspoon dried marjoram, crumbled

½ teaspoon crushed fennel seeds

1 large garlic clove, finely minced

1½ cups bottled marinara sauce

Salt to taste

¼ teaspoon freshly ground black pepper

One 9-ounce package refrigerated Italian Sausage Ravioli with Green Bell Pepper Pasta, cooked al dente by package directions and drained very well

1 cup loosely packed fresh basil leaves, cut into chiffonade (see Tip)

⅓ cup freshly grated Parmesan cheese

continued

1. Heat oil in large, heavy skillet over moderate heat 1 minute. Add green, red, and yellow peppers, marjoram, fennel, and garlic and cook, stirring now and then, until peppers are limp, about 8 minutes.

2. Add marinara sauce, salt to taste, and black pepper and cook, stirring often, until mixture steams, 3 to 5 minutes. Taste for salt and pepper and fine-tune.

3. Bed ravioli on heated deep platter, top with pepper ragu, sprinkle with basil and Parmesan, and serve.

LINGUINE WITH THREE-TOMATO SAUCE

Makes 4 to 6 servings

To chiffonade the basil, wash the leaves and pat dry. Stack eight to ten large leaves, roll into a fat "cigar," then with a large, sharp chef's knife, slice crosswise, spacing the cuts about ⅛ inch apart. Have everything chopped and ready to go before you begin assembling this pasta. And have the pasta water boiling—the pasta should go into it at the outset so it's done the same time the sauce is.

1½ pounds red-ripe tomatoes (about 3 large), peeled, cored, seeded, and coarsely chopped
1 cup loosely packed fresh basil leaves, cut into chiffonade
¼ teaspoon salt
2 tablespoons extra-virgin olive oil
4 medium-size scallions, trimmed and thinly sliced (include some green tops)
½ cup coarsely chopped oil-packed sun-dried tomatoes
2 large garlic cloves, minced
1 whole bay leaf
¼ teaspoon freshly ground black pepper

⅛ teaspoon ground hot red pepper (cayenne)
Two 8-ounce cans tomato sauce or 2 cups Basic Tomato Sauce (page 30)
¾ cup dry white wine, such as Soave or Pinot Grigio
1 pound linguine, cooked al dente by package directions and drained well
1 cup crumbled aged ricotta salata or coarsely shredded Fontina cheese
⅓ cup freshly grated Parmesan cheese

1. Place fresh tomatoes, basil, and salt in large heatproof bowl; set aside.

2. Heat oil in large, heavy skillet over moderate heat for 1 minute. Add scallions, sun-dried tomatoes, garlic, bay leaf, and black and red pepper and cook, stirring, until scallions are limp and golden, 3 to 5 minutes.

continued

THE FASTEST WAY TO PEEL TOMATOES IS TO BLANCH THEM FOR 30 TO 60 SECONDS IN BOILING WATER, THEN TO PLUNGE THEM INTO ICE WATER. THE SKINS WILL LOOSEN AND SLIP RIGHT OFF. TO SEED, HALVE THE TOMATOES CROSSWISE, THEN WORKING OVER THE SINK, SQUEEZE EACH HALF GENTLY, CUT SIDE DOWN. THE SEEDS AND EXCESS JUICE WILL SPURT OUT.

3. Add tomato sauce and wine, raise heat to high, and boil uncovered for 1 minute. Remove bay leaf and add skillet mixture to tomatoes in bowl. Stir to mix.

4. Add hot drained linguine and two cheeses to bowl and toss well. Taste for salt and black pepper, adjust as needed, and serve with additional freshly grated Parmesan.

LINGUINE WITH CHICKEN AND CILANTRO-PEANUT SAUCE

Makes 4 servings

For people who can't get enough Thai food, here's a recipe loaded with all the flavors of Bangkok. And it couldn't be easier to make, thanks to the carved, fully cooked chicken breast strips that have recently come to the supermarket.

1 large garlic clove, finely minced

1 teaspoon finely grated lemon zest

1 cup bottled Thai peanut sauce

1/4 cup creamy peanut butter

One 14-ounce can Thai coconut milk (use light, if you like)

2 tablespoons soy sauce

1 tablespoon fresh lime juice

1/2 teaspoon hot red pepper sauce

Two 10-ounce packages carved, fully cooked chicken breast strips (see Note)

1 pound linguine, cooked al dente by package directions and drained well

1/2 cup coarsely chopped fresh basil

1/2 cup coarsely chopped fresh cilantro

1 large firm-ripe tomato, cored, seeded, and diced but not peeled

1/2 cup coarsely chopped dry roasted peanuts

1. Bring garlic, lemon zest, peanut sauce, peanut butter, coconut milk, soy sauce, lime juice, and red pepper sauce to boiling in a large nonreactive skillet over moderate heat, then boil uncovered, stirring often, until reduced by about one-third, 5 to 8 minutes.

2. Add chicken and cook 3 minutes, stirring now and then.

3. Add linguine, basil, cilantro, and tomato. Toss lightly but thoroughly and serve, topping each portion with chopped peanuts.

NOTE

If you're unable to find the fresh carved, cooked chicken breast strips, substitute frozen cooked chicken strips or cubes. In this recipe, only fresh herbs will do.

CHICKEN AND MUSHROOM PAPPARDELLE WITH CREAMY SPINACH SAUCE

Makes 4 servings

Pappardelle—pasta ribbons about three-fourths inch wide—aren't available everywhere. If you can't find them, substitute tagliatelle, the next widest pasta ribbons, fettuccine, or farfalle (bow-ties). To save time, I use a package of carved, fully cooked chicken breast pieces (either the Italian-flavored or plain roasted), packaged sliced mushrooms, frozen chopped spinach, and to bind everything together, prepared alfredo sauce.

1 tablespoon extra-virgin olive oil

2 tablespoons unsalted butter

One 8-ounce package sliced fresh white mushrooms, coarsely chopped

1 cup fresh or frozen chopped onion (about 1 medium-large yellow onion)

1 large garlic clove, minced

½ teaspoon dried thyme, crumbled

¼ teaspoon salt

¼ teaspoon freshly ground black pepper

One 10-ounce package carved, fully cooked chicken breast (see headnote above)

One 10-ounce package prepared alfredo sauce (from the refrigerator counter; use light, if you like)

One 10-ounce package frozen chopped spinach, thawed and pressed very dry

12 ounces pappardelle, cooked al dente by package directions and drained well

½ cup freshly grated Parmesan cheese

1. Heat oil and butter in large, heavy skillet over moderate heat 1 minute. Add mushrooms, onion, garlic, thyme, salt, and pepper

and cook, stirring often, until mushrooms release their juices and these evaporate, about 5 minutes.

2. Add chicken, alfredo sauce, and spinach; adjust heat so mixture bubbles gently, then cook, stirring frequently, until steaming, about 5 minutes. Taste for salt and pepper and adjust as needed.

3. Add pappardelle and toss lightly. Sprinkle with Parmesan and serve.

LINGUINE WITH ROSY SHRIMP SAUCE

MAKES 4 SERVINGS

Cook the linguine while the sauce simmers.

2 tablespoons extra-virgin
olive oil
4 large scallions, trimmed and
thinly sliced (include some
green tops)
2 garlic cloves, minced
1 pound large uncooked shelled
and deveined fresh or thawed
frozen shrimp, halved
lengthwise
1½ teaspoons minced fresh
rosemary or ¾ teaspoon
dried rosemary, crumbled
1½ teaspoons finely grated
orange or lemon zest
One 1-pound can crushed
tomatoes, with their
liquid

One 8-ounce can tomato sauce
or 1 cup Basic Tomato Sauce
(page 30)
½ teaspoon salt
¼ teaspoon freshly ground
black pepper
¼ teaspoon red pepper flakes
¾ cup heavy cream or a 50/50
mixture of heavy cream and
half-and-half
One 10-ounce package frozen
baby green peas, rinsed under
cool water and drained well
1 pound linguine, cooked al
dente by package directions
and drained well
2 tablespoons coarsely chopped
Italian (flat-leaf) parsley

1. Heat oil in very large, heavy skillet over moderate heat for 1 minute.
Add scallions and cook, stirring, until limp and golden, about 2 minutes.

2. Add 1 garlic clove, shrimp, and ½ teaspoon each rosemary and
orange zest, and cook, stirring, until shrimp turn pink, about 3 minutes. Transfer to large bowl and reserve.

3. Add tomatoes, tomato sauce, salt, black pepper, red pepper
flakes, and remaining garlic, rosemary, and orange zest to skillet.

Adjust heat so mixture barely bubbles and cook uncovered, stirring now and then, until slightly thickened and flavors mingle, about 10 minutes.

4. Return shrimp mixture to skillet, add cream and peas, and simmer uncovered 2 minutes. Taste for salt and adjust as needed.

5. Add linguine and parsley, toss well, and serve.

PAD THAI

Makes 6 to 8 servings

True Pad Thai contains tiny dried shrimp as well as fresh (to save time, have your fishmonger peel and devein the fresh shrimp—or use frozen shelled and deveined shrimp), but dried shrimp are often hard to come by so I've omitted them. If you find them, soften ¼ cup dried shrimp in warm water, drain well, then add along with the fresh shrimp. Your Pad Thai will be all the better.

1 pound dried ⅛-inch-wide rice noodles
¼ cup Asian fish sauce
¼ cup sugar
½ cup rice vinegar
2 tablespoons ketchup
6 tablespoons peanut or vegetable oil
2 large garlic cloves, minced
One 1-inch piece lemongrass, minced, or 1 teaspoon finely grated lemon zest
1 teaspoon finely minced fresh ginger
8 large scallions, trimmed and cut into ½-inch lengths

¾ pound shelled and deveined medium-size raw shrimp
2 extra-large eggs, lightly beaten
1 cup coarsely chopped roasted unsalted peanuts (reserve ¼ cup for garnish)
1 cup coarsely chopped fresh cilantro
¾ pound fresh bean sprouts, rinsed well (reserve ½ cup for garnish)
Juice of ½ lime
1 lime, cut into slim wedges (garnish)

1. Soak noodles in large bowl of warm water for 25 minutes; drain well and set aside. Combine fish sauce, sugar, rice vinegar, and ketchup and set aside.

2. Meanwhile, heat very large, deep skillet over moderately high heat for 1 minute. Add 2 tablespoons oil and swirl to coat skillet bottom and sides. Add garlic, lemongrass, and ginger and cook, stirring, for 30 seconds. Add scallions and cook, stirring, for 30 seconds more. Add shrimp and cook, stirring, just until pink, 1 to 2 minutes. Transfer all to large heatproof bowl.

3. Add eggs to skillet, tilting to cover pan bottom. Scramble until firm, breaking eggs into small clumps; add to shrimp mixture.

4. Add remaining 4 tablespoons oil to skillet and heat over moderate heat for 30 seconds. Add reserved noodles, and using spatula, spread into thin layer covering pan bottom. Cook 5 minutes, scraping up and turning noodles several times until steaming hot. Add reserved fish sauce mixture to skillet and cook noodles 3 to 5 minutes more, turning often.

5. Add $3/4$ cup peanuts, cilantro, shrimp/egg mixture, and all but $1/2$ cup bean sprouts and cook, tossing frequently, for 2 minutes or until heated through.

6. Mound mixture on large heated platter, drizzle with lime juice, then scatter with reserved bean sprouts and peanuts. Garnish with lime wedges and serve.

NOTE

BECAUSE OF THE SALTINESS
OF THE SAUCE, TUNA, AND
OLIVES, THIS RECIPE ISN'T
LIKELY TO NEED SALT. BUT
TASTE BEFORE SERVING.

FUSILLI ARRABBIATA WITH TUNA

MAKES 4 TO 6 SERVINGS

To get the choreography right, cook the pasta while the sauce finishes simmering. And resist the temptation to put out the Parmesan. Italians do not like cheese with seafood pastas.

2 tablespoons extra-virgin
  olive oil
1 large garlic clove, minced
One 28-ounce bottle marinara
  sauce or 3½ cups Basic
  Tomato Sauce (page 30)
⅓ cup dry red wine, such as
  Chianti or Valpolicella
1 whole bay leaf
½ teaspoon red pepper flakes
½ teaspoon dried marjoram,
  crumbled

One 12-ounce can water-pack
  solid white-meat tuna,
  drained well and chunked
½ cup coarsely chopped pitted
  black olives (optional)
¼ cup coarsely chopped fresh
  basil
¼ cup coarsely chopped fresh
  Italian (flat-leaf) parsley
1 pound fusilli pasta, cooked al
  dente by package directions
  and drained well

1. Heat oil in very large, heavy skillet over moderate heat for 1 minute. Add garlic and cook, stirring, until golden, about 2 minutes.

2. Reduce heat to moderately low; add marinara sauce, wine, bay leaf, red pepper flakes, and marjoram and simmer uncovered, stirring now and then, for 10 to 15 minutes to blend flavors.

3. Add tuna and olives, if using, and simmer 2 to 3 minutes more; remove bay leaf. Taste for red pepper and add more if needed—a classic *arrabbiata* sauce doesn't lack for "heat."

4. Add chopped fresh basil and parsley, then hot drained fusilli, toss well, and serve.

Fusilli Arrabbiata with Shrimp: Prepare as directed, substituting 3/4 pound raw, shelled, and deveined fresh or frozen medium-size shrimp for tuna and dry white wine for red. Cook shrimp in sauce just until they turn pink, 3 to 5 minutes.

Fusilli Arrabbiata with Scallops: Prepare as directed, substituting 3/4 pound raw bay scallops for tuna and dry white wine for red. Cook scallops in sauce just until they turn milky, 3 to 5 minutes. If scallops' liquid makes sauce soupy, simmer uncovered several minutes more until consistency of marinara sauce.

NOTE

Because of the saltiness of the cheeses, this recipe is not likely to need additional salt.

FUSILLI, GREEN BEANS, AND TOMATOES WITH TWO CHEESES

Makes 4 servings

Cut green beans are one of the frozen foods I find perfectly acceptable provided they are not overcooked. For this recipe, drop them solidly frozen into lightly salted boiling water and cook just until crisp-tender—2 to 3 minutes is all it takes. With a small strainer or slotted spoon, scoop the beans to a bowl of ice water to stop the cooking. And use the same pot of boiling water to cook the fusilli. Saves time and dishwashing. The two cheeses I like best for this recipe are the Italian Fontina (exquisitely creamy) and ricotta salata, an aged Sicilian sheep cheese with the salty tang of feta. Most high-end groceries and specialty food shops carry both. You can use ricotta salata only. Or you can substitute feta for both cheeses.

One 9-ounce package frozen cut green beans (do not thaw)
¼ cup extra-virgin olive oil (the fruitiest you can find)
2 medium-large yellow onions, coarsely chopped
3 large garlic cloves, finely minced
4 large vine-ripened tomatoes, cored, seeded, and coarsely diced
2 tablespoons white wine vinegar

½ pound fusilli, cooked al dente by package directions and drained well
½ cup finely julienned fresh basil leaves (no substitute)
2 tablespoons coarsely chopped Italian (flat-leaf) parsley
¾ cup each diced Fontina and crumbled ricotta salata (see headnote above)
½ teaspoon freshly ground black pepper

1. Cook beans in large pot of boiling water just until crisp-tender, 2 to 3 minutes. With small strainer or slotted spoon, lift beans to bowl of ice water; set aside. (Use same water for cooking pasta.)

2. Heat oil in large, heavy skillet over moderately high heat 1 minute. Add onions and cook, stirring often, until lightly browned, about 8 minutes. Add garlic and cook and stir 2 minutes. Add tomatoes and vinegar and cook uncovered, stirring now and then, until tomatoes soften slightly, 2 to 3 minutes. Set off heat.

3. Drain green beans well and add to skillet along with hot drained fusilli, basil, parsley, Fontina, ricotta salata, and pepper. Toss well and serve.

SPINACH FETTUCCINE WITH ROASTED EGGPLANT, GARLIC, TOMATOES, PROSCIUTTO, AND SAGE

MAKES 4 SERVINGS

Nothing intensifies the flavor of vegetables like 30 minutes in a hot oven, because roasting caramelizes their natural sugars. For this recipe, the vegetables don't have to be peeled, merely chunked.

1 pound slim young eggplants, trimmed and cut into 1-inch cubes

6 firm-ripe Italian plum (Roma) tomatoes (about 1½ pounds), cored, seeded, and cut into slim wedges

6 large garlic cloves, halved lengthwise

6 large fresh sage leaves or 1 teaspoon rubbed sage

Four 3-inch sprigs fresh lemon thyme or ½ teaspoon dried thyme, crumbled

½ teaspoon freshly ground black pepper

4 to 5 tablespoons extra-virgin olive oil

8 ounces spinach (green) fettuccine

4 ounces thinly sliced prosciutto, slivered (see Tips)

4 to 8 tablespoons hot pasta cooking water

Freshly grated Parmesan cheese

1. Preheat oven to 450°F.

2. Toss eggplants, tomatoes, garlic, sage, thyme, and pepper in 4 tablespoons oil in ungreased 13 × 9 × 2-inch baking pan. Spread evenly in pan and roast uncovered, stirring every 10 minutes, until vegetables are limp and lightly browned, about 30 minutes. Remove thyme sprigs.

3. Toward end of roasting, cook fettuccine al dente by package directions. Balance large fine-mesh sieve over large heatproof bowl, set in sink, and dump pasta and cooking water into sieve (this warms bowl). Lift out sieve of pasta and prop in top of pasta kettle to drain. Reserve ½ cup hot pasta cooking water and discard remainder.

4. Spoon roasted vegetables into warm bowl and scatter prosciutto on top. Dump in hot pasta and toss well, adding extra tablespoon oil, if needed, and enough hot pasta cooking water for good consistency.

5. Serve at once and pass Parmesan separately.

VARIATIONS

Fettuccine with Roasted Zucchini, Yellow Pepper, and Tomatoes: Prepare as directed, but substitute 1 pound trimmed, chunked slim young zucchini for eggplant and add 1 cored, seeded, thinly wedged large yellow bell pepper. Also substitute two 3-inch sprigs fresh rosemary (or ½ teaspoon dried) for sage and plain fettuccine for spinach fettuccine.

Fettuccine with Roasted Broccoli and Red and Yellow Peppers: Prepare as directed, but substitute 1¼ pounds broccoli, trimmed and divided into small florets, for eggplant. Omit tomatoes and add 2 cored, seeded, thinly wedged large bell peppers, one red, one yellow. Also substitute two 3-inch sprigs fresh rosemary (or ½ teaspoon dried) for sage and reduce roasting time to 20 minutes. Finally, use plain fettuccine instead of spinach fettuccine.

FETTUCCINE WITH BROCCOLI, BACON, AND BROWNED BREAD CRUMBS

MAKES 4 SERVINGS

It's important that the broccoli florets be no more than 1 to 1½ inches across the top. Save broccoli stems for soup. To save time, use prepackaged florets from the fresh produce section of your supermarket or from the salad bar.

6 slices lean bacon, snipped crosswise into julienne strips

2 tablespoons extra-virgin olive oil

1 cup soft white bread crumbs

⅓ cup coarsely chopped pine nuts

4 large garlic cloves, minced

⅔ cup coarsely chopped Italian (flat-leaf) parsley

½ teaspoon freshly ground black pepper

One 14½-ounce can chicken broth blended with 2 tablespoons all-purpose flour

1 pound fettuccine

1½ pounds broccoli, trimmed and divided into small florets (about 2 cups florets)

⅔ cup freshly grated Parmesan cheese

1. In very large, heavy skillet over moderate heat, cook the bacon until crisp and brown, 3 to 5 minutes. With slotted spoon, scoop browned bacon to paper towels to drain. Reserve drippings; wipe skillet clean.

2. Add oil to skillet and heat 1 minute over moderate heat. Dump in bread crumbs and pine nuts and cook, stirring, until lightly browned, about 3 minutes. Transfer crumb mixture to paper towels; again wipe skillet clean.

3. Add reserved bacon drippings to skillet and heat 1 minute over moderate heat. Add garlic, parsley, and pepper and cook, stirring,

just until garlic turns golden, 1 to 2 minutes. Add broth mixture and cook, stirring, until mixture thickens and no raw flour taste lingers, 3 to 5 minutes. Set skillet off heat.

4. Cook fettuccine al dente by package directions, adding broccoli florets for last 5 minutes. Drain well and dump into skillet mixture.

5. Add cheese, reserved crumb mixture, and bacon and toss well. Serve with additional grated Parmesan.

VARIATIONS

Fettuccine with Asparagus, Bacon, and Browned Bread Crumbs: Prepare as directed, substituting 2 cups fresh asparagus tips for broccoli and adding to pasta cooking water 3 minutes before pasta is done.

Fettuccine with Broccoli Rabe, Bacon, and Browned Bread Crumbs: Prepare as directed, substituting 2 cups coarsely chopped broccoli rabe for broccoli and adding to pasta cooking water 2 minutes before pasta is done.

10-MINUTE PENNE WITH CAPONATA SAUCE

MAKES 4 SERVINGS

Years ago when I moved from North Carolina to New York, I'd never heard of caponata—an Italian roasted eggplant salad that can now be bought by the can in every supermarket. It was my piano teacher, Stanley Lock, who introduced me to this delicacy. Stanley liked to stir caponata into a chickpea casserole. I've since learned many other uses for it and this one is a favorite (my unorthodox Tex-Mex variation substitutes bottled salsa for caponata).

2 tablespoons extra-virgin olive oil (the fruitiest you can find)
2 medium-size scallions, trimmed and thinly sliced (include some green tops)
1½ cups frozen bell pepper stir-fry mix (red, green, and yellow peppers; do not thaw)
2 large garlic cloves, thinly sliced
Two 7¾-ounce cans caponata, with their liquid

¼ cup chicken broth or water
¼ cup coarsely chopped fresh basil
2 tablespoons coarsely chopped Italian (flat-leaf) parsley
Salt and freshly ground black pepper
½ pound penne or fusilli, cooked al dente by package directions and drained
⅓ cup freshly grated Parmesan cheese

1. Heat oil in large, heavy skillet over moderately high heat for 2 minutes. Add scallions, stir-fry mix, and garlic; reduce heat to moderate and cook, stirring, until scallions are limp and excess pepper juices evaporate, 3 to 5 minutes.

2. Add caponata and broth and simmer uncovered, stirring often, just until flavors mingle, about 5 minutes.

3. Mix in basil, parsley, and salt and pepper to taste. Add penne and toss lightly to coat with sauce, sprinkle with grated cheese, and serve with additional grated Parmesan.

CAVATAPPI SAUCED WITH FRESH ARUGULA, BASIL, TOMATOES, AND BLACK OLIVES

MAKES 4 SERVINGS

Cavatappi are short, tubular pasta curlicues or corkscrews. If you can't find them, substitute penne, fusilli, or medium-size shells. All work well with this out-of-the-garden sauce. The sauce is cold, the pasta hot. Even leftovers are good if you take them from the refrigerator and let stand at room temperature for 30 minutes. Drizzle with a teaspoon or two of olive oil, toss, and serve.

3 cups loosely packed fresh basil leaves, coarsely chopped

1½ cups loosely packed fresh young arugula leaves, coarsely chopped

4 medium-small firm, vine-ripened tomatoes, cored, seeded, and coarsely diced but not peeled (about 1 pound)

½ cup coarsely chopped, pitted oil-cured black olives (about 12 medium-size olives)

3 tablespoons extra-virgin olive oil (the fruitiest you can find)

1 tablespoon dry vermouth

1 large garlic clove, finely minced

¼ teaspoon freshly ground black pepper

12 ounces cavatappi, fusilli, or medium-size shells, cooked al dente by package directions and drained very well

¾ cup freshly grated Parmesan cheese

1. Place basil, arugula, tomatoes, olives, olive oil, vermouth, garlic, and pepper in large bowl.

2. Dump hot drained pasta on top and toss well. Add ¼ cup Parmesan and toss well again. If mixture seems dry, add 1 to 2 tablespoons pasta cooking water, toss and serve. Pass remaining ½ cup grated Parmesan.

TIP

To save time, I processor-chop the arugula and basil together—5 to 6 pulses is all it takes. Then I dump the chopped greens into a large bowl and give the tomatoes four to five zaps in the processor (no need to rinse the work bowl). With the food processor, having a fast trigger finger is everything if you're to dice tomatoes without reducing them to mush. The same holds for processor-chopping herbs, onions, and bell peppers.

NOTE

The way to seed tomatoes is to halve them crosswise, then squeeze gently into the sink—the seeds and excess juice will spurt out. You don't want juicy tomatoes for this recipe. First, they won't processor-chop neatly. And second, they'll water down the sauce—not a good thing.

PASTA SHELLS WITH SAUSAGE, PEAS, AND PORTOBELLOS

<small>MAKES 4 TO 6 SERVINGS</small>

Take advantage of the sliced portobello mushrooms now available in produce sections. Also, put frozen baby green peas to good use; they need only to be thawed and drained. Begin cooking the pasta at the same time you begin reducing the broth.

1 tablespoon extra-virgin olive oil

1 large sweet Italian sausage, removed from its casing (about 6 ounces)

6 large scallions, trimmed and thinly sliced (include some green tops)

Two 6-ounce packages fresh portobello mushroom slices, very coarsely chopped

One and a half 14½-ounce cans chicken broth

1 tablespoon unsalted butter

One 10-ounce package frozen baby green peas, thawed and drained

Salt and freshly ground black pepper

1 pound medium-size pasta shells, cooked al dente by package directions and drained

¼ cup coarsely chopped Italian (flat-leaf) parsley

¼ cup coarsely chopped fresh mint

½ cup freshly grated Parmesan cheese

1. Heat olive oil in very large, heavy skillet over moderate heat for 1 minute. Add sausage and cook, breaking up clumps, until no longer pink, about 3 minutes. Drain excess drippings from skillet.

2. Add scallions and mushrooms to skillet and cook, stirring, until mushrooms give up their juices and these evaporate, 5 to 8 minutes.

3. Add broth and butter, adjust heat so mixture barely boils, and cook, uncovered, stirring often, until liquid reduces by half, about 10 minutes.

4. Add peas and season to taste with salt and pepper. Add pasta, parsley, and mint and toss well. Heat 1 to 2 minutes, just until steaming. Taste for salt and pepper and adjust as needed.

5. Transfer to large heated bowl, scatter cheese on top, and serve.

COUSCOUS WITH CHICKEN, RED AND GREEN VEGETABLES

Makes 6 servings

Couscous, often called the "Moroccan pasta," is so quick, so easy, and such a good backdrop for stews and skillet scrambles that we should use it more often. This particular recipe is a fusion of North African and Mediterranean flavors.

3 tablespoons extra-virgin olive oil

6 large scallions, trimmed and thinly sliced (include some green tops)

1 medium-size green bell pepper, cored, seeded, and coarsely chopped

2 large garlic cloves, finely minced

One 10-ounce package Italian-flavored carved, fully cooked chicken breast

One 10-ounce can diced tomatoes with green chilies, with their liquid

2 tablespoons tomato paste

2 tablespoons sweet paprika

2 whole bay leaves

1 teaspoon dried oregano, crumbled

One 15½-ounce can chickpeas, rinsed and drained well

1 cup dried currants

One 10-ounce package couscous, prepared by package directions (substitute chicken broth for water)

⅓ cup freshly grated Parmesan cheese

¼ cup coarsely chopped Italian (flat-leaf) parsley

1. Heat oil in large, heavy skillet over moderate heat 2 minutes. Add scallions, green pepper, and garlic and cook, stirring often, until scallions are golden, 2 to 3 minutes.

2. Add chicken, tomatoes with chilies, tomato paste, paprika, bay leaves, and oregano; bring to a simmer, adjust heat so mixture bubbles gently, cover, and simmer until flavors marry, about 15 minutes.

3. Add chickpeas and currants and simmer uncovered, stirring now and then, 10 minutes. Discard bay leaves.

4. Bed couscous on heated deep platter, ladle skillet mixture on top, sprinkle with Parmesan and parsley, and serve.

Black Beans 'n' Rice with
Avocado: Prepare as
directed, then fold in,
along with the cilantro,
1 medium-size firm-ripe
Haas avocado that has
been peeled, pitted,
diced, and tossed lightly
with 2 tablespoons fresh
lime or lemon juice.

Black Beans 'n' Rice with
Avocado and Tomatoes:
Prepare Black Beans 'n'
Rice with Avocado as
directed, then fold in,
along with avocado, 2
diced, peeled Italian
plum (Roma) tomatoes.

BLACK BEANS 'N' RICE

Makes 4 servings

As easy as it gets! But plenty satisfying, too.

2 tablespoons extra-virgin olive oil
1 cup fresh or frozen chopped onion (1 medium-large yellow onion)
1 cup frozen chopped green bell pepper
1 large garlic clove, minced
3/4 cup uncooked converted rice
1/2 teaspoon finely grated orange zest
1/2 teaspoon dried oregano, crumbled
1/4 teaspoon dried thyme, crumbled
1/4 teaspoon ground cumin
One 14 1/2-ounce can chicken broth
One 15 1/2-ounce can black beans, rinsed and drained well
Salt and freshly ground black pepper
1/4 cup coarsely chopped fresh cilantro or Italian (flat-leaf) parsley

1. Heat oil in large, heavy saucepan over moderate heat for 1 minute. Add onion and green pepper and cook, stirring, until lightly browned, about 5 minutes.

2. Mix in garlic, rice, orange zest, oregano, thyme, and cumin and cook, stirring, just until rice is nicely glazed, 1 to 2 minutes.

3. Add broth, bring to a boil, adjust heat so mixture bubbles gently, cover, and cook until rice is firm-tender, about 15 minutes. Uncover and cook 5 minutes more.

4. Mix in black beans and salt and pepper to taste, then lightly fold in cilantro and serve.

PROSCIUTTO AND PESTO RISOTTO

Makes 4 servings

Because prosciutto and sun-dried tomatoes are intensely salty, you're not likely to need additional salt in this recipe.

Three 14½-ounce cans chicken broth
3 tablespoons extra-virgin olive oil
1 medium-size yellow onion, coarsely chopped
1 large garlic clove, minced
½ cup dry white wine
½ teaspoon freshly ground black pepper

2 cups Arborio rice
½ cup coarsely chopped dry-pack sun-dried tomatoes
¾ cup coarsely chopped prosciutto
¼ cup bottled pesto sauce
½ cup coarsely chopped fresh basil
¼ cup freshly grated Parmesan cheese

1. Bring broth to boiling in medium-size saucepan, then adjust heat so broth stays at a slow simmer.

2. Heat oil 2 minutes in large, heavy saucepan over moderately low heat. Add onion and cook, stirring, until glassy, 3 minutes. Add garlic and cook, stirring, for 1 minute. Add wine and pepper, raise heat to moderately high and boil, uncovered, until only a glaze remains on pan bottom, 1 to 2 minutes.

3. Add rice, toss to coat, then cook, stirring, until grains are opaque, 2 to 3 minutes.

4. Reduce heat to moderately low, then add tomatoes and ½ cup hot broth. Cook, stirring often, until broth is absorbed. Continue cooking this way, adding broth ½ cup at a time, but only after previous addition is fully absorbed.

5. Add prosciutto with final ½ cup broth and cook and stir until broth is absorbed and rice is tender. From start to finish, it will take 20 to 25 minutes for risotto to cook. Stir in pesto, chopped basil, and cheese. Serve at once in heated soup plates.

SPINACH MADELEINE PIE

Makes 6 servings

I recently stayed at Green Springs, a lovely B & B in St. Francisville, Louisiana, and much to my surprise, my hostess Madeline Nevill was the lady who created that Deep South classic, Spinach Madeleine. (The discrepancy in the spelling of Madeline is intentional; to Madeline, the French spelling—Madeleine—seemed more "gourmet-ish.") Madeline told me she'd tried to develop some breakfast variations because her guests want to taste the dish that made her famous. But none, she admits, was as good as the original. That got me to thinking. Could I work up a main-dish version, a tart that uses Spinach Madeleine as the filling? Here's the result and I think it's delicious. As for Madeline Neville, she has a sense of humor about the recipe she created for *River Road Recipes*, a best-selling cookbook published in 1959 by the Junior League of Baton Rouge. "I sure have made my fifteen minutes of fame last for forty years," she jokes.

2 tablespoons unsalted butter

2 tablespoons finely minced yellow onion

1 small garlic clove, minced

2 tablespoons all-purpose flour

Two 10-ounce packages frozen chopped spinach, thawed and liquid reserved

½ cup spinach liquid plus enough evaporated milk to total 1¼ cups

1 extra-large egg

1 teaspoon Worcestershire sauce

1 teaspoon salt

½ teaspoon freshly ground black pepper

½ teaspoon hot red pepper sauce

One 6-ounce roll jalapeño cheese, cubed

1 frozen 9-inch deep-dish pie shell, thawed and recrimped to form high fluted edge

1 cup Buttered Bread Crumbs (page 36), or 2 slices firm-textured white bread buzzed to crumbs with 1 tablespoon melted butter in food processor or electric blender

1. Set heavy-duty baking sheet on middle rack and preheat oven to 400°F.

2. Melt butter in large, heavy saucepan over moderate heat; add onion and garlic and cook, stirring, just until limp, about 2 minutes. Blend in flour and cook, stirring, for 2 minutes.

3. Add spinach and cook uncovered, stirring often, until very dry, about 5 minutes.

4. Whisk together spinach liquid mixture, egg, Worcestershire sauce, salt, black pepper, and red pepper sauce. Add to spinach and cook and stir just until mixture steams, 2 to 3 minutes; do not boil or mixture may curdle. Add cheese and stir just until melted.

5. Spoon into pie shell (see Tips), mounding slightly in center, and scatter crumbs evenly on top.

6. Set in center of baking sheet in oven and bake uncovered for 20 minutes. If crust is browning too fast, cover with strips of foil.

7. Reduce oven temperature to 325°F. and bake until center is softly set, about 20 minutes. Let stand 15 minutes, cut into wedges, and serve.

TIPS

To thaw frozen spinach quickly, place in large microwave-safe bowl and microwave uncovered 5 minutes on high, breaking up chunks at half time. Because the spinach filling is heavy, set the frozen pie shell, still in its foil pan, in a standard 9-inch pie pan for extra support—good practice whenever you use frozen pie crust. The foil pans are far too flimsy to support most fillings.

CABBAGE, LEEK, AND BACON PIE WITH CARAWAY SEEDS

Makes 6 servings

Coleslaw mixes are a huge time-saver, but I use them more for cooking than for slaw.

6 slices lean bacon, snipped crosswise into julienne strips
6 medium-size leeks, trimmed, washed well, and thinly sliced
One 8-ounce bag coleslaw mix (green and red cabbage plus carrots)
1 teaspoon caraway seeds
1 frozen 9-inch deep-dish pie shell, thawed and recrimped to form high fluted edge
1 cup coarsely shredded Gruyère or Swiss cheese (about 4 ounces)

2 extra-large eggs
One 12-ounce can evaporated milk
2 tablespoons all-purpose flour
1 teaspoon salt
1/4 teaspoon freshly ground black pepper
1/4 teaspoon freshly grated nutmeg

1. Set heavy-duty baking sheet on middle rack and preheat oven to 400°F.

2. Fry bacon in large, heavy skillet over moderate heat until all fat renders out and only crisp brown bits remain, about 5 minutes. Lift bacon bits to paper towels to drain. Pour all drippings from skillet, then spoon 2 tablespoons back in.

3. Add leeks, coleslaw mix, and caraway seeds to skillet and toss in drippings to coat. Reduce heat to moderately low, cover, and "sweat" 10 minutes, stirring halfway through.

4. Set pie shell, still in foil pan, in standard 9-inch pie tin for added support. Spread skillet mixture evenly over bottom of pie shell.

Scatter reserved bacon on top, then shredded cheese, distributing each uniformly.

5. Quickly whisk together eggs, milk, flour, salt, pepper, and nutmeg and pour evenly over mixture in pie shell.

6. Set in center of baking sheet in oven and bake uncovered for 15 minutes. If crust is browning too fast, cover with strips of foil.

7. Reduce oven temperature to 325°F. and bake until center is softly set, about 20 minutes. Let stand 15 minutes, cut into wedges and serve.

VARIATION

Broccoli and Blue Cheese Pie: Prepare as directed, but substitute one 8-ounce bag broccoli coleslaw mix for cabbage slaw mix and 1 teaspoon dill weed for caraway seeds. Also combine 2 ounces finely crumbled blue cheese, Roquefort, or Gorgonzola with ¼ cup shredded sharp Cheddar or Monterey jack and use in place of Gruyère.

NOTE

MOST SLAW MIXES CONTAIN A FEW LARGE PIECES OF CABBAGE. FOR THIS RECIPE THEY MUST BE THINLY SLICED.

DOUBLE CHEESE AND ZUCCHINI QUICHE

Makes 6 servings

Quiches are a splendid way to pile a meal into a single container, in this case a frozen pie crust. Chop the zucchini in a food processor and use frozen chopped onion.

1 frozen 9-inch deep-dish pie shell, thawed and recrimped to form high fluted edge

2 tablespoons extra-virgin olive oil

1 cup fresh or frozen chopped onion (about 1 medium-large yellow onion)

½ pound tender young zucchini, trimmed and coarsely chopped or shredded

½ teaspoon dried oregano, crumbled

¼ teaspoon dried thyme, crumbled

½ cup coarsely shredded Monterey jack cheese (about 2 ounces)

3 extra-large eggs

One 12-ounce can evaporated milk (use skim, if you like)

2 tablespoons freshly grated Parmesan cheese

¾ teaspoon salt

¼ teaspoon freshly ground black pepper

1. Preheat oven to 425°F. Set pie shell, still in foil pan, in standard 9-inch pie tin for added support.

2. Heat oil in skillet over high heat for 2 minutes. Add onion, reduce heat to moderate, and cook, stirring often, until tender. Mix in zucchini, oregano, and thyme and cook, stirring often, until zucchini is tender and almost all liquid has evaporated, about 5 minutes. Spoon evenly into pie shell and sprinkle with Monterey jack.

3. Whisk together eggs, milk, Parmesan, salt, and pepper and pour over zucchini. Bake uncovered 20 minutes. If crust is browning too fast, cover with strips of foil.

4. Reduce oven temperature to 325°F. and bake until center barely quivers when you nudge pan, 20 to 25 minutes. Let stand 10 to 15 minutes, cut into wedges, and serve.

POTATO, PARSLEY, AND GRUYÈRE QUICHE

MAKES 6 SERVINGS

A terrific way to recycle leftover boiled potatoes.

1 frozen 9-inch deep-dish pie shell, thawed and recrimped to form high fluted edge

1½ cups peeled, thinly sliced and cooked red-skin potatoes (about 3 medium-size potatoes)

½ cup coarsely shredded Gruyère or Swiss cheese (about 2 ounces)

2 extra-large eggs

One 12-ounce can evaporated milk (use skim, if you like), or 1 cup half-and-half cream + ½ cup milk

¾ teaspoon salt

½ teaspoon freshly ground black pepper

¼ teaspoon dried thyme, crumbled

¼ teaspoon freshly grated nutmeg

½ cup coarsely chopped parsley

⅓ cup canned diced pimientos, drained

1. Preheat oven to 425°F. Set pie shell, still in foil pan, in standard 9-inch pie tin for added support.

2. Layer half of potatoes evenly in pie shell and sprinkle with cheese.

3. Whisk eggs, milk, salt, pepper, thyme, and nutmeg to blend, then mix in parsley and pimientos. Pour half of mixture evenly over cheese and potatoes.

4. Arrange remaining potatoes on top and pour remaining milk mixture over all, pushing bits of pimiento and parsley down underneath.

5. Bake, uncovered, for 20 minutes. If crust is browning too fast, cover with strips of foil.

6. Reduce oven temperature to 325°F. and bake until center barely quivers when you nudge pan, 20 to 25 minutes. Let stand 15 minutes, cut into wedges, and serve.

HAM AND GREEN PEA QUICHE

Makes 6 servings

An unusual cheeseless quiche that packs plenty of protein with less fat.

1 frozen 9-inch deep-dish pie shell, thawed and recrimped to form high fluted edge

One 10-ounce package frozen green peas, thawed and drained

1¼ cups half-and half cream or evaporated milk (use skim, if you like)

2 medium-size scallions, trimmed and coarsely chopped (include some green tops)

2 tablespoons minced celery

½ teaspoon minced fresh rosemary or ¼ teaspoon dried rosemary, crumbled

⅛ teaspoon freshly grated nutmeg

1 tablespoon unsalted butter

1 cup coarsely chopped baked or boiled ham

2 extra-large eggs

½ teaspoon salt

¼ teaspoon freshly ground black pepper

1. Preheat oven to 425°F. Set pie shell, still in foil pan, in standard 9-inch pie tin for added support.

2. Churn half of peas and ½ cup half-and-half to puree in food processor or electric blender; set aside.

3. Cook scallions, celery, rosemary, and nutmeg in butter in a small skillet over moderate heat, stirring until scallions are limp, about 3 minutes. Mix in ham, spoon evenly into pie shell, scatter remaining whole peas on top, and set aside.

4. Beat eggs with remaining half-and-half, salt, and pepper. Mix in reserved pea puree and pour evenly into pie shell.

5. Bake uncovered for 20 minutes. If crust is browning too fast, cover with strips of foil.

6. Reduce oven temperature to 325°F. and bake until center barely trembles when you nudge pan, 15 to 20 minutes. Let stand 15 minutes, cut into wedges, and serve.

CURRIED TURKEY AND VEGETABLE QUICHE

MAKES 6 SERVINGS

Not the usual way to use up the Thanksgiving bird but an awfully good one. To save vegetable prep time, I use packaged shredded carrots from the produce counter.

1 frozen 9-inch deep-dish pie shell, thawed and recrimped to form high fluted edge
1 cup firmly packed shredded fresh carrots
3 medium-size scallions, trimmed and thinly sliced (include some green tops)
1 small celery rib, trimmed and diced
1 tablespoon minced fresh ginger

2 teaspoons curry powder
2 tablespoons unsalted butter
1 cup finely chopped cooked turkey
2 extra-large eggs
1 cup evaporated milk (use skim, if you like)
½ teaspoon salt
¼ teaspoon freshly ground black pepper
½ cup coarsely shredded Swiss cheese (about 2 ounces)

1. Preheat oven to 425°F. Set pie shell, still in foil pan, in standard 9-inch pie tin for added support.

2. Cook carrots, scallions, celery, ginger, and curry powder in butter in a small skillet over moderate heat, stirring until carrots and scallions are limp, about 5 minutes. Mix in turkey, spoon evenly into pie shell, and set aside.

3. Beat eggs with milk, salt, and pepper. Mix in cheese and pour evenly into pie shell.

4. Bake uncovered 20 minutes. If crust is browning too fast, cover with strips of foil.

5. Reduce oven temperature to 325°F. and bake until center barely trembles when you nudge pan, 15 to 20 minutes. Let stand 15 minutes, cut into wedges, and serve.

VARIATION

CHILI CHICKEN QUICHE: PREPARE AS DIRECTED, BUT SUBSTITUTE COOKED CHICKEN FOR TURKEY, CHILI POWDER FOR CURRY, AND SHARP GRATED CHEDDAR FOR SWISS CHEESE. ALSO, OMIT FRESH GINGER, ADD ⅓ CUP CHOPPED CILANTRO AND, IF YOU LIKE, ¼ CUP COARSELY CHOPPED PIMIENTO-STUFFED OLIVES ALONG WITH CHEESE.

CONFETTI QUICHE

Instead of going to all the trouble of coring, seeding, and chopping red and green bell peppers, I use frozen bell pepper stir-fry mix and chop it solidly frozen. I also use frozen pie crusts—as I do for all my quiches. But I do insist upon fresh garlic and onions, in this case scallions.

1 frozen 9-inch deep-dish pie shell, thawed and recrimped to form high fluted edge

4 slices lean bacon, snipped crosswise into julienne strips

1½ cups frozen bell pepper stir-fry mix (red, green, and yellow peppers; do not thaw), coarsely chopped

3 medium-size scallions, trimmed and thinly sliced (include some green tops)

1 large garlic clove, minced

1 teaspoon chopped fresh thyme or ¼ teaspoon dried thyme, crumbled

½ teaspoon chopped fresh rosemary or ¼ teaspoon dried rosemary, crumbled

One 10-ounce package frozen whole-kernel corn, thawed and drained

2 extra-large eggs

1 cup evaporated milk or ½ cup each half-and-half and heavy cream

½ teaspoon salt

¼ teaspoon freshly ground black pepper

3 tablespoons freshly grated Parmesan cheese

1. Preheat oven to 400°F. Set pie shell, still in foil pan, in standard 9-inch pie tin for added support.

2. Cook bacon in medium-size heavy skillet over moderate heat until crisp, about 5 minutes. With slotted spoon, scoop bacon to paper towels to drain, and reserve.

3. Add stir-fry mix, scallions, garlic, thyme, and rosemary to drippings in skillet and cook, stirring, until vegetables are limp and excess juices have evaporated, about 5 minutes.

4. Pulse corn kernels in food processor or electric blender until consistency of cream-style corn. Stir into skillet mixture and cook over low heat, stirring occasionally, until flavors meld, 5 to 10 minutes.

5. Meanwhile, beat eggs with milk, salt, pepper, and Parmesan.

6. Sprinkle reserved bacon over bottom of pie shell, cover with corn mixture, then pour in egg mixture, distributing evenly and stirring to float red, yellow, and green peppers to top.

7. Bake uncovered for 20 minutes. If crust is browning too fast, cover with strips of foil.

8. Reduce oven temperature to 325°F. and bake until center barely quivers when you nudge pan, about 20 minutes. Let stand 15 minutes, cut into wedges, and serve.

TUNA-NOODLE PIE

MAKES 6 SERVINGS

Everyone's favorite—Tuna-Noodle Casserole—in a new format.

1 frozen 9-inch deep-dish pie
  shell, thawed and recrimped
  to form high fluted edge
½ cup narrow egg noodles,
  cooked by package directions
  and drained
One 3½-ounce can chunk
  white tuna, drained and
  flaked
½ cup frozen baby green peas,
  thawed and drained
1 tablespoon minced parsley
1 tablespoon canned diced
  pimientos, drained

2 extra-large eggs
One 12-ounce can evaporated
  milk or 1½ cups half-and-half
3 tablespoons freshly grated
  Parmesan cheese
¼ teaspoon dried marjoram,
  crumbled
¼ teaspoon dried thyme,
  crumbled
¼ teaspoon salt
¼ teaspoon freshly ground
  black pepper

1. Preheat oven to 425°F. Set pie shell, still in foil pan, in standard 9-inch pie tin for added support.

2. Mix noodles, tuna, peas, parsley, and pimientos in bowl and spoon evenly into pie shell.

3. Beat eggs with milk, cheese, herbs, salt, and pepper; pour evenly over tuna mixture.

4. Bake uncovered 20 minutes. If crust is browning too fast, cover with strips of foil.

5. Reduce oven temperature to 325°F. and bake until center is just set, 20 to 25 minutes. Let stand 15 minutes, cut into wedges, and serve.

RICOTTA-VEGETABLE PIE IN A PASTA CRUST

Use thin spaghetti for this recipe — No. 9 or finer.

6 ounces thin spaghetti, cooked al dente by package directions and drained well

3 tablespoons extra-virgin olive oil

1 tablespoon unsalted butter

⅓ cup freshly grated Parmesan cheese

2 extra-large eggs, beaten until foamy

4 large scallions, trimmed and thinly sliced (include some green tops)

One 16-ounce bag frozen bell pepper stir-fry mix (red, green, and yellow peppers; do not thaw)

1½ cups finely diced zucchini (about 1 medium-size)

2 garlic cloves, minced

1 teaspoon dried marjoram, crumbled

½ teaspoon dried basil, crumbled

½ teaspoon dried rosemary, crumbled

½ teaspoon freshly ground black pepper

One 14½-ounce can crushed tomatoes, with their liquid

3 tablespoons tomato paste

1½ cups firmly packed ricotta cheese

1 cup shredded mozzarella cheese (about 4 ounces)

1. Preheat oven to 350°F. Coat 12-inch pie pan or tart tin with non-stick cooking spray; set aside.

2. Combine spaghetti, 1 tablespoon olive oil, butter, Parmesan, and eggs in large bowl. Transfer to prepared pie pan and shape into "pie crust."

3. Heat remaining 2 tablespoons olive oil in large, heavy skillet over moderate heat 2 minutes. Add scallions, stir-fry mix, zucchini, garlic, marjoram, basil, rosemary, and pepper and cook, stirring often, until vegetables brown lightly, 8 to 10 minutes.

continued

4. Add tomatoes and tomato paste and cook uncovered, stirring now and then, until excess juices evaporate and flavors mingle, about 10 minutes.

5. Spread ricotta over bottom of crust, scatter evenly with $1/2$ cup mozzarella, top with skillet mixture, smoothing to edges, then cover rim of spaghetti crust with foil to prevent overbrowning. Bake uncovered 20 minutes.

6. Scatter remaining $1/2$ cup mozzarella on top and bake just until cheese melts, about 5 minutes more. Cool 15 minutes, then cut into wedges and serve.

CABBAGE AND GORGONZOLA TORTE IN POLENTA CRUST

MAKES 6 SERVINGS

Italians would make this unusual pie with crinkly-leafed Savoy cabbage, and if you can find it, do so. Otherwise, substitute a package of slaw mix. Also use a roll of prepared polenta—most supermarkets carry it.

One 16-ounce roll prepared polenta

3/4 cup freshly grated Parmesan cheese

2 tablespoons cold water

2 tablespoons extra-virgin olive oil

4 large scallions, trimmed and sliced thin (include some green tops)

2 large garlic cloves, minced

Two 8-ounce packages slaw mix

1/4 teaspoon freshly ground black pepper

3/4 cup crumbled Gorgonzola cheese (about 3 ounces)

3/4 cup coarsely shredded Fontina cheese (about 3 ounces)

NOTE

BECAUSE OF THE SALTINESS OF THE GORGONZOLA, THIS RECIPE WON'T NEED SALT. BUT TASTE AND ADD IF IT SUITS YOU.

1. Preheat oven to 375°F. Coat a 9-inch pie pan with nonstick cooking spray. Mix polenta with 1/4 cup Parmesan and 2 tablespoons water, then press into pan, forming a pie shell; set aside.

2. Heat oil in large, heavy skillet over moderate heat 1 minute. Add scallions and cook, stirring, until limp and golden, 3 to 5 minutes. Add garlic and cook, stirring, for 1 minute.

3. Add slaw mix and pepper and cook, stirring, for 2 minutes, turning to glaze cabbage. Reduce heat to lowest setting, cover, and "sweat" for 10 minutes.

4. Off heat, mix in Gorgonzola and Fontina. Taste for salt and pepper and adjust as needed. Turn into polenta shell, spreading to edges.

5. Bake uncovered 20 minutes. Scatter remaining 1/2 cup Parmesan evenly on top and bake until lightly browned, 5 to 8 minutes more. Cut into wedges and serve.

MICROWAVE DINNERS

The reason so many people are disappointed with the microwave oven and have downgraded it to popcorn popper is that in the beginning, they tried to make it do everything.

Alas, it can't. Nor was it ever intended to replace the conventional oven. One of the first things I learned while working with the microwave as a research assistant at Cornell was that this speed demon was basically a giant steamer. It never browned or crisped foods.

What it did do—impressively—was slash cooking time.

For me, the best way to use a microwave oven is in tandem with a standard oven, broiler, or cooktop. Thus, I shortcut tedious cooking jobs by microwave, then do the crisping and browning the old-fashioned way.

Today, thanks to space-age materials, casseroles can move directly from microwave to conventional oven (or cooktop) and vice-versa. Which means you can often combine, cook, and brown everything in a single dish. It goes without saying that any containers and covers you use must be microwave-safe.

The recipes that follow are based on a microwave oven of 600 watts or more (less powerful models are poor candidates for cooking) and use the following power levels:

High = 100% power
Medium-High = 70% power
Medium = 50% power

Medium-Low = 30% power
Low = 10% power

BURGER POT ROAST

MAKES 4 SERVINGS

Okay, so I've cheated by turning hamburger into pot roast. Well, why not? Unless you resort to pressure cooking (a method I personally don't like), you'll never get a real pot roast done in less than two or three hours. I also cut prep time by using packaged, peeled baby-cut carrots and frozen small whole onions. To intensify flavors, I blast my burger pot roast and vegetables in the broiler before sliding them into the microwave to finish cooking.

4 tablespoons extra-virgin olive oil or vegetable oil
1 pound small red-skin potatoes, scrubbed and quartered but not peeled
2 cups frozen small whole onions (do not thaw)
One 1-pound package peeled baby-cut fresh carrots
2 medium-size celery ribs, trimmed and sliced ½ inch thick
4 large whole garlic cloves, peeled
1 ¾ pounds lean ground beef chuck

½ cup canned beef consommé
1 ½ teaspoons dried marjoram, crumbled
½ teaspoon dried thyme, crumbled
1 teaspoon salt
½ teaspoon freshly ground black pepper
2 whole bay leaves
One 14 ½-ounce can beef broth blended with 5 tablespoons all-purpose flour
¼ cup minced parsley

1. Preheat broiler. Toss 2 tablespoons oil with potatoes, onions, carrots, celery, and garlic in 13 ½ × 11 × 2 ½-inch baking dish (4 ½ quarts) until well coated. Wreathe vegetables around edge of dish.

2. Combine ground chuck, 1 tablespoon oil, consommé, marjoram, thyme, salt, and pepper; mound in center of baking dish, then pat into oval 9 inches long, 5 ½ inches wide, and 1 ¼ inches high without compacting meat. Rub with remaining 1 tablespoon oil.

3. Set 6 inches from heat and broil 8 to 10 minutes until meat is richly browned. Remove from oven and stir vegetables well. Tuck in bay leaves.

4. Cover baking dish. (I use a slightly smaller baking dish turned upside-down but a microwave-safe plastic cutting board or tray will also work.) Microwave on High for 20 minutes, stirring vegetables at half-time, until meat is well done (170°F. in the middle).

5. Stir broth mixture into dish and microwave uncovered 10 minutes on High, stirring at half-time, until broth boils and thickens somewhat. Remove bay leaves, taste gravy for salt and pepper, and fine-tune.

6. Sprinkle parsley over vegetables and serve.

FROZEN BELL PEPPER STIR-
FRY MIX IS A TERRIFIC TIME-
SAVER, BUT FOR THIS
RECIPE THE STRIPS SHOULD
BE COARSELY CHOPPED. NO
PROBLEM. ATTACK THE
SOLIDLY FROZEN STRIPS WITH
A CHEF'S KNIFE AND THE
JOB'S DONE IN JIG TIME.

MEAT 'N' MAC 'N' MUSHROOMS

MAKES 6 SERVINGS

This recipe, like many in this chapter, moves from microwave to conventional oven. It's a husky dish that needs only a tartly dressed green salad to accompany.

2 tablespoons extra-virgin
  olive oil
2 cups fresh or frozen chopped
  onions (about 2 medium-large
  yellow onions)
Half of an 8-ounce package
  sliced fresh white mushrooms
1 cup coarsely chopped frozen
  bell pepper stir-fry mix
  (red, green, and yellow
  peppers; do not thaw)
1 large garlic clove, minced
1 pound lean ground beef
  chuck; or ¾ pound lean
  ground beef chuck and
  ¼ pound lean ground pork
  shoulder or sweet Italian
  sausage removed from casings
  and crumbled

2 teaspoons chili powder
1 teaspoon dried oregano,
  crumbled
¾ teaspoon salt
¼ teaspoon freshly ground
  black pepper
1 cup bottled marinara sauce or
  Basic Tomato Sauce
  (page 30)
1 tablespoon tomato paste
5 tablespoons freshly grated
  Parmesan cheese
1¼ cups elbow macaroni
  cooked al dente by package
  directions and drained, or
  3 cups deli macaroni salad,
  well drained

1. Preheat oven to 400°F.

2. Toss oil with onions, mushrooms, stir-fry mix, and garlic in shallow round or oval 2½-quart casserole. Cover with waxed paper and microwave 10 minutes on High.

3. Stir well; add beef, chili powder, oregano, salt, and black pepper. Break meat up as much as possible and spread evenly over bottom of

casserole. Cover with waxed paper and microwave on Medium-High for 5 minutes.

4. Break up meat, mix in marinara sauce and tomato paste, spread evenly, cover with waxed paper, and microwave on High for 10 minutes. Mix in 2 tablespoons cheese, then macaroni.

5. Set uncovered in preheated oven and bake until bubbly, about 10 minutes.

6. Scatter remaining cheese on top and bake 5 minutes more. Serve at once.

TIP

COOK THE PASTA WHILE THE MEAT MICROWAVES. OR TO MAKE LIFE REALLY SIMPLE, SUBSTITUTE A DELI MACARONI SALAD FOR THE ELBOWS.

MICROWAVE VEGETABLE LASAGNE

This lasagne may not cook much faster than the old-fashioned type, but it doesn't dirty half the pans in the kitchen. Using no-cook lasagne noodles, pre-sliced fresh mushrooms, pre-shredded mozzarella, frozen bell pepper stir-fry mix, and bottled marinara sauce is one secret. Here's another: Mix the seasonings into the ricotta and marinara sauce right in their original containers.

3 tablespoons extra-virgin olive oil

1 small eggplant (about ½ pound), trimmed and cut into ½-inch cubes but not peeled

2 young zucchini (about ½ pound), trimmed and thinly sliced

One 8-ounce package sliced fresh white mushrooms

2 cups frozen bell pepper stir-fry mix (red, green, and yellow peppers; do not thaw)

2 large scallions, trimmed and thinly sliced (include some green tops)

2 large garlic cloves, finely minced

2 large whole bay leaves

2 teaspoons dried marjoram, crumbled

2 teaspoons dried basil, crumbled

1 teaspoon salt

½ teaspoon freshly ground black pepper

One 15-ounce container whole-milk ricotta cheese

One 26-ounce bottle marinara sauce

Eight 6¾ × 3½-inch no-cook lasagne noodles (from an 8-ounce package)

One 8-ounce package coarsely shredded mozzarella cheese

8 tablespoons freshly grated Parmesan cheese

I. Place oil in 14 × 11½ × 2¼-inch (or similar size) baking dish. Add all vegetables, half the garlic, both bay leaves, I teaspoon each marjoram and basil, ½ teaspoon salt, and ¼ teaspoon pepper. Toss well, spread evenly, cover with waxed paper and microwave 25 minutes on High, stirring well twice, after IO minutes, then again after 20. Discard bay leaves.

2. Meanwhile, preheat oven to 425°F. Coat 9 × 9 × 2-inch baking dish with nonstick vegetable cooking spray and set aside. Combine ricotta with half the remaining garlic, marjoram, basil, salt, and pepper; set aside. Combine marinara sauce with rest of garlic, marjoram, basil, salt, and pepper; set aside also.

3. Layer ingredients into prepared baking dish this way, each time distributing evenly, laying lasagne noodles side by side and pressing into layer directly below:

1/3 cup marinara sauce

2 lasagne noodles

1/3 vegetable mixture

3/4 cup mozzarella

2/3 cup marinara sauce

2 lasagne noodles

1/2 ricotta mixture

2 tablespoons Parmesan

2/3 cup marinara sauce

1/3 vegetable mixture

2 tablespoons Parmesan

remaining ricotta mixture

2 lasagne noodles

1/3 cup marinara sauce

2 tablespoons Parmesan

remaining vegetable mixture

3/4 cup mozzarella

2 lasagne noodles (press firmly into layers below)

remaining marinara sauce

4. Cover snugly with plastic food wrap and microwave 15 minutes on Medium-High, turning 180° at half time. Let stand, still covered, in turned-off microwave 5 minutes.

5. Remove plastic wrap and set lasagne on large baking sheet. Sprinkle remaining 2 tablespoons Parmesan and remaining mozzarella evenly on top, set uncovered in preheated oven, and bake until cheese melts and bubbles, 8 to 10 minutes.

6. Remove from oven, let stand 10 minutes, then cut into large squares and serve.

SHEPHERD'S PIE

Makes 4 to 6 servings

This no-sweat Shepherd's Pie begins in the microwave and finishes in a very hot oven so the potato topping (frozen hash browns) turns richly golden.

2 cups fresh or frozen chopped onions (2 medium-large yellow onions)

One 8-ounce package fresh shredded carrots

1 large bay leaf, crumbled

1/2 teaspoon dried thyme, crumbled

2 1/2 tablespoons bacon drippings, melted butter, or vegetable oil

1 pound lean ground lamb shoulder or lean ground beef chuck

1 cup frozen green peas (do not thaw)

4 cups frozen hash brown potatoes (do not thaw)

One 10 1/2-ounce can beef consommé blended with 5 tablespoons all-purpose flour, 1 tablespoon each Worcestershire sauce and steak sauce, 1/2 tablespoon bacon drippings, 1 teaspoon salt, and 1/2 teaspoon freshly ground black pepper

1. Preheat oven to 450°F. Toss onions, carrots, bay leaf, and thyme in 1 1/2 tablespoons drippings in shallow round or oval 2 1/2-quart microwave-to-oven casserole.

2. Crumble in lamb, add peas, and toss again. Top with potatoes, distributing evenly.

3. Cover with plastic food wrap and microwave on High for 15 minutes.

4. Uncover, pour consommé mixture evenly over potatoes, then drizzle with remaining 1 tablespoon drippings.

5. Transfer to oven and bake uncovered until bubbly and potatoes are tipped with brown, 25 to 30 minutes. Serve at once.

SAUERKRAUT, POTATO, AND KIELBASA CASSEROLE

Makes 4 to 6 servings

If you can get fresh sauerkraut (many delis and deli counters sell it), by all means use it. If not, use a good canned sauerkraut that's not too sharp or salty. The one I like is a mild Bavarian sauerkraut with caraway seeds. It's a national brand and widely available.

1 tablespoon vegetable oil
½ pound kielbasa, half thinly sliced, half quartered lengthwise
1 large yellow onion, halved vertically then each half thinly sliced
2 cups frozen hash brown potatoes (do not thaw)

½ teaspoon caraway seeds
¼ teaspoon fennel seeds
¼ teaspoon freshly ground black pepper
Two 15-ounce cans mild Bavarian sauerkraut with caraway seeds, drained
2 tablespoons minced parsley

1. Place oil, sliced kielbasa, onion, hash browns, caraway seeds, fennel seeds, and pepper in shallow round or oval 2 ½-quart casserole; toss to mix and distribute evenly. Cover with waxed paper and microwave on High for 12 minutes.

2. Stir well, spoon sauerkraut over all, and space quartered kielbasa evenly on top. Cover with plastic food wrap and microwave on High for 15 minutes.

3. Let stand, still covered, 2 minutes. Sprinkle with parsley and serve.

HURRY-UP PASTITSIO

By using the microwave to make the meat filling, I've trimmed the cooking time of this classic Greek casserole by more than half. I further cut kitchen time by using deli macaroni salad for the pasta layer and bottled alfredo sauce for the cheese-custard topping. To give the *pastitsio* the proper finish, I bake it at 375°F—but for 25 to 30 minutes only.

1 cup fresh or frozen chopped onion (about 1 medium-large yellow onion)

1 large garlic clove, minced

2 tablespoons extra-virgin olive oil

1 pound lean ground lamb shoulder or lean ground beef chuck

1 teaspoon dried oregano, crumbled

1 teaspoon salt

1/4 teaspoon freshly ground black pepper

1/4 teaspoon ground cinnamon

1 cup Fine Dry Bread Crumbs (page 37)

One 8-ounce can tomato sauce or 1 cup Basic Tomato Sauce (page 30)

1 cup bottled alfredo sauce blended with 1/4 cup thawed frozen egg product, 2 tablespoons each milk and freshly grated Parmesan cheese, and 1/4 teaspoon ground nutmeg

2 cups macaroni salad, drained well and mixed with 1/4 cup freshly grated Parmesan cheese

3 tablespoons freshly grated Parmesan cheese (topping)

1. Preheat oven to 375°F.

2. Mix onion, garlic, and oil in shallow round or oval 2 1/2-quart casserole, cover with waxed paper, and microwave on High for 5 minutes.

3. Add lamb, oregano, salt, pepper, and cinnamon, breaking meat into small pieces, mixing well with onion mixture, and spreading evenly over bottom of casserole. Cover with waxed paper and microwave on Medium-High for 5 minutes. Stir well, again breaking up meat.

4. Mix in crumbs and tomato sauce, spread evenly in casserole, cover with waxed paper, and microwave 5 minutes on High. Mix in $1/4$ cup alfredo sauce mixture and again spread evenly.

5. Mix $1/2$ cup alfredo sauce mixture into macaroni mixture and spread over meat layer. Pour remaining alfredo sauce mixture evenly over all and scatter grated Parmesan on top.

6. Set, uncovered, in preheated oven and bake 25 to 30 minutes until topping is set like custard and lightly golden. Let stand 10 to 15 minutes, then serve.

CASSEROLE OF COLLARDS, CORN, AND KIELBASA

Makes 2 servings

This homespun recipe is something I rustled up one day when I had to produce a hearty lunch in half an hour. Not counting salt and pepper, it contains three ingredients only (all of them staples in my freezer). You can, if you like, add a pinch of crumbled dried rosemary and/or thyme at the outset but neither one is necessary. You can also microwave 1 cup fresh or frozen chopped onion (about 1 medium-large yellow onion) in 1 ½ tablespoons bacon drippings, butter, or vegetable oil 5 minutes on High before step 1 (the casserole should be covered with waxed paper). That'll ratchet up the flavor but it's really a matter of taste.

One 10-ounce package frozen cream-style corn with low-fat sauce (do not thaw)
2 cups frozen chopped collards or turnip greens (do not thaw)

½ teaspoon salt
¼ teaspoon freshly ground black pepper
½ pound fresh or frozen kielbasa, halved crosswise (no need to thaw)

1. Place frozen block of corn, then collards in lidded 1 ½-quart round casserole and sprinkle evenly with salt and pepper.

2. Prick kielbasa well with fork and lay on top of collards (this way drippings will trickle down, flavoring both collards and corn). Cover with lid and microwave on Medium-High for 20 minutes.

3. Transfer casserole to counter and let stand, still covered, for 3 minutes. Stir corn and collards well, spoon onto heated plates, and top each portion with kielbasa.

MICROWAVE SUCCOTASH SALAD

Makes 4 to 6 servings

Succotash may seem an odd choice for salad, but with ham and bacon it's excellent. I like it hot, but it's also good at room temperature.

4 slices lean smoky bacon, sliced crosswise at ½-inch intervals

4 medium-size scallions, trimmed and thickly sliced (include some green tops)

One 10-ounce package frozen baby lima beans, large clumps broken up

One 10-ounce package frozen whole-kernel corn, large clumps broken up

Two 3-inch sprigs fresh rosemary, bruised, or ½ teaspoon dried rosemary, crumbled

¼ teaspoon freshly ground black pepper

1 cup finely diced baked or boiled ham

2 cups Al Dente Make-Ahead Rice (page 35), at room temperature

¼ cup extra-virgin olive oil or corn oil

2 to 3 tablespoons cider vinegar

½ teaspoon salt

½ cup chopped parsley or fresh cilantro or ¼ cup each

1. Spread bacon over bottom of lidded shallow 3-quart casserole, cover with waxed paper, and microwave 4 ½ minutes on High. Scoop browned bacon bits to paper toweling to drain and reserve.

2. Add scallions and limas to casserole, stir to coat with drippings, cover with lid, and microwave 5 minutes on High.

3. Add corn, rosemary, and pepper; mix well, cover with lid, and microwave 10 minutes on High.

4. Discard rosemary sprigs; add reserved bacon, ham, rice, olive oil, 2 tablespoons vinegar, salt, and parsley and toss well. Taste for vinegar, salt and pepper, adjust as needed, and serve.

FIVE-CORN PUDDING WITH SUMMER SQUASH, SMITHFIELD HAM, AND LOVAGE

MAKES 6 SERVINGS

Lovage is a leafy wild celery that looks for all the world like Italian flat-leaf parsley. But its flavor is pure celery with none of the bitterness of celery leaves. Many farmer's markets now sell lovage, as do specialty grocers; if you should find it, by all means try it in this casserole. If not, substitute fresh cilantro or Italian parsley.

2 tablespoons unsalted butter, cut into bits
6 medium-size scallions, trimmed and sliced about ¼ inch thick (include some green tops)
4 small-to-medium zucchini or yellow squash, trimmed and cut into ½-inch cubes (about 1 ¼ pounds)
2 cups frozen baby gold and white corn (do not thaw)
One 10-ounce package frozen cream-style corn (do not thaw)
One 10-ounce package frozen Southwestern-style corn with roasted red peppers (do not thaw)
¾ teaspoon salt
¼ teaspoon freshly ground black pepper

2 tablespoons all-purpose flour
Three-fourths of an 8-ounce package light cream cheese (Neufchâtel), cubed
1 cup moderately coarsely chopped fully cooked Smithfield ham (about 4 ounces)
½ cup evaporated skim milk or half-and-half cream
2 tablespoons coarsely chopped fresh lovage or ¼ cup coarsely chopped fresh cilantro or Italian flat-leaf parsley
One 6-ounce package corn bread stuffing mix tossed with 2 tablespoons melted unsalted butter (save stuffing seasoning packet to use another time)

1. Mix butter, scallions, and zucchini in shallow 2- to 2 ½-quart casserole. Spread evenly over bottom, cover with waxed paper, and microwave on High for 15 minutes.

2. Meanwhile, pulse frozen gold and white corn in food processor until texture of coarse meal. Also preheat oven to 400°F.

3. Mix processed corn into casserole along with cream-style corn, Southwestern-style corn, salt, and pepper. Cover with waxed paper and microwave on High for 12 minutes.

4. Mix in flour, then cream cheese, and when it melts, stir in ham, evaporated milk, lovage, and ½ cup stuffing mix. Scatter remaining stuffing mix evenly on top.

5. Transfer to oven and bake uncovered until bubbling and browned, about 15 minutes. Serve at once.

TIPS

I PROCESSOR-CHOP THE SOLIDLY FROZEN WHOLE-KERNEL CORN TO MAKE THE CASSEROLE CREAMIER. I ALSO PROCESSOR-CHOP THE HAM AND LOVAGE (OR CILANTRO OR PARSLEY). HERE'S THE TECHNIQUE FOR LEAFY HERBS: PULL OFF THE LEAVES BUT DO NOT WASH, THEN PULSE IN THE FOOD PROCESSOR (FOR HERBS I USE A MINI-CHOPPER) UNTIL AS COARSE OR FINE AS YOU LIKE. DUMP CHOPPED HERBS INTO A SMALL FINE-MESH STRAINER, RINSE PROCESSOR WORK BOWL AND BLADE DIRECTLY INTO STRAINER, THEN SET STRAINER UNDER COLD WATER TAP. ONCE HERBS ARE WASHED, WRING DRY IN SEVERAL THICKNESSES PAPER TOWELING. BUNDLE IN PAPER TOWELING, POP INTO A PLASTIC BAG, AND SET IN REFRIGERATOR. STORED THIS WAY, HERBS (EXCEPT MINTS AND BASILS) STAY FRESH FOR FOUR TO FIVE DAYS, PARSLEY EVEN LONGER.

MUSHROOM-SPINACH RAGOUT WITH BROILED POLENTA TOPPING

Makes 6 to 8 servings

I find this a wonderful party dish—perfect for a buffet—for two reasons: it couldn't be easier and it can be prepared through step 4 well ahead of time. To intensify the mushroom flavor, I use four different mushrooms— two dry, two fresh, both of these now available pre-sliced at the produce counter. Additional time-savers are prepared polenta (I used dried tomato polenta here, but plain is equally good) and frozen chopped spinach, which only needs to be thawed and pressed dry in a fine sieve.

One ½-ounce package dried porcini mushrooms
One ½-ounce package dried shiitake mushrooms
2 cups boiling water
3 tablespoons melted unsalted butter
1 tablespoon extra-virgin olive oil
One 8-ounce package sliced fresh white mushrooms
One 6-ounce package sliced fresh portobello mushrooms, coarsely chopped
6 medium-size scallions, trimmed and thinly sliced (include some green tops)
2 large garlic cloves, minced
1½ teaspoons chopped fresh lemon thyme or ½ teaspoon dried thyme, crumbled

One 10-ounce package frozen chopped spinach, thawed and pressed dry (see Tips)
½ pound cooked Smithfield ham, moderately coarsely chopped
¾ cup mushroom soaking water blended with ½ cup sour cream, 3 tablespoons all-purpose flour, 1 teaspoon salt, and ½ teaspoon freshly ground black pepper
Half of an 8-ounce package light cream cheese (Neufchâtel), cubed
One 1-pound roll dried tomato polenta, ends removed and roll cut into rounds ½ inch thick
½ cup freshly grated Parmesan cheese

1. Soak dried porcini and shiitake mushrooms in boiling water 20 minutes.

2. Meanwhile, mix 2 tablespoons melted butter and olive oil with sliced white mushrooms, portobellos, scallions, garlic, and thyme in shallow 2- to 2 1/2-quart casserole. Cover with waxed paper and microwave 7 minutes on High.

3. Drain dried mushrooms, reserving soaking water. Coarsely chop shiitakes and mix into casserole along with porcini. Re-cover with waxed paper and microwave 8 minutes on High.

4. Mix spinach, ham, and soaking water mixture into casserole, cover with waxed paper, and microwave 5 minutes on High. Mix cream cheese into casserole, stirring until melted.

5. Top casserole with polenta rounds, cover with plastic food wrap, and microwave on Medium-High 8 minutes. Meanwhile, preheat broiler.

6. Brush polenta rounds with remaining 1 tablespoon melted butter and sprinkle generously with Parmesan.

7. Slide into broiler, setting 5 inches from heat, and broil until bubbly and tipped with brown, 3 to 4 minutes. Serve at once.

ALMOST INSTANT BRUNSWICK STEW

Makes 6 servings

Old-fashioned Brunswick stew cooks forever. This microwave version is ready in less than 45 minutes.

6 golfball-size red-skin potatoes, scrubbed and quartered but not peeled
1 pound chicken drummettes
2 small celery ribs, trimmed and thinly sliced
3 tablespoons bacon drippings or vegetable oil
2 cups fresh or frozen chopped onions (2 medium-large yellow onions)
One 9- or 10-ounce package frozen baby lima beans, thawed and drained
1 teaspoon poultry seasoning
One 14 ½-ounce can chicken broth
One 9- or 10-ounce package frozen whole-kernel corn (do not thaw), large clumps broken up
One 14 ½- or 15-ounce can crushed tomatoes, with their liquid, blended with 2 tablespoons all-purpose flour
One 8-ounce can tomato sauce or 1 cup Basic Tomato Sauce (page 30)
Salt and freshly ground black pepper

1. Toss potatoes, chicken, and celery in drippings in deep, lidded round or oval 4½-quart casserole, cover, and microwave 15 minutes on High; stir well at half-time.

2. Mix in onions, limas, and poultry seasoning; cover and microwave on High for 10 minutes.

3. Add chicken broth and corn, set lid on askew, and microwave 10 minutes on High.

4. Mix in tomatoes, tomato sauce, and salt and pepper to taste, set lid on askew, and microwave on High until vegetables are tender and chicken is done, 5 to 7 minutes.

5. Let stand, covered, 2 minutes, taste for salt and pepper, adjust as needed, and serve.

CHICKEN DIVAN

MAKES 4 SERVINGS

This 1930s recipe from Mid-Manhattan's late lamented Divan Parisienne Restaurant remains hugely popular because it's a nifty way to recycle leftovers. My microwave version uses raw chicken cutlets (thin slices of breast meat), fresh broccoli, and to bind everything together, prepared alfredo sauce from the supermarket refrigerator counter. To give my Divan the correct bubbly brown finish, I slide it under the broiler just before serving. Check the variations and give them a try, too.

1 pound boneless, skinless chicken cutlets, cut crosswise into ¾-inch-wide strips
¼ cup water
4 cups medium-size broccoli florets (about ¾ pound untrimmed broccoli)
¼ teaspoon freshly ground black pepper
6 tablespoons freshly grated Parmesan cheese

One 10-ounce refrigerated container alfredo sauce blended with ¼ cup freshly grated Parmesan, 2 tablespoons each mayonnaise and dry sherry, and ¼ teaspoon freshly grated nutmeg

1. Arrange chicken strips spoke-fashion and not overlapping in 10-inch pie plate, quiche dish, or shallow round casserole coated with nonstick vegetable cooking spray. Pour in water.

2. Cover with plastic food wrap and microwave on Medium for 5 minutes. Lift chicken to plate and reserve; pour all liquid from pie plate, then spoon 2 tablespoons back in.

3. Arrange broccoli florets spoke-fashion in pie plate, not overlapping and with stems pointing outward. Fill center, again not overlapping, with smaller florets.

4. Cover with plastic food wrap and microwave on High for 4 minutes. Pour any liquid from pie plate. Preheat broiler.

continued

5. Sprinkle $1/8$ teaspoon pepper and 2 tablespoons grated Parmesan evenly over broccoli. Arrange chicken strips on top and sprinkle with remaining pepper and 2 tablespoons grated Parmesan. Pour alfredo sauce mixture evenly over all, spreading to edge and smoothing top.

6. Cover with waxed paper and microwave 5 minutes on Medium. Sprinkle remaining 2 tablespoons grated Parmesan evenly on top.

7. Slide into broiler, setting 4 inches from heat, and broil just until bubbly and dappled with brown, about 2 minutes. Serve at once.

VARIATIONS

Turkey Divan with Asparagus: Prepare as directed, substituting turkey cutlets for chicken and fresh asparagus spears or tips for broccoli. Also microwave asparagus 3 minutes instead of 4.

Cauliflower Divan with Cheddar Sauce: Prepare as directed, using chicken or turkey and substituting small cauliflower florets for broccoli. Also microwave cauliflower 5 to 6 minutes until crisp-tender. Omit alfredo mixture and substitute one thawed 10-ounce package frozen Welsh rarebit blended with 2 tablespoons each mayonnaise and medium-dry Madeira or sherry and $1/4$ teaspoon freshly grated nutmeg. Otherwise, proceed as directed.

Ham and Vegetable Divan with Cheddar Sauce: Prepare Chicken Divan as directed, omitting chicken and microwaving broccoli florets (or asparagus tips or cauliflower florets) until crisp-tender as directed in steps 3 and 4. In step 5, substitute $1/2$ pound thinly sliced baked or boiled ham for chicken, omit alfredo mixture, and top instead with one thawed 10-ounce package frozen Welsh rarebit blended with 2 tablespoons each mayonnaise and tawny Port, medium-dry Madeira or sherry and $1/4$ teaspoon freshly grated nutmeg. Complete recipe as directed in steps 5, 6, and 7.

Seafood Divan: Prepare Chicken Divan as directed, omitting chicken and microwaving broccoli florets (or asparagus tips) until crisp-tender as directed in steps 3 and 4. In step 5, substitute 1 pound cooked shelled and deveined medium-size shrimp or 1 pound flaked and picked-over lump crab for chicken, then complete recipe as directed in steps 5, 6, and 7. (In alfredo sauce mixture, use dry white wine or dry vermouth in place of sherry, if you like.)

NOTE

BECAUSE OF THE SALTINESS OF THE SAUCE AND CHEESE, THIS RECIPE NEEDS NO SALT.

ZIP-QUICK CHICKEN COUSCOUS

MAKES 6 SERVINGS

Who'd have thought that couscous could be made by microwave? Once the initial stove-top browning of chicken, onions, and seasonings is done, the microwave takes over and trims cooking time of this Moroccan classic to just 30 minutes. The couscous grains need only to be covered with boiling chicken broth and left to stand 5 minutes. To pare prep time, I use packaged, peeled baby-cut fresh carrots, canned tomatoes, and canned chickpeas.

3 tablespoons extra-virgin olive oil
1 pound chicken drummettes
2 cups fresh or frozen chopped onions (about 2 medium-large yellow onions)
2 large garlic cloves, minced
1/2 teaspoon ground turmeric
1/2 teaspoon ground cumin
1/2 teaspoon freshly ground black pepper
1/4 teaspoon ground cinnamon
1/4 teaspoon ground hot red pepper (cayenne)
1/4 teaspoon saffron strands, crumbled into 1/3 cup hot water

1 1/2 cups peeled baby-cut fresh carrots, sliced 1/2 inch thick
One 14 1/2-ounce can diced tomatoes, with their liquid
1/3 cup dried currants
1 1/2 teaspoons salt
1 medium-size zucchini, trimmed, halved lengthwise, then each half sliced 1/2 inch thick
One 14 1/2-ounce can chicken broth + enough water to total 2 cups
One 1-pound 3-ounce can chickpeas, rinsed and drained
One 10-ounce box quick-cooking plain couscous

1. Heat oil in lidded, flameproof 2 1/2-quart round or oval casserole over high burner heat 1 minute. Add chicken, turning to coat with oil, reduce heat to moderately high, cover with lid, and brown 5 minutes.

2. Turn chicken, mix in onions, garlic, turmeric, cumin, black pepper, cinnamon, and cayenne; cover and brown for 5 minutes.

3. Off heat, mix in saffron mixture, carrots, tomatoes, currants, and salt. Cover with lid and microwave on Medium-High for 20 minutes.

4. Stir well, add zucchini, pushing down into liquid, cover, and microwave on High for 5 minutes. Meanwhile, bring broth mixture to boiling in medium-size saucepan over high heat.

5. Add chickpeas to casserole, distributing evenly and pushing down into liquid. Cover and microwave 5 minutes on High.

6. Meanwhile, take boiling broth mixture off heat, add couscous, stir once, cover, and let stand 5 minutes.

7. To serve, fluff couscous with fork, mound in deep heated platter, and spoon chicken mixture on top.

VARIATION

Microwave Couscous with Lamb: Omit chicken and substitute 1 pound lean ground lamb shoulder. Heat oil as directed in step 1, add lamb, and brown 5 minutes over high heat, breaking meat into walnut-size chunks. Drain excess drippings from casserole, then spoon 3 tablespoons back in. Proceed as recipe directs, but in step 3, add 2 large whole bay leaves and two 3-inch strips orange zest along with saffron mixture and other ingredients. Follow steps 3 through 7, but discard bay leaves and orange zest before serving.

ASOPAO (PUERTO RICAN CASSEROLE OF CHICKEN AND RICE, GREEN PEAS AND OLIVES)

MAKES 6 SERVINGS

I've speeded up this Puerto Rican classic by substituting chicken drumsticks for a stewing hen, frozen green peas for fresh, and bottled olive salad for whole green olives. Finally, I cook the whole thing by microwave, which trims cooking time by at least half.

3 strips lean smoky bacon, cut crosswise into ½-inch strips
2 tablespoons vegetable oil
1½ pounds chicken drumsticks (6 drumsticks)
1 tablespoon fresh lime juice
1 teaspoon crumbled dried oregano mixed with 1 teaspoon each salt and sweet paprika and ½ teaspoon freshly ground black pepper
1 cup fresh or frozen chopped onion (about 1 medium-large yellow onion)
Half of a 1-pound bag frozen bell pepper stir-fry mix (red, green, and yellow peppers; do not thaw)

2 large garlic cloves, finely minced
½ cup finely diced baked or boiled ham
½ cup olive salad (chopped green olives and pimientos)
¾ cup uncooked converted rice
2 cups chicken broth or water
One 10-ounce can diced tomatoes with green chilies, with their liquid
1 tablespoon small capers, well-drained
One 10-ounce package frozen tiny green peas, thawed and drained
¼ cup minced Italian flat-leaf parsley

1. Spread bacon in lidded 3-quart shallow casserole, cover with waxed paper, and microwave on High until crisp, about 3 minutes; with slotted spoon, lift bacon to paper toweling to drain. Add vegetable oil to casserole drippings.

2. Rub drumsticks with lime juice, then with oregano mixture. Add drumsticks to casserole, turning in dripping mixture to coat evenly, then arrange spoke-fashion with meaty portions pointing outward. Cover with waxed paper and microwave 5 minutes on High.

3. Mix in onion, stir-fry mix, garlic, and ham; cover with waxed paper and microwave 5 minutes on High.

4. Mix in olive salad, rice, chicken broth, tomatoes with chilies, and capers; cover with lid and microwave 20 minutes on High or until rice is al dente. Add peas, distributing evenly, cover with lid, and microwave 5 minutes on High. Let stand, still covered, 3 minutes.

5. Use fork to mix in parsley and reserved bacon and serve.

VARIATION

Asopao with Shrimp: Follow step 1 as directed. In step 2, substitute 1 pound shelled and deveined medium-size raw shrimp for chicken drumsticks and halve each lengthwise. Toss shrimp with 2 table-spoons fresh lime juice, then sprinkle evenly with oregano mixture. Add shrimp to casserole, tossing in dripping mixture to coat evenly, then spread over casserole bottom. Cover with lid and microwave 1 minute on High; stir well, again spread in casserole, and microwave 3 minutes on Medium. Lift shrimp to large plate and reserve. Proceed as directed in steps 3 and 4, but use a half-and-half mixture of chicken broth and clam juice. Also, when adding peas to casserole in step 4, add shrimp, distributing evenly and pushing down into rice. Finish as directed in step 5.

TOMATO-WHITE WINE RISOTTO WITH BLACK OLIVES

The olives and prosciutto are so salty this recipe needs no additional salt. A dry—but not too dry—white wine is best for cooking the risotto. A Pinot Grigio, for example, or a Soave.

4 tablespoons (½ stick) unsalted butter (no substitute)

1 ½ cups coarsely chopped yellow onion (about 1 large)

1 large garlic clove, minced

Two 3-inch sprigs fresh rosemary or ½ teaspoon dried rosemary, crumbled

1 large whole bay leaf

1 ½ cups Arborio (short-grain) rice (no substitute)

½ cup slivered, pitted oil-cured black olives

One 14-ounce can crushed tomatoes with their liquid

One 14 ½-ounce can chicken broth + enough white wine to total 2 ¼ cups combined with ¼ teaspoon freshly ground black pepper

½ cup freshly grated Parmesan cheese

½ cup coarsely chopped Italian flat-leaf parsley

4 ounces thinly sliced prosciutto, finely slivered

1. Place butter in middle of shallow round or oval 2 ½- to 3-quart casserole, cover with waxed paper, and microwave 1 minute on High to melt.

2. Add onion, garlic, rosemary, and bay leaf, tossing to coat with butter. Cover with waxed paper and microwave 10 minutes on High.

3. Mix rice and olives into casserole, stirring to coat with butter; add tomatoes and broth mixture, cover snugly with plastic wrap, and microwave 10 minutes on High. Stir rice mixture, cover with plastic

wrap, and microwave 15 minutes on High. Let stand, still covered, 3 minutes.

4. Remove bay leaf and rosemary sprigs. Fork up risotto, taste, and if not creamy and al dente, cover with plastic wrap and microwave 3 minutes longer on High.

5. Add cheese and as soon as it melts, fork in parsley and prosciutto and serve.

TURKEY SHORTCAKE

MAKE 4 TO 6 SERVINGS

Though not an everyday user of frozen foods, I do find them valuable whenever I need to get dinner fast. This is something I slung together one hurried evening — and my friends loved it.

FOR THE TURKEY
Four 9 ⅜-ounce packages
   frozen reduced-calorie home-
   style turkey with vegetables
   and pasta
1 cup frozen whole-kernel corn,
   clumps broken up

1 cup frozen tiny green peas,
   clumps broken up
Two ¾-inch pats Duxelles
   (page 33)
½ cup bottled alfredo sauce
¼ cup minced parsley

FOR THE SHORTCAKE
1 ½ cups Dumpling/Biscuit
   Topping Mix (page 31)

¾ to 1 cup milk

1. For the turkey, place frozen turkey, corn, and peas in lidded shallow 2 ½- to 3-quart casserole, cover with lid, and microwave on Medium-High for 20 minutes.

2. Meanwhile, prepare shortcake. Preheat oven to 425°F. Place dumpling/biscuit mix in large bowl, then use fork to mix in just enough milk to make a dough soft enough to drop from a spoon.

3. Mix duxelles, alfredo sauce, and parsley into turkey mixture, then drop biscuit dough in pretty pattern over surface.

4. Bake uncovered until mixture bubbles and biscuit topping is tipped with brown, about 20 minutes. Serve at once, first giving each person a portion of biscuit, then a ladling of the turkey mixture, then a second bit of biscuit.

RISOTTO WITH BROCCOLI AND SHRIMP

MAKES 4 TO 6 SERVINGS

While developing recipes for our book *Micro Ways*, my co-author Elaine Hanna developed a fast, foolproof way to cook risotto by microwave. This recipe, wholly my own, uses her technique. To trim prep time, I use broccoli coleslaw mix (julienned broccoli stems plus shredded carrot).

2 ½ cups broccoli coleslaw mix (about half of a 1-pound package)

1 cup fresh or frozen chopped onion (about 1 medium-large yellow onion)

1 medium-size celery rib, trimmed and finely diced

1 large garlic clove, minced

1 large whole bay leaf

One 3-inch sprig fresh rosemary or ½ teaspoon dried rosemary, crumbled

3 tablespoons extra-virgin olive oil

1 cup Arborio (short grain) rice

One 14 ½-ounce can chicken broth + enough dry white wine or dry vermouth to total 2 ¼ cups combined with 1 teaspoon salt and ¼ teaspoon freshly ground black pepper

¾ pound shelled and deveined, medium-size raw shrimp

½ cup freshly grated Parmesan cheese

1. Toss broccoli mix, onion, celery, garlic, bay leaf, and rosemary in oil in shallow round or oval 2-quart casserole to coat well. Spread evenly in casserole, cover with waxed paper, and microwave on High for 10 minutes.

2. Mix rice into casserole, stirring to coat with oil; add broth mixture, cover snugly with plastic wrap, and microwave on High for 10 minutes. Reduce power level to Medium and microwave for 5 minutes.

3. Mix in shrimp, distributing evenly, cover with plastic wrap, and microwave on Medium for 5 minutes. Let stand, still covered, 3 minutes.

4. Remove bay leaf and rosemary sprig, fork in grated Parmesan, and serve.

NOTE

THOUGH IT'S UNORTHODOX TO ADD CHEESE TO A SEAFOOD RISOTTO, I DO SO TO HEIGHTEN THE CREAMINESS.

NOTE

I usually avoid frozen asparagus because it tends to go mushy. Not so with frozen asparagus cuts prepared this way.

TIP

The fastest way to sliver prosciutto is to stack the slices, halve the stack crosswise, stack the two halves, then with a sharp chef's knife slice straight through them—again crosswise—at $1/4$-inch intervals.

RED WINE RISOTTO WITH MUSHROOMS, ASPARAGUS, AND PROSCIUTTO

Makes 4 to 6 servings

The microwave makes such good risotto I rarely bother to prepare it the time-honored way. This particular risotto is one of my all-time favorites.

3 tablespoons unsalted butter (no substitute)
$1/2$ cups coarsely chopped red (Italian) onion (about 1 large)
1 large garlic clove, minced
One 8-ounce package sliced fresh white mushrooms
Two 3-inch sprigs fresh lemon thyme or $1/2$ teaspoon dried thyme, crumbled
1 large whole bay leaf
1 cup Arborio (short-grain) rice
One 14 $1/2$-ounce can beef broth + enough dry red wine to total 2 $1/4$ cups combined with $1/2$ teaspoon salt and $1/4$ teaspoon freshly ground black pepper

One 9-ounce package frozen asparagus cuts (do not thaw but do separate into individual pieces)
$1/2$ cup freshly grated Parmesan cheese
4 ounces thinly sliced prosciutto, finely slivered (see Tip)

1. Place butter in middle of shallow round or oval 2-quart casserole, cover with waxed paper, and microwave on High for 1 minute to melt.

2. Add onion, garlic, mushrooms, thyme, and bay leaf, tossing to coat with butter. Cover with waxed paper and microwave on High for 10 minutes.

3. Mix rice into casserole, stirring to coat with butter, add broth mixture, cover snugly with plastic wrap, and microwave on High for 10 minutes. Stir rice mixture, cover with plastic wrap, and microwave on Medium for 10 minutes.

4. Distribute asparagus evenly on top of rice mixture, cover with plastic wrap, and microwave on High for 5 minutes. Let stand, still covered, 3 minutes.

5. Remove bay leaf and thyme sprigs. Mix in grated Parmesan and as soon as it melts, fork in slivered prosciutto and serve.

CREAMY PESTO RAVIOLI

Two kinds of ravioli, two kinds of pasta sauce. Put them together with broccoli florets from the salad bar or produce section, top with cheese, then microwave. Now that's dinner on a deadline!

Two 9-ounce packages refrigerated ravioli (one beef-and-garlic, one four-cheese)
2 cups small broccoli florets (from salad bar or prepared produce section)
1/2 cup refrigerated, prepared reduced-fat pesto with basil

One 10-ounce package refrigerated alfredo sauce
1 1/2 cups shredded mozzarella or mixed Italian cheeses (about 6 ounces)

1. Cook ravioli in salted water according to package directions, adding broccoli for last 3 minutes. Meanwhile, lightly grease shallow 2 1/2-quart flameproof casserole.

2. Drain ravioli and broccoli very well. Place in prepared casserole, toss with pesto, then top with alfredo sauce and cheese.

3. Microwave uncovered 8 to 10 minutes on High until mixture bubbles. Meanwhile, preheat broiler.

4. The minute casserole comes from microwave, slide into broiler, setting 5 to 6 inches from heat. Broil until tipped with brown, 1 to 2 minutes, and serve.

THAI SHRIMP WITH SNOW PEAS AND PEANUT SAUCE

MAKES 4 SERVINGS

If you use packaged shredded fresh carrots as I do and sweet-talk your fishmonger into shelling and deveining the raw shrimp for you, this dish is ready in record time.

4 large scallions, trimmed and finely chopped (include some green tops)
1 garlic clove, minced
1 cup coarsely shredded fresh carrots
2 tablespoons peanut or vegetable oil
1 pound shelled and deveined large raw shrimp
4 ounces snow peas, trimmed and strings removed
1 teaspoon salt
⅛ teaspoon ground hot red pepper (cayenne)
¼ cup canned Thai coconut milk (use light, if you like)

2 tablespoons chicken broth or water
⅓ cup creamy-style peanut butter
1 tablespoon finely minced lemongrass stalks or 1 teaspoon finely grated lemon zest
1 tablespoon fresh lime juice
1 teaspoon finely minced fresh ginger
⅛ teaspoon red pepper flakes
3 cups Al Dente Make-Ahead Rice (page 35), reheated
½ cup coarsely chopped dry-roasted peanuts

1. Toss scallions, garlic, and carrots with oil in shallow 2-quart round or oval casserole. Spread evenly, cover with waxed paper, and microwave on High for 5 minutes.

2. Arrange shrimp spoke-fashion around edge of casserole with tails pointing inward, cover with waxed paper, and microwave on High for 2 minutes.

continued

3. Add snow peas, placing in center of casserole; cover with waxed paper and microwave on High just until shrimp turn pink and snow peas are crisp-tender, about 2 minutes. Sprinkle with salt and cayenne and let stand 2 minutes. With slotted spoon, transfer casserole contents to bowl.

4. Add all remaining ingredients except rice and chopped peanuts to casserole, blend well, cover with waxed paper, and microwave on Medium for 2 minutes.

5. Return shrimp, vegetables, and accumulated juices to casserole and toss well to coat with sauce. Cover with waxed paper and microwave on Medium for 1 minute.

6. To serve, mound rice on heated deep platter, spoon hot shrimp mixture on top, and sprinkle evenly with chopped peanuts.

VARIATIONS

Thai Chicken with Snow Peas and Peanut Sauce: Prepare as directed, omitting shrimp and substituting 1 pound ($^1/_4$-inch-thick) chicken (or turkey) cutlets that have been cut crosswise into $^1/_4$-inch-wide strips. In step 2, microwave chicken 4 minutes. Otherwise, proceed as directed.

Thai Beef with Snow Peas and Peanut Sauce: Prepare as directed for Thai Chicken, substituting 1 pound ($^1/_4$-inch-thick) slices rib eye or beef tenderloin that have been cut crosswise into $^1/_4$-inch-wide strips. In sauce, use beef broth instead of chicken and add 1 tablespoon teriyaki sauce. In step 2, microwave beef 3 minutes instead of 4; proceed as directed.

GEORGIA'S SPICY SEA SCALLOPS WITH SCALLION COUSCOUS

Makes 4 servings

My friend Georgia Downard, a single working mom with two hungry adolescents, relies on her microwave to get food on the table fast. Once an editor at *Gourmet* and now culinary director of the TV Food Network, Georgia says her kids also like this dish made with shrimp (see variation).

FOR THE SCALLOPS
1 cup chopped yellow onion (about 1 medium-large onion)
1 cup chopped green bell pepper (about 1 medium-large)
½ cup chopped celery (about 1 small rib)
2 garlic cloves, minced
2 to 3 teaspoons Creole seasoning
1 tablespoon extra-virgin olive oil

One 14 ½-ounce can stewed, chopped tomatoes, with their liquid
1 tablespoon cornstarch blended with 3 tablespoons cold water
Salt and freshly ground black pepper
1 pound sea scallops, drained and halved horizontally, if large
1 tablespoon fresh lemon juice
2 tablespoons minced Italian (flat-leaf) parsley

FOR THE COUSCOUS
2 cups boiling canned chicken broth or water
2 large scallions, trimmed and thinly sliced (include some green tops)

1 tablespoon unsalted butter
1 cup quick-cooking plain couscous

1. To prepare the scallops: Combine onion, green pepper, celery, garlic, and Creole seasoning with oil in shallow 2-quart casserole,

stirring well to coat with oil. Spread evenly in casserole, cover with waxed paper, and microwave on High for 5 minutes, stirring halfway through cooking time.

2. Mix in tomatoes and their liquid, cornstarch mixture, and salt and pepper to taste; cover with lid or plastic food wrap and microwave on High for 5 minutes, again stirring halfway through.

3. Add scallops to casserole, distributing evenly, cover with lid or plastic food wrap, and microwave on Medium-High until cooked through, 3 to 4 minutes.

4. Meanwhile, prepare couscous. Remove boiling broth from heat and stir in scallions, butter, and couscous; cover, and let stand off heat 5 minutes.

5. As soon as scallops are done, stir in lemon juice and parsley. Taste for salt, pepper, and lemon juice and adjust as needed. Also taste couscous for salt and add, if needed.

6. To serve, fluff couscous with fork, then mound on heated deep platter and ladle scallops mixture on top.

VARIATION

Cajun Shrimp with Scallion Couscous: Prepare as directed, substituting 1 pound shelled and deveined large raw shrimp for scallops and microwaving just until shrimp turn pink, 3 to 4 minutes. Also, if you like, substitute Cajun seasoning for Creole.

MAKE IT SNAPPY BEEF AND VEGETABLE SOUP

Makes 6 servings

Don't be put off by the length of the ingredients list—this soup is on the table in 40 minutes. Much of what goes into it is frozen. No problem. Set the frozen packets in the fridge in the morning and they'll be thawed by dinner time. Because frozen vegetables have less flavor than the fresh and because a 40-minute soup lacks the richness of one simmered for hours, I've pumped up the seasonings and used richly flavored canned consommé to intensify the beef flavor—broth alone doesn't do it. I've also added a couple of tablespoons of creamy peanut butter, which pulls flavors together nicely and mellows the soup.

1 tablespoon extra-virgin olive oil

2 tablespoons unsalted butter

6 large scallions, trimmed and thinly sliced (include some green tops)

1 large celery rib, thinly sliced (include some leafy tops)

1 large garlic clove, finely minced

2 large whole bay leaves

1 teaspoon dried marjoram or oregano, crumbled

½ teaspoon dried thyme, crumbled

One 9-ounce package frozen seasoned beef strips, thawed

One 14½-ounce can beef broth

One 10½-ounce can beef consommé

2 large parsley sprigs

One 10-ounce package frozen succotash, thawed and drained

2 cups frozen O'Brien potatoes, thawed

1 cup frozen cut green beans, thawed and drained

2 tablespoons creamy-style peanut butter

One 14½-ounce can diced tomatoes, with their liquid

One 8-ounce can tomato sauce

Salt and freshly ground black pepper

1. Place oil, 1 tablespoon butter, scallions, celery, garlic, bay leaves, marjoram, and thyme in 5-quart round or oval lidded casserole and

toss well. Spread evenly, cover with waxed paper, and microwave on High for 10 minutes.

2. Mix in beef strips, broth, consommé, and parsley; cover with lid and microwave on High for 5 minutes.

3. Add succotash, potatoes, and beans; cover with lid and microwave on High for 10 minutes.

4. Add peanut butter and stir until melted. Mix in tomatoes, tomato sauce, and salt and pepper to taste; cover with lid and microwave on High for 10 minutes. Let stand, still covered, 5 minutes.

5. Stir in remaining 1 tablespoon butter and when it melts, discard bay leaves and parsley sprigs. Ladle soup into large heated bowls and serve.

VARIATION

Jiffy Chicken Soup with Seven Vegetables: Prepare as directed but substitute one thawed 9-ounce package frozen cooked chicken breast strips for beef and one 14 $\frac{1}{2}$-ounce can chicken broth for beef broth (keep beef consommé, however). Omit green beans and in step 4, after tomatoes, tomato sauce, salt, and pepper have microwaved 8 minutes on High, add one thawed and drained 10-ounce package frozen tiny green peas, distributing evenly. Cover and microwave 2 minutes on High. Proceed as directed in step 5.

HADDOCK AND VEGETABLE CHOWDER

MAKES 4 SERVINGS

Fish chowder by microwave? Why not? It cooks fish to perfection. This recipe is the New England classic—with carrots added to make it a more nutritionally balanced meal.

2 ounces salt pork or smoked slab bacon, cut into ¼-inch cubes

1 cup chopped fresh or frozen onion (about 1 medium-large yellow onion)

2 medium-size all-purpose potatoes (about ¾ pound), peeled and cut into ½-inch cubes

1 cup peeled baby-cut fresh carrots, sliced ½ inch thick

1 cup water

1 teaspoon salt

¼ teaspoon freshly ground black pepper

1 pound skinned fresh haddock, cod, or halibut fillets

1 cup milk (at room temperature)

1 cup light cream or half-and-half (at room temperature)

1 tablespoon unsalted butter

1. Spread salt pork in lidded 2½-quart casserole, cover with waxed paper, and microwave on High until crisp, about 5 minutes; with slotted spoon, lift pork to paper towels to drain.

2. Add onion, potatoes, and carrots to drippings and toss to coat. Add water, salt, and pepper; cover with lid and microwave 20 minutes on High until vegetables are tender.

3. Lay fish on vegetables, add milk and cream, cover with lid, and microwave 8 minutes on Medium-High until fish nearly flakes. Taste for salt and pepper and fine-tune.

4. Add butter, cover with lid, and let stand 3 minutes; break fish into chunks.

5. Ladle into heated soup plates and scatter reserved salt pork over each portion.

continued

Fish Chowder with Corn and Parsley: Prepare as directed but in step 2, add 1 cup frozen whole-kernel corn (no need to thaw but do break up chunks and distribute evenly) along with onion, potatoes, and carrots. Proceed as directed in steps 2, 3, and 4. In step 5, after ladling chowder into soup plates, scatter 1 tablespoon freshly minced parsley over each portion along with salt pork.

Chili Chowder with Cilantro: Prepare Fish Chowder with Corn and Parsley as directed above, but in step 2, add 1 teaspoon chili powder and $1/4$ teaspoon each ground cumin and hot red pepper (cayenne) along with frozen corn. In step 3, use 2 cups light cream instead of 1 cup each milk and light cream. Proceed as directed in steps 3, and 4. In step 5, after ladling chowder into soup plates, scatter 1 tablespoon minced fresh cilantro instead of parsley over each portion along with salt pork.

Salmon Chowder with Peas and Fresh Mint: Prepare Haddock and Vegetable Chowder as directed, but substitute 1 pound fresh skinless salmon fillets for haddock. In step 2 after onion, potatoes, and carrots have microwaved 15 minutes, add 1 cup frozen green peas (no need to thaw but do break up chunks and distribute evenly). Cover with lid and microwave on High for 5 minutes longer. Proceed as directed in steps 3 and 4. In step 5, after ladling chowder into soup plates, scatter 1 teaspoon freshly minced mint over each portion along with salt pork.

INDEX